Event Mobilities

Events from a mobilities perspective attend to moments in which individual networks coalesce in place but are not isolated in their performance as they often foster far-reaching and mobile networks of community. In so doing, individuals travel from varying distances to participate in localized performances. However, events themselves are also mobile, and events affect mobility. Mobile events serve as contexts that provide meanings and purpose articulated in relation to, and as, a series of other social actions. They further highlight the role of the body and embodied practices in the performance of events.

Building on Sheller and Urry's (2004) seminal work *Tourism Mobilities*, the purpose of this book is to further develop event studies research within mobilities studies so as to challenge the limits set by dichotomous understandings of home/away, work/leisure and host/guest. Simply put, events are always already place-based and political in the sense that they can both inspire mobility as well as lead to various immobilities for different social groups. The title addresses everyday as well as extraordinary events, shining an empirical and theoretical light onto the political, economic and social role of events in numerous geographic and cultural contexts. It stretches across academic disciplines and fields of study to illustrate the advantages of an interdisciplinary conversation on mobilities.

This groundbreaking volume is the first to offer a conceptualization and theorization of event mobilities. It will serve as a valuable resource and reference for event, tourism and leisure studies students and scholars interested in exploring the ways the everyday and the extraordinary interlace.

Kevin Hannam is Professor of Tourism in the Business School at Edinburgh Napier University, UK. Previously he was at Leeds Beckett University, UK. He is also a Visiting Research Fellow at the University of Johannesburg, South Africa. He is co-editor of the Routledge journals *Mobilities* and *Applied Mobilities*.

Mary Mostafanezhad is an Assistant Professor in the Department of Geography at the University of Hawai'i at Mānoa, USA.

Jillian Rickly is an Assistant Professor in the Business School at the University of Nottingham, UK.

Routledge Advances in Event Research Series

Edited by Warwick Frost and Jennifer Laing
Department of Marketing, Tourism and Hospitality,
La Trobe University, Australia

Events in the City
Using public spaces as event venues
Andrew Smith

Event Mobilities
Politics, place and performance
*Edited by Kevin Hannam, Mary
Mostafanezhad and Jillian Rickly*

Forthcoming:

**Approaches and Methods in Event
Studies**
Edited by Tomas Pernecky

Visitor Attractions and Events
Locations and linkages
*Edited by Adi Weidenfeld, Richard Butler
and Allan Williams*

Critical Event Studies
Karl Spracklen and Ian Lamond

Festival Events
Theoretical perspectives in festival events
and social cohesion
Judith Mair and Michelle Duffy

Royal Events
Rituals, innovations and meanings
Warwick Frost and Jennifer Laing

Event Mobilities

Politics, place and performance

Edited by Kevin Hannam, Mary Mostafanezhad and Jillian Rickly

Routledge
Taylor & Francis Group

LONDON AND NEW YORK

First published 2016
by Routledge

2 Park Square, Milton Park, Abingdon, Oxfordshire OX14 4RN
711 Third Avenue, New York, NY 10017

Routledge is an imprint of the Taylor & Francis Group, an informa business

First issued in paperback 2018

British Library Cataloguing in Publication Data
A catalogue record for this book is available from the British Library

Library of Congress Cataloging in Publication Data
Names: Hannam, Kevin, editor. | Mostafanezhad, Mary, editor. | Rickly-
Boyd, Jillian M., editor.
Title: Event mobilities : politics, place and performance / edited by Kevin
Hannam, Mary Mostafanezhad and Jillian Rickly-Boyd.
Description: Abingdon, Oxon ; New York, NY : Routledge, 2016.
Series: Routledge advances in event research series
Includes bibliographical references and index.
Identifiers: LCCN 2015041554
Subjects: LCSH: Special events–Social aspects–Case studies.
Festivals–Social aspects–Case studies.
Spatial behavior–Social aspects–Case studies.
Movement (Philosophy)
Classification: LCC GT3405 .E93 2016 | DDC 394.2–dc23
LC record available at http://lccn.loc.gov/2015041554

ISBN: 978-1-138-90186-5 (hbk)
ISBN: 978-1-138-59246-9 (pbk)

Typeset in Times New Roman
by Cenveo Publisher Services

Contents

Contributors

Ali Abdallah is a Senior Lecturer and Programme Leader of Tourism Management Studies at Stenden University Qatar. His research interests include the development of tourism in the Middle East, hospitality and the Lebanese Diaspora. Ali is completing a PhD on the Lebanese Diaspora at Leeds Beckett University.

Lisa C. Braverman is a PhD candidate in Communication and Culture at Indiana University Bloomington. Her work focuses on rhetoric and public culture, and more specifically how definitions of the term 'genocide' are changing in an age of digital media.

Julie Cidell is a native of the Chicago area with a PhD in geography from the University of Minnesota. She has published on military base conversion, airport expansion, the suburban logistics landscape, the geography of chocolate, green buildings, and the mobilities of road races. She has worked as a transportation engineer in Boston, but currently, she is an Associate Professor of Geography and GIS at the University of Illinois at Urbana-Champaign. Her two main areas of study are the role of local governments in urban sustainability, and mobilities. For the former, she asks how local governments and individual actors matter in struggles over large-scale infrastructure and policy development and the corresponding urban environments that are produced. With regards to mobilities, her interests include the political and social aspects of airports, railroads, and logistics hubs and how they intersect with neighbourhoods and household activities. Personal involvement in the mobilities of running and road races has led to research on that topic as well.

Chris Gibson is Editor of *Australian Geographer*, and Professor of Human Geography and Director of the Global Challenges Program at the University of Wollongong, Australia. From 2005–2010 he was the lead chief investigator of the largest ever study of the social, cultural and economic significance of festivals for rural and regional communities in Australia – a project funded by the Australian Research Council that attracted the involvement of over 400 festivals and events, and spawned many books and papers including *Festival Places: Reinventing Rural Australia* (Channel View, 2011) and *Music Festivals and Regional Development in Australia* (Ashgate, 2012).

Kevin Hannam is Professor of Tourism at Edinburgh Napier University, UK and a research affiliate at the University of Johannesburg, South Africa. Previously he was at Leeds Beckett University and the University of Sunderland, UK. He is founding co-editor of the journals *Mobilities* and *Applied Mobilities* (Routledge), co-author of the books *Understanding Tourism* (Sage, 2010) and *Tourism and India* (Routledge, 2010) and co-editor of the *Routledge Handbook of Mobilities* (Routledge, 2013) and *Moral Encounters in Tourism* (Ashgate, 2014). He has extensive research experience in South and South-East Asia. He has a PhD in geography from the University of Portsmouth, UK and is a Fellow of the Royal Geographical Society (FRGS), member of the Royal Anthropological Institute (RAI) and Vice-Chair of the Association for Tourism and Leisure Education and Research (ATLAS).

Elizabeth Louis is a Senior Research and Evaluation Specialist at Landesa, a research and advocacy organization working on land rights for the rural poor, based in Seattle. Elizabeth earned a PhD in human geography from the University of Hawai'i at Mānoa in 2012. Her research areas are the political ecologies of land and agriculture, alternative food and agricultural movements, and the political ecologies of sanitation, with a regional focus on South Asia. Her dissertation research examined the local outcomes of a global movement for food sovereignty in addressing the interrelated issues of rural distress and food security among poor *Dalit* (untouchable) farmers in the rural Telengana region of India. She then did a two year post-doc on the political ecologies of sanitation access among rural communities in India. Elizabeth is currently conducting research on the gendered and diverse outcomes of land titling on landless households in West Bengal and Odisha states of rural India.

Angela Montague is a Post-Doctoral Teaching Scholar in the Department of Anthropology at the University of Oregon. She is a cultural anthropologist and has been conducting research in Mali, West Africa since 2004. Working closely with Kel Ansar Tuareg from the region of Timbuktu, she has been focusing on the uses of cultural productions and tourism for social, political, and economic purposes. Dr Montague's dissertation research shed light on issues of competing global discourses and contested nationalism in Northern Mali, particularly through an ethnographic investigation of the Festival in the Desert (Essakane). Her current research is on tourism development in post-conflict areas and theories of (im)mobilities.

Mary Mostafanezhad is an Assistant Professor in the Department of Geography at the University of Hawai'i at Mānoa. Mary's research interests lie at the inter-section of critical geopolitics and cultural, development and tourism studies. Her current research examines contemporary forms of market-based development and humanitarian interventions. Through this research she theorizes the implica-tions of these practices for the ongoing redefinition of the relationship between the so-called global North and global South and draws connections between popular culture, political economy and geopolitical imaginaries. Mary is the author of *Volunteer Tourism: Popular Humanitarianism in Neoliberal Times* (Ashgate, 2014) and co-editor of *At Home in the Field: Ethnographic Encounters in Asia and the Pacific Islands* (University of Hawai'i Press, 2015), *Moral Encounters in Tourism* (Ashgate, 2014), *Political Ecology of Tourism: Communities, Power and the Environment* (Routledge, 2016), and *Tourism and Leisure Mobilities: Politics, Work and Play* (Routledge, 2016). She is also a board member of the Association of American Geographers Recreation, Tourism and Sport and Cultural and Political Ecology Specialty Groups, the co-founder of the Critical Tourism Studies Asia-Pacific Consortium, affiliate faculty in the Thai Studies Department at the University of Hawai'i at Mānoa, and an affiliated researcher in the Research Network on Celebrity and North-South Relations.

Peter Peters is Assistant Professor in the Department of Philosophy of the Faculty of Arts and Social Sciences at Maastricht University, the Netherlands. He is trained as a sociologist and holds a PhD for his dissertation on mobilities in technological cultures, in which he combines insights from social theory and science and technology studies to analyse practices of travel. From 2008 to 2013 he was Professor in the research centre 'Autonomy and the Public Sphere in the Arts' at Zuyd University, Maastricht. Here, he developed research on artistic research and its relation to science and technology studies, as well as site-specific art, and art in the public sphere. His current research focuses on how knowledge, techniques and craftsmanship are developed in historical and contemporary practices of organ building. He is interested in how the organ, as a complex technology endowed with artistic qualities, can be seen as a site of knowledge generation and exchange. Peters is author of *Time, Innovation and Mobilities* (Routledge, 2006). He has published his work in journals including *Interdisciplinary Science Reviews*, *Research Policy, Configurations*, and *Mobilities*. He is a member of the editorial board of *Mobilities* (Sage) and review editor of the journal *Time & Society* (Sage).

Jillian Rickly is an Assistant Professor of Tourism Marketing and Management in the Nottingham University Business School at the University of Nottingham. She is a tourism geographer working in the areas of geohumanities and mobilities studies. Her work weaves together environmental perceptions, identity and bio-politics, and performance theories to consider the relations between travel motivation and experience. From this foundation, she has published widely on the concept of authenticity in tourism studies and has contributed a series of chapters to edited volumes regarding tourism mobilities as well as landscape perspectives for tourism studies. Dr Rickly is a co-author of *Tourism, Performance, and Place: A Geographic Perspective* (Ashgate, 2014) and a co-editor of *Tourism and Leisure Mobilities: Politics, Work and Play* (Routledge, 2016). She earned her PhD in Geography from Indiana University.

Tani H. Sebro is a PhD candidate and lecturer in the Department of Political Science at the University of Hawai'i at Mānoa. Her research and teaching interests span the subdisciplines of political ethnography, critical political theory, and international relations with a particular emphasis on refugee politics in Southeast Asia. She has been working on issues related to refugees in the Thai-Burma border zone since 2005, and has served as an Immigration Consultant to the Norwegian Ministry of Foreign Affairs. Her dissertation addresses the relationship between ethnic nationalism, mobility, and the biopolitics of exile amongst Burmese refugees in Thailand. Tani H. Sebro is also an avid dance practitioner and is currently exploring how kinaesthetic methodologies both disrupt and enhance the field of political ethnography.

Rebecca Sheehan is a member of Oklahoma State University's Department of Geography faculty. Her research examines cultural landscapes, especially concerning intersections of identity, public space, tourism, and marginalized as well as non-mainstream groups. She has done extensive place-based research employing ethnography, participant observation, interview, survey, and archival methods. Her past research in Jackson Square examines ideas of inclusion and exclusion especially concerning concepts of home and belonging. She continues to have ongoing research projects in New Orleans, most recently concerning 1) how processes of gender identity, sexuality, and New Orleans's relatively new parading tradition of all-female marching groups inform individual, group, and city identity and 2) how animal 'nuisances', pets, and legislation shape and impart meaning to public space in the city. Her past research in Oklahoma shows how community is formed and what it does in the state's panhandle and how roller derby in the Bible Belt makes steps toward greater recognition of diverse genders and sexualities. Her new project in Oklahoma City explores how the annual international PARK(ing) Day event informs notions of public space and identity, especially regarding junctures of the local and global. Dr Sheehan's work is informed by feminist theory, especially performativity.

Karl Spracklen is a Professor of Leisure Studies at Leeds Beckett University, UK, and the principal editor of the journal *Metal Music Studies*. His work on leisure uses history, philosophy, and sociology to understand the meaning and purpose of leisure: how free leisure choices are, and how much modern leisure is a product of constraints. He has published four key monographs on leisure theory: *The Meaning and Purpose of Leisure* (2009); *Constructing Leisure: Historical and Philosophical Debates* (2011); *Whiteness and Leisure* (2013); and *Digital Leisure* (2015). Professor Spracklen has published widely on leisure with over seventy publications. He is interested in subcultures, identities, spaces and hegemonies of leisure - his research on tourism, folk music and morris, Goth, heavy metal and sport is all underpinned by a concern with the problem of leisure. His research is influenced by Habermas, Adorno, Gramsci, Bourdieu, and Marx. Professor Spracklen has been the Chair of the Leisure Studies Association from 2009 to 2013. From 2014 Professor Spracklen has been the Vice-President of Research Committee 13 (Sociology of Leisure) of the International Sociological Association. Professor Spracklen is the joint editor (with Professor Karen Fox) of a book series for Palgrave Macmillan: Leisure Studies in a Global Era.

Rodanthi Tzanelli is Associate Professor of Cultural Sociology at the University of Leeds, UK. She works with globalization and mobility theory with current focus on the axiological basis of worldmaking processes as these are filtered through media and tourism. She serves on the international advisory committee of EUMEDNET (Malaga), the Global Studies Community (Illinois) and the ICSPR (Ikaria, Greece) and is on the editorial board of several journals, including *Cultural Sociology* (BSA, Sage), *Anuario de Turismo y Sociedad* (Colombia), *Athens Journal of Social Sciences* (Athens) and the *International Journal of Tourism Anthropology* (Inderscience). Rodanthi has been visiting scholar in Anthropology at Oxford and Sociology at CEMORE, Lancaster. She is author of over 60 articles and 8 monographs, including the latest *Mobility, Modernity and the Slum: The Real and Virtual Journeys of Slumdog Millionaire* (2015).

1 Introduction

Towards an agenda for event mobilities research

Kevin Hannam, Mary Mostafanezhad, and Jillian Rickly

The Slovenian philosopher and cultural critic, Slavoj Žižek describes an event as 'an amphibious notion with even more than fifty shades of grey' (Žižek 2014: 3). He goes on to suggest that 'An "[E]vent" can refer to a devastating natural disaster or the latest celebrity scandal, the triumph of the people or a brutal political change, an intense experience of a work of art or an intimate decision' (ibid). Thus, Žižek describes an event as '*the effect that seems to exceed its causes*–and the *space* of an event is that which opens up by the gap that separates an effect from its causes' (italics in original, 2014: 5). Chapters in this collection integrate the philosophy of event (Badiou 2007a, 2007b, 2013; Bassett 2008; Colwell 1997; Deleuze 1993; Deleuze and Conley 1992; Zourabichvili 2012) with emerging work in the mobilities paradigm as a way to examine the connections and interconnections between people, place, politics and experience. Scholars working in the mobilities paradigm have examined the relationship between large-scale movements of people, objects, capital, and information across the world with more localized processes of daily circulation, movement through public space, and the everyday travel of material things (Hannam et al. 2006). On the other hand, philosophers such as Žižek have described an event as something extraordinary that happens beyond sufficient reason and that has the potential to change or shatter our perceptions of reality (2014: 7). Addressing the relationship between the ordinary and the extraordinary event – or how the ordinary becomes extraordinary and vice versa – is a critical goal of this collection. Further, its authors are concerned with the politics of performing events – both the spectacular and the mundane. Understood in this way, events can tell us much about the way they become ordinary or extraordinary as well as how this classification is historically, politically, and culturally produced. Collectively, the chapters in this collection represent an attempt to map out an emerging 'event mobilities' framework from which to better understand events, not as mobilities but rather, mobilities as assemblages of events.

This framework builds on recent work in tourism mobilities which scholars often conceptualize in terms of involving the interconnections of various movements: the movement of people, the movement of material things, the movement of more intangible thoughts and fantasies, and the use of old as well as new technologies (Sheller and Urry 2004; Hannam et al. 2014). Importantly, scholars argue that it is not just that tourism is a form of mobility, like other forms of mobility such as commuting or migration, but that different mobilities inform and are informed by tourism (Sheller and Urry 2004). This conceptual framing fore-shadows the approach to event studies represented in the chapters in this collection. As events are informed by a range of mobilities, we emphasize how, rather than think in terms of event mobilities, it may be more useful to, conversely, conceptualize mobilities as consisting of networks of events. By focusing on mobilities as networks of events, we open the door for new considerations of the relationships between people, places, and politics at the myriad conjunctures in which they collide.

This collection offers an 'event mobilities' framework from which to analyse diverse 'mega' as well as 'minor' events. For example, rather than focus on spec-tacular mega-events such as the recent Olympic Games in London (Boyle and Haggerty 2009), mobilities scholars have tended to focus on momentary or temporary events, or a series of memorable events: walking, driving, running, flying, cycling, commuting, busking, sailing, boating, skiing, or hunting (Myers and Hannam 2012). Thus, the act of mobility can become the actual event itself (Cidell 2014). Mobilities are articulated in relation to, and as a series of, other sorts of social functions and pursuits, from travelling to work and numerous leisure activities, to going on holiday, leaving a country in search of work or sanctuary, or to hopping on a bus to get to the supermarket. Mobile events might appear to serve as contexts that provide meanings and purpose to a distinct action – from frantically leaving one's home to escape a mudslide to embarking on a protest march. Events are also how mobilities become articulated as meaningful activi-ties within different systems and categories of knowledge. Indeed, place identi-ties, as well as personal identities, are frequently communicated in terms of narratives of events – moments in time-space through which they become linked.

On the one hand, when we consider mobilities as events we also enable mobil-ity to be understood as much more than an undifferentiated flow and instead as a series of identifiable activities. Weddings, for example, routinely involve complex orderings of mobility and proximity in the social, familial and religious obligations to travel to the event (Urry 2002; Sattar et al. 2013). Weddings are also ritualistic and representative of personal identity transformations from (at least) 'unmarried' to 'married'. But frequently such events also involve multiple governance assemblages – for example when a non-EU or non-US citizen seeks to marry an EU or US citizen. This can lead to the reconfiguring of a wedding as a series of multiple events, of multiple weddings in different geographical loca-tions to gain the necessary paperwork rather than an event as a single point in time. Events of love, for example, are institutionalized by the state (Mai and King 2009). Analysing the mobilities of events allows us to make sense of the human and technological systems that societies produce and reproduce. What follows is a review and development of mobilities approaches to researching events. We begin by outlining some of the key concepts in mobilities. We then develop these concepts in terms of event mobilities. Finally, we consider how event mobilities can be conceptualized as interruptions, transitions, framings, and materialities.

Mobilities

Mobilities scholars examine movements of people, objects, capital, and information across the world in ways that emphasize the complexities of mobility and the corollary reconfiguration of geopolitical discourses (Hannam et al. 2006; Hannam 2013). International relations can have profound effects on when, who, and for what reason people are able to freely move across international borders. Geopolitical discourses or 'scripts', as shown in any variety of institutional and popular media, work to divide up the world in ways that can lead to conflicts over space and resources (O'Tuathail 2002). Global media representations contribute to the ongoing ordering of social life and the ways in which people and things move across space and borders. However, mobilities scholars seek to understand how such ordering is also networked with everyday mobilities, developing the notion of performativities and the 'more than representational'. Thus, conceptualizing mobilities is not just about recognizing the interconnections between different forms of mobility such as travel and migration, but developing a more nuanced epistemology of the movements of people, places, and things. Scholars have sought to develop the notion of 'performativity' in relation to mobilities (Nash, 2000; Hannam 2006).

Performativity scholars seek out 'a more embodied way of rethinking the relationships between determining social structures and personal agency' (Nash, 2000: 654). In non-representational theory, meanwhile, scholars examine physical or emotional behaviours that are not necessarily understood through conventional models of human behaviour. Non-representational theories challenge the status of social constructionist understandings of the world by highlighting some of the limitations of representational approaches and suggesting insights from actor-network theory concerning the complex relationships between humans and the material worlds they encounter – often through specific events.

Nigel Thrift (1997: 126–127) explains how non-representational theory is about 'practices, mundane everyday practices, that shape the conduct of human beings toward others and themselves at particular sites.' It is not 'concerned with representation and meaning, but with the performative "presentations", "showings", and "manifestations" of everyday life'. Non-representational theorists examine the ways in which ordinary people appreciate 'the skills and knowledges they get from being embodied beings'. Drawing upon Thrift's work, Nash, meanwhile, argues that the notion of performativity:

> is concerned with practices through which we become 'subjects' decentred, affective, but embodied, relational, expressive and involved with others and objects in a world continually in process. ... The emphasis is on practices that cannot adequately be spoken of, that words cannot capture, that texts cannot convey – on forms of experience and movement that are not only or never cognitive.
>
> (2000: 655)

Thus, the emphasis on pre-linguistic experience is relevant to the analysis of the bodily experience of events.

A crucial complement to understanding the world as 'more than representational' is, therefore, attending to the agency of other people, non-human beings, materialities, and mobilities. With the performative turn, attention to embodiment as well as agency expands enquiries to include relations of power between the actors involved. In the case of a mobilities perspective on events, one need not look further than the use of information technologies (mapping applications, social media, mobile banking, among many others) as changing the conditions of tourism and events mobilities, as well as the way we think about events (see Cresswell and Martin 2012).

The notion of performativity is thus concerned with the ways in which people know the world without knowing it, the multi-sensual practices and experiences of everyday life as such proposes a post-humanistic approach to the understanding of social life. As Peter Adey (2009: 149) notes: '[t]his is an approach which is not limited to representational thinking and feeling, but a different sort of thinking-feeling altogether. It is a recognition that everyday mobilities such as walking or dancing involve various combinations of thought, action, feeling and articulation.' Recently, 'more than representational theory' has been put forward, as a way of analysing the coupling of representations to the non-representational embodied practices discussed above (Adey 2010). Mobilities research thus examines the embodied nature and experience of different modes of travel, seeing these modes in part as forms of material and sociable dwelling-in-motion, places of and for various activities. These 'activities' can include specific forms of talk, work, or information-gathering, but may involve simply being connected, maintaining a moving presence with others that holds the potential for many different convergences or divergences of global and local physical presence (Hannam et al. 2006).

Conceptualizing mobilities also entails attention to how distinct social spaces or 'moorings' orchestrate new forms of social and cultural life (Hannam et al. 2006). Examples include stations, hotels, motorways, resorts, airports, leisure complexes, beaches, galleries, roadside parks, and so on. Understanding mobilities in this context requires a place-based perspective. Places are thus not so much fixed but are implicated within complex networks through which 'hosts, guests, buildings, objects and machines' are contingently brought together to produce certain performances (Hannam et al. 2006: 13). Moreover, places are also 'about proximities, about the bodily co-presence of people who happen to be in that place at that time, doing activities together, moments of physical proximity between people that make travel desirable or even obligatory for some' (Hannam et al. 2006: 13). In their discussion of Singapore as the archetypal 'mobile city', for example, Oswin and Yeoh argue that the:

> mobile city approach understands the city as much more than a calculation of border-crossing labour and capital inputs and outputs. A process-orientation enables examination of interrelationships of movements of people, objects, capital and ideas in and through the overlapping scales of the local, the bodily, the national, and the global.
>
> (2010: 170)

Although mobilities researchers often emphasize multi-scalar relationality (Oswin and Yeoh 2010), in what follows we outline an agenda for place-based research into event mobilities. We also consider how events and the mobilities that make up events also make places through the performativities discussed above.

Conceptualizing event mobilities

Adey et al. (2013) ask: 'How do different events of moving, slowing, staying, passing, pausing, or rushing inform the meaning and experience of mobility?' This question is in part engaged with by Žižek's (2014) who reflects on the philosophical consequences of events. Significantly, Žižek (2014) begins by asking us to take a risk by attempting to define an 'event'. Thus, as we have boarded this train, we are already on the move. As noted above, an event is commonly understood as, at least, something out of place, something shocking that interrupts the normal flow of things that comes out of the blue such as the events of the 'Arab Spring' – a synergy that nobody can actually explain fully. Events then are somewhat enigmatic and imaginative in that, as Žižek contends, they seem to exceed their causes and (2014: 3). Events can be considered as traumatic, life-changing experiences such as the 'intrusion of something new which remains unacceptable for the predominant view' (Žižek 2014: 77). Events, from this perspective are always political, charged with notions of 'freedom' and significantly often involve a degree of excess, violent or otherwise, in the social encounters formed by such events (Badiou 2007a, 2007c, 2013; Heidegger 2012; Zourabichvili 2012).

An event can also be conceived as a change: a change in terms of the ways in which reality may appear to us as well as a transformation of the self. An event thus produces something new and heralds a symbolic transition as social anthropologists have recognized in terms of progression through the human life course in diverse societies (Turner 1969). Žižek (2014) considers the motion of events as 'a change of the very frame through which we perceive the world and engage in it' (Žižek 2014: 10). This alludes to the ways in which films and other media commonly saturate our understandings of events and the places of events as has been demonstrated in analyses of films such as *Slumdog Millionaire* in Mumbai where tourists seek to re-perform significant events from the film while on tour (Diekmann and Hannam 2012) or where Chinese tourists in northern Thailand re-enact scenes from the Chinese blockbuster hit, *Lost in Thailand*, at Chiang Mai University (Mostafanezhad and Promburom 2015). Fundamentally, fiction and reality thus become blurred through touristic events.

Finally, we might also conceptualize events as 'extremely fragile moments' which may be initially memorable but which can easily be forgotten – hence an emphasis on the materialities of events as means through which we attempt to remember them. Time, in terms of past, present and future, then, is an important aspect of events such that many governments and communities now think of their material legacies as much as the events themselves when planning them.

Contra Žižek's (2014) philosophical reflections, events often consist of every-day, mundane mobilities (Edensor 2007). For example, the packing of luggage for an event involves various technologies, while producing worries of loss. Lightness and the use of specially designed travel materials mark the holiday as a special event, one requiring specialised 'skills, routines and reflexes'. The timing of mobility for events is equally informed by more routine moves. How and when people go to work, whether they work from home, and how they use their time while commuting are all 'kinds of event-in-progress' (Adey et al. 2014).

Building off the integration of analytical frameworks drawn from philosophies of event and mobilities literature we outline emerging conceptualizations of an 'event mobilities' framework. In the discussion below we address four dimensions of the 'event in transition' namely, 'interruptions', 'transitions', 'framings', and 'materialities'. Discussion of these dimensions is tempered by the acknowl-edgement that such mobilities are frequently grounded in the more routine aspects of social lives.

Interruptions

Mobilities scholars have conceptualized events as interruptions of mobility. Disaster events, for example, bring to the fore the astounding fragility of complex mobility systems (Hannam et al. 2006). The attacks of 9/11 – an event which many people still find hard to comprehend – embedded into the global conscious-ness not only a massive loss of human life, but also a vision of simultaneous destruction of multiple mobility systems and a disruption of the global discourse of unfettered mobility as a way of life. As Hannam et al. (2006: 7) note, for example:

> A huge node in the global financial trading system was shut down. A major station in the metropolitan transportation system was obliterated. A signifi-cant hub in the telephonic and electronic communications systems fell silent, while the mobile phone network was overwhelmed. And the crucial channels of governmental emergency coordination of police and fireman faltered. Bridges and tunnels were closed to traffic, crowds had to flee Manhattan on foot unable to contact loved ones, and air traffic was placed on an emergency footing. The attacks were perceived as targeting not just the United States at a national scale, but also specifically New York City as a 'global city' of transnational mobility of capital, information and people.

This event was both a significant interruption but also significantly traumatic and clearly led to a further series of events and repercussions that could never have been envisaged or imagined.

The impact of Hurricane Katrina on the US Gulf Coast in September 2005 brought another major American metropolitan area to the point of chaos and total systems failure. The dysfunctional evacuation of New Orleans exacerbated differential mobility empowerments (Tesfahuney 1998). Once the storm hit and flooded out bridges, roads and the power grid, government coordination and civil order collapsed along with communications systems. Simultaneous to these happenings, the ensuing media mobilization of reporters, cameras and satellite-broadcast images revealed to the world the trauma. In addition to other complex issues being brought to the fore, this event ultimately underlined the dependence of the urban USA on complex and tightly interlocking systems of mobility, transportation, and communication to sustain contemporary urban life (Hannam et al. 2006). In their research, Cook and Butz (2015) focus on the Attabad landslide, which destroyed a large section of the arterial roadway in the Gojal district of northern Pakistan, stranding those living north of the landslide. They argue that state 'disaster management strategies enact domination, but also render visible pre-existing relations of domination that were established in the context of road infrastructure development and the region's political liminality' (Cook and Butz 2015: 1).

Birtchnell and Buscher (2011) have commented on the impact of the eruption of the Eyjafjallajökull volcano in Iceland which was measured not in lives lost but in flights lost. The event was not a humanitarian catastrophe, but a logistical calamity, exposing fault-lines in the 'contours of the risk society' (Beck 1992: 19). But this event was significant as it caused an interruption which caused travellers to pause momentarily and reconsider the complex interconnections of aeromobility systems, and debate and formulate alternative imaginaries (Birtchnell and Buscher 2011). Similarly, the more recent 2015 bombing in Bangkok shed light on the role traumatic events can have on perceptions of vulnerability among tourist pedestrians. Located in a major tourist centre, the explosion killed 20 individuals including many international tourists. Media reports focused on the affect the event was anticipated to have on the tourism industry given emergent associations of the city with the bombing. Thus, it interrupted international tourist flows to the country as well as flows of tourist pedestrians who avoided the megacity because of emergent affiliations with pedestrian mobility and risk.

Transitions

To illustrate the notion of the event as mobile transition we can call upon numerous anthropological studies of various rites of passage; the passage from youth to adulthood for instance. From this framework, we could, for example, examine student's gap years, educational exchanges or volunteering experiences as mobile events which are all concerned with transitions. Indeed, many universities and travel companies highlight the need for students to engage with such life-changing events for their future careers. To travel as part of education has been recognized by most cultures around the world and was an integral part of the Grand Tour (Urry 2002). In the 1500s, French writer Montaigne argued that students needed 'some direct adventuring with the world, a steady and lively interplay with common folk, supplemented and fortified with trips abroad' (Brodsky-Porges 1981). Holdsworth (2009: 1852) adds that '[s]tudents are constantly on the move: between halls; from place of residence (which may be halls of residence, privately rented accommodation, or parental home) to campus; as well as from "home" to university'. Engaging in transitional events has arguably led to new cultural forms, including new cultural identities and subjectivities as students travel, for example, as part of the New Zealand overseas experience (OE) (see Conradson and Latham 2007; Cohen 2010; Haverig 2011).

Framings

Contemporary events are also 'framed' by global media systems. Events are nothing without publicity and both cinematic events and events portrayed on social media have significant effects. Drawing upon the concept of performativities, discussed above, the relations between media and mobilities are not determined by each other, rather, they co-exist as relational 'more-than representational mobilities' (Adey 2010: 146). For instance, in their analysis of touristic mobilities in India's slums Diekmann and Hannam (2012) examine the coupling of Western representations of mobilities in films that focus on India's slums with the practices of walking tours as experienced by mostly Western tourists in the slums of Mumbai. They argue that a mobilities approach aids the analysis of the connections between cinematic events such as films and touristic events such as guided tours as more than representational – as simultaneously both visually engaged with, and also embodied through, the concept of performativity.

Regarding mega-events, Rodanthi Tzanelli (2015) offer a mobilities-informed analysis of the ethics and aesthetics of the Football World Cup held in Brazil in 2014. She notes that, '[t]he 2014 mega-event's opening ceremony and the Brazilian mourning of football defeat become chrono-spatial windows to the Brazilian culture's emotional and material movements in the world. Performed Brazilian-style, these movements are recorded in music, rhythm, theatrical performance and (un)choreographed protest in equally important ways ...' (Tzanelli 2015: 6). She goes on to discuss the new technologies that were introduced to frame the World Cup for audiences around the world using over 37 television cameras for each match. Moreover, she further notes that the British football commentators' presentations 'were framed around discourses of travel and mobility: the slum and Carnival capital for Rio; the coastal artistic metropolis for Recife; the country's power base for Brasilia; the Amazonian beautiful but progressively industrialised Manaus; the home of African capoeira for Salvador; and the industrious, concrete but cosmopolitan São Paulo' (Tzanelli 2015: 17). Thus, experiences often become events through global media framing.

Materialities

Material 'stuff' helps to constitute events and this 'stuff' is always in motion, being assembled and reassembled in changing configurations (Sheller and Urry 2006). In their seminal paper, Cook and Crang (1996) discuss how rather than being spatially fixed, the material geographies of food are mobilized within circuits of culinary culture, outlining their production and consumption through processes of commodity fetishism. Cook et al. (1998) then examine how food geographies are the result of 'locally circulated' global flows of agents and knowledge. They suggest that the analysis of the geographies and biographies of food is a vital component of any food analysis, as it illustrates the inter-connectivity between the mobilities of food paths (Cook et al. 1998). And, as we know, food is a core component of the hospitality afforded at events.

However, many events are materializations of past events – heritage – rather than current ones, materials such as food are used to remember past events as Marcel Proust importantly pointed out in his remembrance of taste. The mobile materialities of heritage thus involve complex 'hybrid geographies' (Whatmore 2002) of humans and non-humans that contingently enable people and things to move and to hold their shape as they transit across various regions, both physically and imaginatively. Therefore, there is a complex materiality to being on the move, as heritage events and the things that constitute heritage itself engage with all sorts of materials that enable their movement. Crucial to the recognition of these materialities is an understanding of the corporeal body as an affective vehicle through which we sense place and movement, and construct emotional geographies (Rodaway 1994; Crouch 2000; Bondi et al. 2005). Community traditions often involve the active development and performances of memorable events. Moreover, significant events in people's lives are often ascribed to moving – moving in terms of transitions in life phases and moving more literally in terms of migration.

Basu and Coleman (2008: 317) go on to discuss the idea of 'materialities' in more depth as follows:

> We use the term 'materiality' straightforwardly to refer to physical objects and worlds, but also to evoke more varied – multiple – forms of experience and sensation that are both embodied and constituted through the interactions of subjects and objects. Such interactions are often both moving, in the sense that they stir the emotions, and, indeed, moving, insofar as they entail the movement of both people and things, subjects and objects.

The event of moving home, then, is about encountering a new world, new experiences and a sense of adventure with all the anxieties that this may endure. For many migrant populations there are many material things that become heritage in the present day. Basu and Coleman (2008) emphasize the notion that heritage moves people, physically as well as emotionally and imaginatively to think about their own pasts through different sensations which themselves can be both tangible and intangible – something we can often see in the re-enactment of the past through living history events (Crang 1996; Hannam and Halewood 2006).

Content of the book

The first contribution to this book by Angela Montague examines the mobile imaginaries at work at the Festival in the Desert, Mali. Based upon her fieldwork, she argues that this festival is an event which has become framed by wider geopolitical events but the music continues to be on the move through various cosmopolitan actions. Peter Peters continues the musical theme by focusing on the mobilities of the Dutch violinist and composer André Rieu and his Johan Strauss Orchestra (JSO) – one of the most successful musical touring groups in the world. He further develops the concept of event mobilities in terms of aesthetics of adaptation: acoustic mobilities involve the movement of music as live produced sound and lived experiences, as well as the movement of the various apparatus that enables the performance of music. Next, Karl Spracklen takes us into the world of heavy metal music festivals, connecting ideas concerning events as transition and framing in the context of pilgrimage to the Bloodstock festival. Drawing upon Habermas and Baudrillard he concludes that there are conflicting instrumental rationalities at work around music festivals where the language of global festivals works to stretch the event into a mediatized simulacrum.

Rodanthi Tzanelli takes us further into the mediatization of events in her analysis of the television series *Game of Thrones* (GoT). She notes how as an assemblage of film fans/tourists, digital and cinematic technologies, and natural landscapes, GoT events mobilities (the story, the filmed landscapes' staged tourisms and the fans' actual pilgrimages to them) are subject to multiple interpretations. She argues that the combined epic and mundane mobilities of GoT are not disconnected but part of global cultural and political complexities such that the interplay between these two mobility modes (one slow and mythical, the other fast and everyday) helps to define the motion of events. Rebecca Sheehan takes us away to the circus but in doing so she again links the epic with the mundane by focusing on everyday events for circus performers and how they conceptualize home while being on the move and performing events. She draws upon Ralph and Staeheli's (2011) argument that 'home' may be 'accordion-like', stretching and squeezing people and their materialities in and through different event spaces, such as funerals.

Julie Cidell then considers road races for runners, specifically half marathons, as events that generate unique materialities, mobilities, and immobilities because of their temporalities. Gathering people for the event, carrying out the event itself, and dispersing during and afterwards all involve combinations of bodily mobilities and event mobilities which involve a degree of choreographing. Tani H. Sebro examines the antagonisms between events and mobilities in her study of necromobilities on the Thai/Burma border. She focuses on the choreographing or what she terms the choreomobility of bodies through funerary events which, she argues, involve processes and performances of becoming: vibrant mobilities arise after the death of the body. Funerals as death-events may be punctures in the seemingly stable world of everyday lives but also help with social transitions even in the face of violence. Theoretically such events problematize the geographies of the 'more than representational' by further disturbing notions of temporality such that '[s]paces and times are folded, allowing distant presences, events, people and things to become rather more intimate' (Maddern and Adey 2008: 292). The ways in which space and time are folded and refolded to reconnect memories is further explored by Lisa C. Braverman in her chapter. She integrates mobilities with rhetorical theory, to advance the notion that 'slogans of mobility' help frame event mobilities. The events of the Holocaust are thus mapped and brought to political life in the present through contemporary social media discussions using #WeAreHere.

While food has been widely theorized as a key element of contemporary mobilities, Elizabeth Louis, examines how the media has been prominent in organizing 'Food Sovereignty Galas' – events which range from small localized struggles to large international events like the Slow Food Movement. She argues that food sovereignty events serve as important points of juncture or puncture where discourses collide, mediate events and are then re-presented by attendees. Thus, ideas of food sovereignty have become as mobile as the world-travelling celebrities that develop this mode of advocacy but this celebrity ultimately dislocates them from the contexts that they seek to promote. The final chapter discusses the dislocations involved in food mobilities in a rather different context. Ali Abdallah and Kevin Hannam reflect on the development of Lebanese cuisine in London through the experiences of Lebanese migrants. They argue that Lebanese culture has placed great emphasis upon the production of food as a key but arguably quixotic event in Lebanese social life and as such this has played a significant part in the development of its global diaspora identity.

Conclusions

In an age of intensified mobilities where people continuously schedule more events into their electronic calendars on their smartphones, tablets, and laptops, it perhaps seems self-evident that events lead to even more events (Urry 2007). This introduction has sought to provide a framework for what we are calling a mobilities approach to the study of events. In doing so, we have developed conceptual dimensions of event mobilities in terms of interruptions, transitions, framings and materialities.

In conclusion we note that a mobilities approach to events might require the use of more innovative methodologies to understand and capture the movement involved in any event. Doing mobilities research thus involves paying attention to how people, things, and seemingly intangible entities such as ideas are on the move, as well as how environments themselves make a difference. Law and Urry (2004: 403) have argued that existing methodologies:

> deal, for instance, poorly with the fleeting – that which is here today and gone tomorrow, only to re-appear again the day after tomorrow. They deal poorly with the distributed – that is to be found here and there but not in between – or that which slips and slides between one place and another. They deal poorly with the multiple – that which takes different shapes in different places. They deal poorly with the non-causal, the chaotic, the complex.

If we are to adequately understand the ontology of contemporary mobilities then we also need to have mobile methodologies not necessarily to 'capture' but to keep pace with the fluid (dis)order and (dis)embeddedness of (de)territorialized social life (D'Andrea 2006). Specific methods of data collection require a more 'flexible, informal and context dependent [approach], partly mimicking mobile subjects being studied in their own suppleness' (D'Andrea 2006: 113; see also Adey et al. 2013; Merriman 2014). As the chapters in this collection demonstrate, an 'event mobilities' framework opens up new possibilities for understanding the ways in which events are mediated by the politics of place and performance.

References

Abbott, A. (2001) *Time Matters: On Theory and Method.* Chicago: University of Chicago Press.

Adey, P. (2009) *Mobility.* London: Routledge.

Adey, P., Bissell, D., Merriman, P., Hannam, K. and Sheller, M. (eds.) (2013) *The Routledge Handbook of Mobilities.* London: Routledge.

Basu, P. and Coleman, S. (2008) Introduction: Migrant worlds, material cultures. *Mobilities* 3(3): 313–330.

Beck U. (1992) *Risk Society: Towards a New Modernity.* London: Sage.

Birtchnell, T. and Büscher, M. (2011) Stranded: An Eruption of Disruption. *Mobilities*, 6(1): 1–9.

Badiou, A. (2007a) *Being and Event*: London: Continuum.

Badiou, A. (2007b) The event in Deleuze. *Parrhesia*, 2, 37–44.

Badiou, A. (2013) *Philosophy and the Event.* New York: Polity.

Bassett, K. (2008) Thinking the event: Badiou's philosophy of the event and the example of the Paris Commune. *Environment and Planning D: Society and Space*, 26(5): 895–910.

Bondi, L., Smith, M. and Davidson, J. (eds.) (2005) *Emotional Geographies.* Farnham: Ashgate.

Boyle, P. and Haggerty, K. (2009) Spectacular security: Mega-events and the security complex. *International Political Sociology*, 3(3): 257–274.

Brodsky-Porges, E. (1981) The Grand Tour: Travel as an educational device, 1600–1800. *Annals of Tourism Research*, 8(2): 171–186.

Cidell, J. (2014) Running road races as transgressive event mobilities. *Social and Cultural Geography*, 15(5): 571–583.

Cohen, S. A. (2010) Personal identity (de)formation among lifestyle travellers: a double-edged sword. *Leisure Studies*, 29, 289–301.

Colwell, C. (1997) Deleuze and Foucault: Series, event, genealogy. *Theory and Event*, 1(2).

Conradson, D. and Latham, A. (2007) The affective possibilities of London: Antipodean transnationals and the overseas experience. *Mobilities*, 2(2): 231–254.

Cook, I. and Crang, P. (1996) The world on a plate: Culinary culture, displacement and geographical knowledges. *Journal of Material Culture*, 1(2): 131–153.

Cook, I., Crang, P. and Thorpe, M. (1998) Biographies and geographies: Consumer understandings of the origins of foods. *British Food Journal*, 100(3): 162–167.

Cook, N. and Butz, D. (2015) Mobility justice in the context of disaster. *Mobilities*, DOI: 10.1080/17450101.2015.1047613

Crang, M. (1996) Magic kingdom or a quixotic quest for authenticity. *Annals of Tourism Research*, 23(2): 415–431.

Cresswell, T. (2006) *On the Move: Mobility in the Modern West.* New York: Routledge.

Cresswell, T. and Martin, C. (2012) On turbulence: Entanglements of disorder and order on a Devon beach. *Tijdschrift voor economische en sociale geografie*, 105, 516–529.

Crouch, D. (2000) Places around us: Embodied lay geographies in leisure and tourism. *Leisure Studies*, 19(2): 63–76.

D'Andrea, A. (2006) Neo-nomadism: A theory of post-identitarian mobility in the global age, *Mobilities*, 1(1), 95–119.

Deleuze, G. (1993) *The Fold: Leibniz and the Baroque*: Minneapolis: University of Minnesota Press.

Diekmann, A., and Hannam, K. (2012) Touristic mobilities in India's slum spaces. *Annals of Tourism Research*, 39(3): 1315–1336.

Edensor, T. (2007) Mundane mobilities, performances and spaces of tourism. *Social and Cultural Geography*, 8(2): 199–215.

Graham, S. and Marvin, S. (2001) *Splintering Urbanism: Networked Infrastructures, Technological Mobilities and the Urban Condition*. London: Routledge.

Hall, C. M. (2006) Urban entrepreneurship, corporate interests and sports mega events: the thin policies of competitiveness within the hard outcomes of neoliberalism. *The Sociological Review*, 54(2): 59–70.

Hannam, K. (2006) Tourism and Development III: Performance, performativities and mobilities. *Progress in Development Studies*, 6(3): 243–249.

Hannam, K. (2013) 'Shangri-La' and the new 'great game': Exploring tourism geopolitics between China and India. *Tourism, Planning and Development*, 10(2): 178–186.

Hannam, K. and Halewood, C. (2006) European Viking festivals: An expression of identity. *Journal of Heritage Tourism*, 1(1): 17–31.

Hannam, K., Butler, G., and Paris, C. (2014) Developments and key concepts in tourism mobilities. *Annals of Tourism Research*, 44(1): 171–185.

Hannam, K., Sheller, M. and Urry, J. (2006) Mobilities, immobilities and moorings. *Mobilities*, 1(1): 1–22.

Haverig, A. (2011) Constructing global/local subjectivities – The New Zealand OE as governance through freedom. *Mobilities*, 6(1): 102–123.

Heidegger, M. (2012) *Contributions to Philosophy (of the Event)*. Bloomington: Indiana University Press.

Holdsworth, C. (2009) 'Going away to uni': mobility, modernity, and independence of English higher education students. *Environment and Planning A* 41(8): 1849–1864.

Law, J. and Urry, J. (2004) Enacting the Social. *Economy and Society*, 33(3): 390–410.

Maddern, J. and Adey, P. (2008) Editorial: spectro-geographies. *Cultural Geographies*, 15(3): 291–295.

Mai, N. and King, R. (2009) Love, sexuality and migration: Mapping the issue(s). *Mobilities*, 4(3): 295–307.

Merriman, P. (2014) Rethinking Mobile Methods. *Mobilities*, 9, 167–187.

Mostafanezhad, M., and Promburom, T. (2015). *Lost in Thailand: The Popular Geopolitics of Chinese Film Tourism in Northern Thailand*. Paper presented at the International Conference on Tourism and Ethnicity in ASEAN and Beyond, Chiang Mai, Thailand.

Myers, L. and Hannam, K. (2012) Adventure tourism as a series of memorable events: women traveller's experiences of New Zealand. In Shipway, R. (ed.) *International Sports Events*. London: Routledge.

Nash, C. (2000) Performativity in practice: some recent work in cultural geography. *Progress in Human Geography*, 24(4): 653–664.

Oswin, N. and Yeoh, B. (2010) Introduction: Mobile city Singapore. *Mobilities*, 5(2): 167–175.

O'Tuathail, G. (2002) Post-cold war geopolitics: Contrasting superpowers in a world of global dangers. In R. J. Johnson, P. Taylor, and M. Watts (eds), *Geographies of Global Change* (2nd edn). Oxford: Blackwell.

Ralph, D. and Staeheli, L. (2011) Home and migration: Mobilities, belongings, and identities. *Geography Compass*, 5(7): 517–530.

Rodaway P. (1994) *Sensuous Geographies: Body, Sense and Place*. London: Routledge.

Sattar, Z., Hannam, K. and Ali, N. (2013) Religious obligations to travel. *Journal of Tourism and Cultural Change*, 11(1–2): 61–72.

Sheller, M. and Urry, J. (eds) (2004) *Tourism Mobilities: Places to Play, Places in Play*. London: Routledge.

Tesfahuney, M. (1998) Mobility, racism and geopolitics. *Political Geography*, 17(5): 499–515.

Thrift, N. (1997) The still point. In: Pile, S., Keith, M. (eds) *Geographies of Resistance*. London: Routledge, pp. 124–151.

Turner, V. (1969) *The Ritual Process: Structure and Anti-Structure*. London: Aldine.

Tzanelli, R. (2015) *Socio-Cultural Mobility and Mega-Events: Ethics and Aesthetics in Brazil's 2014 World Cup*. London: Routledge.

Urry J. (1995) *Consuming Places*. London: Routledge.

Urry, J. (2002) *The Tourist Gaze*. London: Sage.

Urry, J. (2007) *Mobilities*. London: Sage.

Veijola, S. and Jokinen, E. (1994) The body in tourism. *Theory, Culture and Society*, 11(3): 125–151.

Whatmore S. (2002) *Hybrid Geographies: Natures, Cultures and Spaces*. London: Sage.

Žižek, S. (2014) *Event: Philosophy in Transit*. Harmondsworth: Penguin.

Zourabichvili, F. (2012) *Deleuze, a Philosophy of the Event: Together with the Vocabulary of Deleuze*: Edinburgh: Edinburgh University Press.

2 All the way to Timbuktu

Mobilizing imaginaries in the globalized space of the Festival in the Desert, Mali

Angela Montague

Heralded as the most remote music festival in the world, the Festival in the Desert[1] is a globally recognized event held annually outside the city of Timbuktu in Mali, West Africa. Conceived of by members of the Tuareg rock band, Tinariwen, it is described as a melding of 'modernity and tradition' – essentially a world music festival grafted onto nomadic gatherings of Malian Tuareg.[2] Organizers of the Festival had many hopes and, until recently, it had many positive outcomes for Tuareg groups, the state of Mali, and tourists. But from the start it was a fragile enterprise fraught with contradictions. Born out of the 1990s' Tuareg rebellion,[3] the Festival stood as an emblem of peace and diplomacy in the region. That is until 2012 when it was displaced by a renewed rebellion that catapulted the region into chaos. As the city of Timbuktu fell into the hands of supporters of Al-Qaeda of the Islamic Maghreb (AQIM), Shari'a law was instituted, outlawing secular music and celebrations in many cities in Northern Mali. Locals, including musicians and the Festival itself, were forced into exile. As of this writing, Timbuktu is no longer occupied by AQIM and in June 2015, Tuareg 'rebels' signed a peace deal with the government giving partial autonomy to the north of the country. The Festival in the Desert, however, has not returned since 2012.

The festival provides a rich case study of the benefits and perils of tourism in postcolonial multicultural nations and in wider globalizing frames.[4] It emblemizes new directions in tourism and mobility studies as it provides a necessary counter-narrative to the notion that host and guest relations are necessarily polarized. For hosts are also guests, and tourists are also toured at events such as festivals. As will become apparent in this chapter, global forces shed light on several so-called dualisms, however instead of favouring one over the other (global over local, for instance), they become reconstituted in and through tourism. In a matrix of 'urban' centres (Bamako, Timbuktu, etc.), and differing cosmopolitanisms (tourists, refugees, nomads and urbanites), we see that tourism development complicates the classic divides between urban and rural, traditional and modern, host and guest, because each necessitates the other.

Popular understandings of globalization view it as a process of increased interconnectedness and global cultural flows, while cosmopolitanism could be seen as the effect, response, or perhaps the lived experience of those who engage with these processes. It involves those who 'seek human solidarities beyond national loyalties' (Glick Schiller 2010: 414); it is a mode of 'dealing with diversity' (Nowicka 2012: 3), as well as 'a dynamic between universalisms and diversity, constructed in encounters between people' (Salazar 2010: 56). With the festival now in exile, renamed the 'Caravan for Peace', organizers are working to bring its message of peace and intercultural dialogue to the world. These processes create several types of cosmopolitanisms, including: tourism as cosmopolitanism in practice (cf: Salazar 2010), nomads as 'ironic cosmopolitans' (Silverman 2012), and refugees as perhaps forced or ambivalent cosmopolitans. Although these movements bring people together from all walks of life, one must not lose sight of power differentials by simply celebrating mobility (Glick Schiller and Salazar 2013). In all of these examples, one side of the equation will quite often have more power in terms of who can travel, why they travel, and whose travel is seen as prestigious.

Kalashnikovs and electric guitars

On the first full moon of 2001, in the village of Tin Essako, thousands of kilometres from the capital of Bamako, the Festival in the Desert was born. This was only a few years after an armed rebellion led by a group of Tuareg revolutionaries, known as *ishumar*, took place against the state of Mali from 1990–1995. Roughly defined as Tuareg intellectuals, *ishumar* were often refugees in Libya and Algeria having fled Mali after the 1960s' rebellion against the newly independent state of Mali, others during the drought of the 1980s. Perhaps derived from the French *chômeur* (an unemployed person), *ishumar* were also made up of young men seeking livelihoods as well as exile in the more prosperous nations of North Africa. Many *ishumar* had become politicized in their feelings of abandonment by the state of Mali. Counted among them were members of the Grammy Award winning Tuareg rock band Tinariwen, who claim they met in a refugee camp in Libya where they had learned to use Kalashnikovs and electric guitars (Tinariwen 2001: 4–5). In fact, at the time of the 1990s' rebellion, owning Tinariwen cassettes could lead to imprisonment as their songs carried messages of the separatist movement (Lecocq 2004: 97). The rebellion ended in 1996 after peace negotiations took place, finalized with a symbolic burning of (Tuareg) weapons known as the *Flame de la Paix* [Flame of Peace]. The Festival in the Desert has been described as a manifestation of what was envisioned in the Flame of Peace, namely the integration of all Malians into one unified nation.

The envisioning of the Festival came in the late 1990s when Tinariwen and the French fusion band Lo'Jo played together in Bamako. Lo'Jo subsequently invited Tinariwen to perform at Les Nuits Toucouleurs Festival in France soon afterward. Manny Ansar (who was their manager at the time, and is the current Festival producer and director) said that performing at this festival reminded them of gatherings that used to happen in their own villages back home. It is from this that they began formulating the idea for a festival in the desert. Its first year, organizers estimated that there were close to 3,000 nomads in attendance along with a few hundred tourists (including Malians from the south) (Ansar interview,

February 2011). The initial idea was for the Festival to be nomadic like the Tuareg, moving each year to a different Tuareg village in Northern Mali, leaving behind a trail of economic development. But this proved too challenging given the logistics of staging such a large event in remote areas. Beginning in 2003, it was held in Essakane, an oasis village just sixty kilometres from Timbuktu. Essakane is a traditional meeting point for nomads according to Manny, and it is also home to his clan (*tewsit*), the Kel Ansar (Kel Antessar alternately).

The *Festival in the Desert* took place each January (until recently) and incorporates three days of musical acts from around the world, with particular emphasis on Tuareg and Malian musicians. There are two stages. The 'Scène Traditionnelle' (also called the small stage), is dedicated to Tuareg traditional music such as the *tendé*, which describes the instrument (a mortar drum) as well as the genre of music. These performances take place during the day and are part of other traditional festivities such as poetry and dance contests and camel races. The other stage, the 'Grande Scène', is a large concert stage with lights and amplification where evening performances by world-famous Malian, Tuareg, and international musicians[5] take place. While the smaller stage is specifically reserved for 'traditional' music, the internationally acclaimed band Tartit, who plays what is considered 'traditional' Tuareg music, performs on the main stage. Thus the divide is not absolute.

For over a decade, the festival was a way in which organizers attempted to use the globalized space provided by tourism to promote peace and intercultural dialogue, and as I argue, to stake a claim to their place within the nation of Mali. The festival was born out of the 1990s' rebellion, yet under the direction of Manny, positioned itself within the goals of peace and reconciliation, promoting Malian music at an otherwise Tuareg event. The festival is thus an attempt at democratic peace brokering and diplomacy in a multicultural context, and, as such, fits well within the rubric of other world music festivals that promote music as the 'weapon of peace'. Similarly, tourism has been described as the 'largest peaceful movement of people across cultural boundaries in the history of the world' (Lett 2012: 275). However, as with many projects of multiculturalism, there are multiple layers of conflict that cannot be ignored by the supposed panacea of music or tourism.

Festivalizing tourism

Events such as festivals are found in nearly every society and are increasingly staged as a means to attract tourists to specific locations. Festivals are a perfect site for investigating the spatial-temporal aspects of tourism mobilities and highlighting the interconnectivity of hosts and guests. Festivals are the perfect distillation of local culture, making visible the social life of foreign places in ways that a tourist could not see or participate in on any given day. As Kirshenblatt-Gimblett states: 'The foreign vacationer at a local festival achieves perfect synchrony: everyone is on holiday, or so it seems … To festivalize culture is to make every day a holiday' (1998: 62). Since the late 1960s there has been a steady increase in newly created festivals around the world, some with long histories that have been 'rediscovered,' reinvigorated, or reinvented; others newly created, 'often as a response to a myriad of social, political, demographic and economic realities' (Picard and Robinson 2006: 2).

Overall, this 'proliferation' of festivals, although part of a complex process, has been interpreted as a means by which communities seek to 're-assert their identities in the face of a feeling of cultural dislocation brought about by rapid structural change' (ibid; see also De Bres and Davis 2001). Picard and Robinson contend that the growing number of festivals reflects a 'feeling of crisis in situations where recognized systems of symbolic continuity are challenged by the realities of new social, economic, and political environments' (2006: 2). Many Tuareg throughout North and West Africa have seen their traditional nomadic lifestyles upset. Beginning with European colonization at the end of the nineteenth century, this disruption has been continuing since independence in the 1960s when national borders cut off their traditional routes, followed by drought and desertification, which decimated their herds in the 1970s and 1980s.

Historically, Tuareg would meet after seasonal migrations and celebrate with music, poetry, camel races and other festivities. Largely abandoned due to forced sedentarism, exile, political and economic upheaval, the Festival in the Desert was, for twelve years, a way to fight back against disenfranchisement. In my interviews with Malian attendees, festival organizers, and tour operators at the Festival, I asked what the purpose of the festival was and why it is important to Tuareg, specifically. Their answers to these questions can be roughly categorized into three types: recognition, bridge building, and preservation. Many of these same sentiments can be found in this quote from the Festival website that describes its purpose:

> The organization of the Festival, with its focus on combining modernity and tradition, is driven by a strong desire to open its doors to the outside world, while still preserving the cultures and traditions of the desert; for some this signifies being listened to and then recognized, for others it is a way to discover the desert through the inhabitants' values of hospitality and tolerance.
>
> ('History: Festival Au Désert' 2013)

Recognition is key for many subaltern subjects, and so-called 'branding' in tourism is one way to achieve recognition. Situated within neoliberal development strategies, tourism is promoted as a way for communities in low-income nations to enter into the global economy without competing with larger economies' commodities. The Festival is a way that Tuareg can essentially brand their culture for sale on the world market. The idea is to show who the Tuareg are, invite outsiders to see their culture, and hope foreigners pay attention when they are experiencing hardship (perhaps in the form of aid). Issa Dicko, one of the initial organizers, said that the rebellion of the 1990s was one way to bring international attention to the 'drastic situation of the Tuaregs of Mali'. His feelings were that if the world knew who the Tuareg were they would come to their aid during times of crisis. 'Thanks to the festival', he says, 'Tuareg culture is being promoted across the world ... It's a very strong message of peace addressed to the people of Africa and the world' (interview in Brouet 2004).

Tuareg participants feel that the Festival is a way of reaching out to the global community, creating intercultural dialogue, and building bridges between cultures. For many Malians, tourism provides a rare opportunity to interact with outsiders and learn about their cultures. In effect, it is a way to have a cosmopolitan experience without having to travel. It is a venue that brings people together from all walks of life to share, celebrate, and by extension consume, Tuareg culture. In his memoirs, Intagrist el Ansari, a Tuareg journalist, says that at the Festival, 'One can cross both ministers, ambassadors, Princess Caroline of Monaco, a billionaire owner of the famous MTV, and a shepherd who supports his eight children with five goats, or a craftsman who offers his crafts; all so different and so similar, taking place on the same large white dune, of fine and pristine sand' (El Ansari 2010). In these 'contact zones,' diverse people come together and interact over the course of the festival, perhaps seeking understanding of each other (cf: Pratt 1992). Cultural tourism is like a dialogue between different groups who are seeking common ground, i.e. cosmopolitanism in practice (Salazar 2010). We are reminded here of Victor Turner's term *communitas* – that point in ritual when all distinctions of difference are stripped down and a sort of unity is achieved. Those with whom I spoke in Mali felt that intercultural dialogue, stemming from tourism, was essential to breaking down barriers of difference. At the 2011 Festival, announcers frequently described the Festival as a 'bridge between cultures', much to the chagrin of cynical tourists. Are the differences really stripped down when so much of cultural tourism is about exotification?

Tuareg participants had hoped to make a lasting impression on visitors' lives at the Festival. But how much do tourists' experiences change them? As Edward Bruner concludes in his article, 'Transformation of Self in Tourism', the tourist probably changes very little, whereas the 'toured' (particularly in 'Third World' destinations) often experience profound changes, not all positive (1991; see also Graburn 2004). Tuareg who promote tourism in Mali mentioned that some of the changes they hoped for were monetary, but they also hoped that through 'intercultural dialogue' visitors would appreciate Tuareg culture. The idea was to 'promote and preserve' Tuareg culture through gaining attention of those in wealthy nations, which by extension, would hopefully bring economic development to the area.

Unfortunately, the cost of organizing the Festival is purportedly very high. Because it is literally in the middle of the desert, everything has to be brought in – toilets, water, electricity – and this is no small feat in a nation lacking such infrastructure for many of its own citizens. Manny stated that Festival organizers have always made sure to balance the numbers of attendees, to simultaneously 'grow the festival, without losing its intimacy', he said. By making only 1,000 tickets available for sale, they hoped to keep it from being overrun by outsiders, although they do allow all Africans, not just Malians, free admission. As already mentioned, a major goal of the Festival was to bring economic development to northern communities, which it had done to a certain extent. Since its inception, the Festival has helped renovate several classrooms near Essakane, pay the salary of a teacher, cover full board for nomadic students in Bamako, provide books and other materials to students, deepen wells, and provide malaria drugs in nomadic camps, according to the website. In contrast, Manny said that the Festival rarely carried any profit and had never reached its ideal of bringing sustainable development to Tuareg communities in the north. Some Tuareg with whom I spoke complained that overall there were never enough paying attendees. Others complained that there were too many non-Tuareg Malians in attendance, especially in the later years when it was closer to Timbuktu. Due to travel advisories regarding potential terrorist attacks in areas around the Festival, it was moved from its location in Essakane to just 10 kilometres outside Timbuktu beginning in 2010. Manny said that moving closer to Timbuktu (for the supposed safety of the tourists) meant that it was too far for many nomads to travel. In 2011, several of my Tuareg consultants felt that in general the Festival was losing its traditional aspects, which they saw as essential for preserving their culture. Many felt that this is what the (mostly European) tourists wanted. 'They came for the nomads not the city-dwellers', said one consultant.

Mobilizing imaginaries

In order to understand the mobility of tourism imaginaries, I suggest that we view tourism as part of a discursive practice between sending and receiving nations whereby the social relations between the tourist and the toured are constituted in a set of hierarchical, historic relations stemming from colonial and Orientalist imaginaries (Said 1979). I take tourism marketing to be a prime example of Western discourse about the 'Other'. In this, the so-called 'West' has historically created an image of Africa that is then adopted by Africans through a practice of self-exotification that they then 'perform' for contemporary tourists through the process of branding themselves as an exotic culture. Thus, ontologically speaking, tourists go in search of an Africa already constructed in and through their own social histories in what has been called the 'tourism imaginary', a sort of social practice that creates a tourist destination as 'credible' by appealing to preconceived notions of a destination and its people (Urry 1990; see also Salazar 2012). I found it apparent in my research that tourists seemed to be in search of confirmation of what they expected a destination *should* be. Furthermore, Africans themselves use these stereotypes to perform back tourists' expectations.

During my 2005 research trip to Mali, I acted as a tour guide for four Americans associated with an import store in the Pacific Northwest. The destination they most anticipated was the Festival in the Desert, and specifically travelling to the fabled city of Timbuktu. The thought of going to Timbuktu carries with it a wide array of predetermined mental imagery – one tourist stated that it was the most intriguing part of the trip. Timbuktu is the quintessential out-of-the-way place, colloquially equivalent to 'the middle of nowhere'. It represents a challenge and holds an aura of escape. Once fabled as the 'El Dorado of Africa', Timbuktu is conceived of as any distant or outlandish place. Once a major cosmopolitan city, many outside of Africa do not in fact know that it is a real city in the nation of Mali. Even fewer will make the journey there. However, Timbuktu is a prime destination for some travellers. As a UNESCO World Heritage Site, tourism makes up a large part of its economy. Until recently, daily lines formed outside the Ministry of Tourism where one could have their passport stamped with the city's seal. As the mayor of the city put it, 'Our asset is our name'. According to Aminata Traoré, Mali's Minister for Culture and Tourism between 1997 and 2000 and a former co-ordinator of the United Nations Development Programme, 'The word "Timbuktu" says something to everybody, even to those who couldn't find Mali on a map' (Mail & Guardian, 2003).

How do Tuareg at the Festival capitalize on this appeal? Through branding themselves as nomads. There is much romanticism attached to Tuareg nomadism that dates back several centuries when they were regarded by the French as the last of the noble savages. I have found that Tuareg are savvy to these clichés and actively seek to capitalize on them through self-exotification. For instance, while attending the Festival, I was frequently approached by men in indigo veils (*tagelmoust*) who introduced themselves by saying, 'Je suis Tuareg; je suis nomad'. Nomadism is perhaps the most prominent stereotype of Tuareg, eclipsing even the romantic moniker 'Blue Men of the Desert'. In fact, much of Tuareg identity rests on being nomadic. I asked several of my consultants and friends what it means to be Tuareg, and nearly everyone responded first, 'to be a nomad'. Even if they live in the city full time, this is still an important facet of Tuareg identity. One consultant, a development worker, said 'I still go visit my herds several times a year, and if I can't, I rearrange my furniture. You see: I am still on the move!'

Throughout my fieldwork in 2011, I worked with several individuals whose work centred on the goal of 'preserving and protecting' Tuareg heritage or *toumast*. Manny said that producing the Festival is about preserving as well as promoting Tuareg intangible cultural heritage. Throughout the day, conferences were held at the Festival on topics ranging from education to health to culture. In conferences attended by more urban, cosmopolitan Tuareg, the topic of preserving Tuareg heritage was explicitly discussed, such as one I attended that was hosted by members of the band Tartit, who were promoting their school for traditional Tuareg music. In contrast, conferences that were attended by largely rural and nomadic Tuareg, elders discussed topics such as how to build wells and create jobs in nomadic areas. I noticed that the latter were not focused on preserving their culture; instead they spoke of possible solutions to pragmatic problems. What I contend is that, those who are further from their culture, those who no longer live it daily, are the ones who are most set on its safeguarding. In effect, it is cosmopolitan, urban Tuareg who act as 'culture brokers'[6] (Kurin 1997). Thus, we see how urban practices do not take over or erase the rural, or nomadic; one's existence relies on the other. Urban Tuareg see themselves as the guardians of

Tuareg heritage and identity that resides in rural/nomadic areas of Mali. The Festival in the Desert acts as a showcase of nomadic culture, preserving local culture, while also being a novel invention set on bringing economic development to nomads, and creating what organizers deemed spaces of intercultural dialogue. However, these processes are predicated on an imaginary, where both sides take part in distilling the story of the 'Other.'

Conclusion

As I have argued, tourism imaginaries are dialogic, part of a back-and-forth discourse that both expands in its reach and contracts in its story over time. This process is not unidirectional. I view it as part of a complex matrix of overlapping *scapes* (Appadurai 1990), where global flows are part of a shifting world navigated by multiple actors where understanding is articulated within 'contact zones' (Pratt 1992). As Marta Amico says of the Festival, '[It] is a powerful means for staging identity, which transforms the festival into a social space where people define themselves in a game of *reciprocal* gazes' (2014: 98, emphasis added). Both sides take part. However, these contact zones are never power-neutral. Pratt defines contact zones as 'social spaces where cultures meet, clash, and grapple with each other, often in contexts of highly asymmetrical relations of power ...' (1992: 43). Tourists as 'global nomads' gain prestige through their travels and choose when and where they go, and what they believe is 'authentic'. Most Tuareg as 'pastoral nomads' have found their movements stunted by national borders, their livelihoods reshaped by the global economy, and their movements often criminalized. Recently, as refugees, many Tuareg have been forced out of their homes and away from their culture and livelihoods, into neighbouring countries where they may or may not be warmly welcomed. In all, the binaries of urban/rural, traditional/modern, global/local, are not broken down in these touristic spaces as much as they are imbricated, one on top of the other, layered, without ever losing sight of each other, creating new forms of mobility where the global and the local are both 'cosmopolitan'.

Notes

1. Anglicized from the French: *Le Festival au Désert*.
2. Tuareg is an outsider term for an internally stratified group of pastoral nomads who refer to themselves as Kel Tamasheq, or 'those who speak Tamasheq', a Libeo-Berber language. I use the term Tuareg (alternately Touareg) to be consistent with other American anthropological works on this group.
3. There have been a series of revolts by Tuareg separatists against the state of Mali following independence from French colonial rule in 1960. Tuareg grievances include loss of land and livelihood, lack of infrastructure and development, and little to no representation in national government.
4. Information for this chapter is based on ethnographic fieldwork conducted between 2004–2005 and 2010–2011 in Bamako and Timbuktu where I lived with Kel Ansar families from Goundam. In 2005 and 2011, I attended the Festival and interviewed participants.

5. Malian musicians include Oumou Sangaré, Khaira Arby, Habib Koyate, Ali Farka Touré, Salif Keita, Bassekou Kouyaté among others. Tuareg musicians include Bombino, Tartit, Tinariwen. International musicians include Robert Plant, Jimmy Buffet, and in 2012 Bono finally made an appearance.
6. Kurin describes a cultural broker as someone who is charged with representing and interpreting someone, someplace, or something through cultural programmes such as museums and festivals for those outside of that culture.

References

Amico, M. (2014) The staged desert: Tourist and nomad encounters at the Festival au Desert. In Kruger, S. and Trandafoiu, R. (eds) *The Globalization of Musics in Transit: Music, Migration and Tourism*. London: Routledge, pp. 86–100.

Appadurai, A. (1990) Disjuncture and difference in the global cultural economy. *Theory, Culture & Society*, 7(2): 295–310.

Brouet, L. (2004) *Festival in the Desert*. [DVD] World Village: USA.

Bruner, E. M. (1991) Transformation of self in tourism. *Annals of Tourism Research*, 18(2): 238–50.

De Bres, K. and Davis, J. (2001) Celebrating group and place identity: A case study of a new regional festival. *Tourism Geographies*, 3(3): 326–337.

El Ansari, I. (2010) Memoir: 'Le Festival Au Désert'. Available online: http://www.afri-cultures.com/php/?nav=article&no=9796.

Glick Schiller, N. (2010) Old baggage and missing luggage: A commentary on Beck and Sznaider's 'Unpacking cosmopolitanism for the social sciences: a research agenda'. *British Journal of Sociology*, 61(S1): 413–420.

Glick Schiller, N. and Salazar, N. B. (2013) Regimes of mobility across the globe. *Journal of Ethnic and Migration Studies*, 39(2): 183–200.

Graburn, N. H. (2004) Secular ritual: A general theory of tourism. In S. Gmelch (ed.) *Tourists and Tourism: A Reader*. Illinois: Waveland Press Inc., pp. 23–34.

Kirshenblatt-Gimblett, B. (1998) *Destination Culture: Tourism, Museums, and Heritage*. Berkeley, CA: University of California Press.

Kurin, R. (1997) *Reflections of a Culture Broker: A View from the Smithsonian*. Washington, D.C.: Smithsonian Institution Press.

Lecocq, B. (2004) Unemployed intellectuals in the Sahara: The Teshumara Nationalist Movement and the revolutions in Tuareg society. *International Review of Social History*, 49, 87–109.

Lett, J. (2012) Epilogue. In V. Smith (ed.) *Hosts and Guests: The Anthropology of Tourism*. Philadelphia: University of Pennsylvania Press, pp. 275–279.

Mail & Guardian (2003) Timbuktu: Sages, camel trains and sand dunes. Available online: http://mg.co.za/article/2003-10-23-timbuktu-sages-camel-trains-and-sand-dunes Accessed 26 November 2014.

Nowicka, M. (2012) Cosmopolitans, spatial mobility and the alternative geographies. *International Review of the Social Research*, 2(3): 1–16.

Picard, D. and Robinson, M. (2006) Remaking worlds: Festivals, tourism and change. In D. Picard and M. Robinson (eds) *Festivals, Tourism, and Social Change: Remaking Worlds*. Clevedon: Channel View Publications, pp. 1–31.

Pratt, M. L. (1992) *Imperial Eyes: Travel Writing and Transculturation*. London: Routledge.

Said, E. W. (1979) *Orientalism*. New York: Vintage.

Salazar, N. B. (2010) Tourism and cosmopolitanism: A view from below. *International Journal of Tourism Anthropology*, 1(1): 55–69.

Salazar, N. B. (2012) Tourism imaginaries: A conceptual approach. *Annals of Tourism Research*, 39(2): 863–882.

Silverman, C. (2012) *Romani Routes: Cultural Politics and Balkan Music in Diaspora.* New York: Oxford University Press.

Tinariwen (2001) *The Radio Tisdas Sessions.* [CD] Liner Notes. World Village: USA.

Urry, J. (1990) *The Tourist Gaze: Leisure and Travel in Contemporary Societies.* London: Sage.

3   Waltzing around the world

Musical mobilities and the aesthetics of adaptation

Peter Peters

Seen from the outside, the recording studio of the Dutch violinist and conductor, André Rieu, is hard to distinguish from other buildings in the small industrial area near Maastricht, the Netherlands.[1] A remote-controlled gate gives access to a small car park. The heart of the building is a tall space where chandelier-style lamps illuminate the white curtains that are hung along the walls. From behind a large recording console in a soundproof room, the sound engineer can look through a window into the studio. Each instrument has its own microphone position. These microphones record the music that travels from this anonymous-looking building to millions of listeners all over the world.

André Rieu and his Johan Strauss Orchestra (JSO) are among the most successful musical touring groups in the world. Rieu has sold 5.7 million tickets in the past ten years (personal communication, André Rieu Productions). Pollstar, a leading trade publication for the concert tour industry, has consistently ranked Rieu among the top 20 global concert tours since 2005. Its highest ranking was in 2009, when the orchestra grossed approximately $90 million from its tour operations, placing it sixth in the world (Peterson and Kara 2013: 1–2). Rieu and his orchestra gave concerts in Europe, the US, Mexico, Brazil, Chile, Peru, Colombia, South Africa, Japan, China and Australia. On tour, the fifty performers are supported by more than seventy people, about thirty of whom work at the company headquarters in Maastricht, while the others accompany the performers to set the stage. The open-air concerts that Rieu organizes every summer in Maastricht attract audiences from all over the world. Giving an average of hundred performances annually and being on tour for ten months of each year, Rieu's travelling orchestra offers a rich case study in mobile music events. In this chapter, I examine how Rieu is successful in reaching global audiences with his idiosyncratic repertoire, mixing Viennese waltzes, classical music, and opera arias with local folk music and popular sing-along songs. I argue that ideas from mobilities studies can help to understand the mobile musical events that Rieu and his orchestra organize.

In recent years, it has been claimed that new research methods are needed to study current mobility practices, discourses and materialities. Next to more traditional social science methods, mobile methods have included participatory observation, virtual and autoethnographies, and various kinds of mapping (Büscher et al. 2011).

Drawing on ethnographic research, this chapter seeks to elucidate the orchestration of the apparatus of Rieu's orchestra by 'traveling along' with it. Over a period of two years, I had open interviews with Rieu, some of his key advisors, as well as orchestra musicians, technicians and office staff. I observed recording and editing sessions in the Rieu studio in Maastricht and visited concerts in Maastricht and Amsterdam, both as a member of the audience and back stage. Finally, I accompanied the orchestra on concert tours to Istanbul and London.

In analysing the musical performance practice of Rieu, I follow Christopher Small's (1998) argument that music is more than what can be known through analysing the score: musical style, harmonic and rhythmic structure, and formal aspects. Turning the noun music into a verb, Small focuses on practices of 'musicking'. The meaning of a musical performance is created in a context to which not only the score or the musicians belong, but also the public. It presupposes not just the music as it is played, but also the technology to amplify the sound, and the space, as well as its acoustics, in which the music sounds. For a music performance, we need composers and musicians, but also 'support personnel' (Becker 2008) such as sound engineers, marketing staff, stage managers, and truck drivers. In a musical performance the participants follow conventions and habits that often arose long ago. They make aesthetic judgements that cannot be dissociated from the practice to which they relate.

Considering the musicking of André Rieu as a social and material practice enables it to be studied as an exemplar of a fascinating category of event mobilities, the movement of music as live produced sound and lived experience, as well as the apparatus that enables the performance of this music. In this chapter, I focus on the question how Rieu's music is performed, as a mobile event, in the practice of travelling around the world.

Mobile music events

Music is probably the most ubiquitous of all arts. We listen to art music in concert halls, to rock stars in football stadiums, to muzak in the elevator, to our iPods on the train. As DeNora (2000) has argued, music is a constitutive feature of human agency as well as an important dimension of social order and organization in late modern societies. The analysis of music used to be the domain of musicologists, who studied the complex systems of notations that were developed in art music and, in doing so, analysed its formal characteristics such as harmonies, rhythms, melodies, and dynamics. Since the 1970s, musicologists have begun to question this focus on the 'music itself'. New musicology analyses music making and music listening as situated activities, drawing upon social and cultural theories from other disciplines, including sociology, cultural studies, geography and anthropology. Understanding music as a material social practice shifts the focus from the musical composition as an elitist artwork, to the actual work necessary to produce, perform and distribute music, as well as the materiality of musical performance and experience (Horner 1998; Connell and Gibson 2003).

Since the mid-1990s, scholars have explored a multitude of issues around musical practices and cultures. Geographers have studied the production and consumption of music in different places and at different historical moments, music regions and the evolution of a music style in relation to places, the role of music in creating a sense of place, the spatial organization of the music industry, the links between music and nation-state citizenship, or the global music industry (Carney 1990; Leyshon et al. 1998; Carney 1998; Anderson et al. 2005). In sociology, cultural studies, and anthropology, musical practices have been examined in a variety of contexts, such as the politics of composition, performance and reception (Leppert and McClary 1987), the social construction of musical meaning (Martin 1995), the relations between ethnicity, identity, place and music (Stokes 1994; Saldanha 2002), and the role of music in transformations of public and private experience (Born 2013). More recently the fields of science and technology studies and sound studies have focused on ways in which recordings influence the study of music performance and the nature of musical experience (Bayley 2010), on how technobiographies of musical instruments such as the Moog synthesizer are shaped by path dependency (Pinch and Trocco 2009), and on the music cultures and technologies of everyday life (Bull and Back 2003; Katz 2004; Beer 2010; Sterne 2012).

Whereas these bodies of literature provide valuable starting points for the analysis of musical cultures and practices in their relation to spaces, infrastructures, and materialities, the more ephemeral and experiential qualities of music making and listening as performed events can be theorized in the context of the performative turn. As a concept, performance can not only refer to musical and artistic performances, such as theatrical events and performance art, but also to other types of social, political and religious events. Drawing on the work of Austin, Butler, Schechner, Auslander, and others, Fischer-Lichte (2008) has used the metaphor of the theatre to analyse how performances, both artistic and in everyday life, are staged, experienced, and interpreted. Approaching the world as 'performative' enables us to see it in the making, emerging over time as a result of situated ways of knowing and doing (Salter 2010). As such, musicking can be theorized in a non-representational register, focusing on how musical events are enacted or performed (Morton 2005; Thrift 2007).

Within the 'new mobilities paradigm' (Hannam et al. 2006; Urry 2007), places as well as events are analysed as networked and performed in and through various mobilities. As Urry has claimed, '[p]laces are intertwined with people through various systems that generate and reproduce performances in and of that place (and by comparison with other places)' (Urry 2006: vii–viii). Instead of having intrinsic or essential characteristics and values, places such as urban centres, cultural heritage sites and wilderness landscapes are performed through specific mobile practices (Peters 2012). Practices of travel can thus be thought of as a way of performing places and times (Edensor 2001; Jóhannesson 2005; Bærenholdt and Haldrup 2006; Walsh and Tucker 2009). Analogous to places, events can be said to be performed through mobile practices. Particular mobilities such as travelling by bus, or walking in the city 'can become articulated as meaningful activities within different systems and categories of knowledge' and thus as events (Adey et al. 2014: 15). On the other hand, we could ask how particular events are constituted through 'the performative practice of mobile actions' (2014: 15).

Whereas site-specific arts and performances have been extensively researched and theorized (see Kwon (2002) for an overview), relatively little work exists on the question of what happens when artistic events travel. As Merriman and Webster argue, there is a long history of artists exploring 'the aesthetics, sensations and kinaesthetic dimensions of moving through the landscape' (2009: 525), but this relates more to performing the movement as an artistic event, e.g. in art walking. Questions such as how an artistic or musical performance changes its meaning when it becomes mobile are under-researched. Within theatre and performance studies, however, the relationship between performance, place and travel is gaining scholarly interest (Rogers 2012). In a recent article, Nóvoa (2012) studies how musicians produce and reproduce their identities while on the move, but it does not address the question how the actual practice of travel could be seen as a performance of their musical practice.

When answering how Rieu's music is performed, as a mobile event, in the practice of travelling around the world, we can draw on an extensive body of literature addressing 'the materials, meanings, production, experience, and doing of music (Wood et al. 2007: 867). To understand how Rieu's musicking is related to the mobile practices of his orchestra, I will focus on four aspects. First, I will discuss his work as a musician: how does he make his music? Second, I will describe the materialities and mobilities of his concert tours: performing his music all over the world assumes that he is able to make it transportable. Third, I will focus on his shows: what characterizes the performance of his concerts as events? Fourth, I will reflect on the 'geographies of affect' of the concerts: how is Rieu successful in creating musical events that millions of his fans experience as deeply moving, seemingly regardless of the local contexts in which he performs?

Adaptations

On a sunny Wednesday morning in September 2014, the orchestra rehearses in the recording studio between half past nine and twelve o'clock. The rehearsal program includes a number of songs with the Berlin Comedian Harmonists, a close harmony group that follows in the footsteps of the famous eponymous company from Berlin in the 1920s and early 1930s. André Rieu sits on a high swivel chair, overlooking the orchestra. He wears headphones and speaks through a microphone. He welcomes the Harmonists and informs the orchestra about the program of the upcoming tour to Brazil. Jokes are made, Rieu counts down and the orchestra starts an up-tempo 'Happy birthday'. Someone in the orchestra celebrates her birthday.

(Field notes)

André Rieu knows the culture of classical music as an insider; his father conducted symphony and chamber orchestras. He began playing violin at a young age and in the biography written by his wife Marjorie Rieu we read that the family Rieu resembled a small conservatory: all family members were expected to play a musical instrument (Rieu 2013). He studied at the conservatories in Liège, Maastricht and Brussels. For thirteen years, Rieu was a violinist in the Limburg Symphony Orchestra, based in Maastricht, the Netherlands. He admires the Royal Concertgebouw Orchestra and considers the Concertgebouw in Amsterdam to be 'the most beautiful concert venue in the world' (personal communication, André Rieu).

By being a member and later leader of a salon orchestra in the 1970s, he expanded his repertoire of serious music with lighter music. 'I hardly knew what a salon orchestra was, but went for a trial rehearsal to *I Glissandi* [the first name of the salon orchestra]. When playing Lehárs *Gold und Silber* it was as if I stepped into a new world. I was immediately struck by what would later become my life's rhythm: the waltz' (2013: 60). The concerts of the Maastricht Salon Orchestra marked the beginning of a performance practice, a style of musicking that is unique in the world. His repertoire is extremely hybrid: he combines waltzes and operetta, arrangements of classical composers ranging from Beethoven to Orff and Rodriguez, world music, gospel songs, opera arias, pop music by Abba and local sing-alongs. With his orchestra he plays all his music in such a way that it is immediately recognizable as music by Andre Rieu. How does he do that?

At first glance, Rieu's ensemble looks like a medium-sized symphony orchestra. In the recording studio, the musicians all have a small private locker with sheet music in front of them. These sheets tell a lot about the way the orchestra works and how it is different from traditional symphony orchestras. Orchestra musicians normally play from their own parts and the conductor overlooks the score. Rieu's musicians rarely perform from written out individual parts. Instead, they all play from the same piano excerpt. This shows the melody, the chords and the bass line of a piece. For Rieu's orchestra members, it is the most natural thing in the world that they derive their own part from the excerpt.

The piano excerpts are at the heart of a performance practice that does not focus on rendering a musical score as faithfully and accurately as possible, but one that is based on making adaptations. All music that Rieu plays is an adaptation of the original – whether it is the *Concierto de Aranjuez* by Joaquín Rodrigo or *Waterloo* by Abba. Rieu makes his adaptations together with the violinist, Frank Steijns, who has been a member of the JSO for twenty years. The practice of adapting music goes back to the unorthodox composition of the salon orchestra: to perform music at all, it had to be arranged. Steijns knows from experience that the orchestra sound that Rieu wants has an emphasis on the melody and the bass. With five cellos, three double basses, tubas, trombones and a bass trombone, the lower voices are well represented. Eleven first violins, three second violins and high woodwind and brass instruments play the melodies. Whereas in the classical music of the nineteenth century the middle voices became increasingly important, Rieu sacrifices harmonic complexity in favour of the clarity of the sound.

Playing from piano excerpts presupposes a long experience with the musicians. Steijns writes the piano excerpts in such a way that the orchestra can interpret them in ways that fit the needs of Rieu. Because they play from under-notated music – indications about dynamics, phrasing and articulation are usually missing – they developed their own way of interpreting. The orchestra begins to play and just 'knows what André wants' (personal communication, Frank Steijns). It has a collective memory that goes back many years – most musicians have been working with Rieu for a long time, some even from the days of the salon orchestra. Precisely because the musicians do not play from their own parts, they are relatively free to improvise. Because of this flexibility, the arrangements of Rieu grow organically during rehearsals. The orchestra plays, Rieu provides guidance on the changes he wants: 'That clarinet should sound more like a horny countess'. If he is happy with the result, he says: 'That's nice. We're going to record'. In the afternoon he listens to the recorded material at home and changes details during the next recording day. From any original to a performance by Rieu, the music is adapted to a piano excerpt, performed in an improvisatory way by musicians who have a longstanding experience of Rieu's preferences, and only slightly polished in the recording studio. This process builds on decades of experience and can be understood as 'collective tacit musical knowledge' (Collins 2001).

Mobilities

The small departure hall of Maastricht Aachen Airport is empty. Above the check in counter a screen indicates the flight number: DNM5855 13:30 Luton Rieu and Orchestra. The aircraft is chartered, as with all flights in Europe. The orchestra members line up, there is talking and laughter. As Chief Operations Officer of André Rieu Productions, Frans Neus is a spider in the web of agreements, schedules and contracts necessary to allow the orchestra to travel around the world. He distributes the boarding passes to the orchestra members. For some of them with passports from non-EU countries such as Russia, there are visas. After the luggage is checked in, the security check follows and minutes later we are on an airport bus to a Fokker 100 of Greenland Express. Rieu arrives in his car at the nosewheel of the plane. His chauffeur drove him here directly from home and his personal assistant, who takes care of his luggage both figuratively and literally on every journey, arranged with the airport authorities a seamless connection on the platform.

We arrive on time at Luton Airport. Outside the airport, the blue buses of the Johann Strauss Orchestra are waiting. The chairs are in groups of four and two, and can be lowered to a horizontal position. Each orchestra member has his or her own place. The orchestra is traveling in these buses on trips in Europe, at distances that are too short to fly. We drive into London, along the low houses of the Wembley area, towards the SSE Arena, near the famous stadium. The buses maneuver into the concrete catacombs of the hall and park next to a row of trucks in which the flight cases with musical instruments, costumes and technical equipment are transported. The orchestra members walk inside, through a long, bare corridor to their dressing rooms. At five they are expected on stage for the sound check. Then there is a joint dinner, after which the orchestra members have time to prepare for the concert. Some stay in the canteen, some find an empty space to practice on their instrument, others follow the example of Rieu and take a nap. (Field notes)

Rieu reaches his audiences through the CDs and DVDs his company produces. It has a longstanding business relation with Universal, the biggest record company in the world. Next to that, he organizes concert tours to perform his music – sometimes days in a row in different locations. Orchestrating the apparatus that enables him and his musicians to travel the world assumes both standardization and improvisation. Talking with the orchestra members and the technicians, the phrase 'well-oiled machine' is often mentioned. The orchestra has been travelling for almost thirty years, initially mainly in the Netherlands, later in Europe and from the late 1990s all over the world. Travelling with the orchestra discloses the routines and habits that facilitate handling all those movements.

A change in the organization of concert tours came in 2004. Like most itinerant performing artists, Rieu worked with local agents and production companies until then. They arranged the hotel rooms, technical support, and ticket sales. Because of bad experiences during a tour to the United States in 2002, it was decided to no longer make use of the services of local promoters but instead do business with the venues directly. Letting his own staff take over the role of the intermediary is not only more efficient, it is also more profitable. As well, Rieu has created the possibility of checking the logistics of his performances in every detail.

A regular tour begins with an assessment of the market for Rieu's music. This depends not only on his fame and popularity in a country, but also on the presence of a middle class prosperous enough to pay for the tickets, and the availability of the type of venue that suits the concerts that Rieu gives: at least six thousand seats, space for the public to dance in the aisles, and plenty of room for the technical equipment. After choosing the concert dates and planning the tour, the contracts with the venues are drafted, and publicity is generated, for ex ample by arranging interviews with Rieu at local and national television and radio stations. Frans Neus points at the importance of having a standardized product. 'It is a universal formula. I cannot think of a country where it does not work. If you would only see the concert and not the city, then you would not know what country you are in' (Personal communication, Frans Neus). A universal formula in terms of programming of concerts goes hand in hand with a standardization of the movements of the apparatus that makes these concerts possible.

For an international tour, the orchestra members and soloists travel, as well as their instruments. This also applies to the technical crew and a large part of the equipment needed for the concert. To be able to work on multiple continents in a short span of time, the company has four complete sets of musical instruments, costumes and technical equipment – one at home in Maastricht, in Europe, America and Asia. This reduces the risk that, for example, musical instruments will not make it on time. A complete set consists of seven truckloads of light, sound, video equipment, musical instruments and costumes. The accompanying technical crew travels in three converted buses, each with twelve beds.

The company not only brings the instruments and technical equipment, but also the washing machines used to wash the clothes of the musicians after each concert. Two chefs ensure that every evening there is an extensive buffet for the musicians and crew. They cook with fresh local products. On intercontinental tours, Rieu and his orchestra are accompanied by a general practitioner, who has a big suitcase with medication, but more importantly knows where to find good hospitals in a city. During a recent tour to Istanbul, Rieu took three judo mats so he could do his daily workout in his hotel room, under the guidance of his personal trainer.

A peak in logistic complexity was reached in 2007 when Rieu decided to tour the world with a replica of Schönbrunn Palace in Vienna, Austria. The orchestra was staged before a copy of the main entrance of the palace. On either side of the stage were two ice rinks with figure skaters. Behind the orchestra the audience saw a ballroom where dancers waltzed. In between the audience, there were large fountains like those in the gardens of the Viennese palace. Six huge video screens embedded in the walls of the palace showed the images of all those playing, skating and dancing.

The idea behind the replica was not just artistic; by doing mega-events for audiences of up to 38,000 visitors, as was the case in Melbourne, Australia in 2008, the company hoped to reduce the number of concerts and still remain profitable. Hence the financial risks that were taken. To construct, deconstruct and transport the fake palace, more than five hundred people were needed. Unexpected problems had to be solved, sometimes at high costs. In the warm Australian summer it was not possible to skate on real ice. The two rinks had to be provided with a thick layer of special plastic that mimics the properties of ice. One of the Australian concerts almost had to be cancelled because of a thunderstorm. Eventually, the company had four copies of the Schönbrunn palace: two for indoor and two for outdoor concerts. It proved to be too much. The logistic of transporting not just the music from nineteenth-century Vienna, but also the material context in which it arose was no longer controlled. Rieu almost went bankrupt.

Performances

The concert in Istanbul starts at exactly nine o'clock. During the concert most people respond or laugh immediately after the English texts, even before they are translated. A latecomer is addressed quasi-sternly: 'You are too late!' Laughter. 'Is that normal in Istanbul?' The audience responds: Yes. 'Traffic?' Applause. 'We have time.' The orchestra plays the 'Second Waltz' by Shostakovitch, the music that made Rieu and his orchestra famous. Later in the program, he invites his audience to dance. The interpreter descends from the stage in a cobalt blue dress and starts to walk across the hall, inviting men to waltz with her. Cameras follow her journey through the hall and show it on the big screens beside the stage. There are, however, few people who take the initiative to get up from their seats to dance. When a Turkish song is performed on authentic musical instruments, everyone sings along.

(Field notes)

Any live musicking takes place in the moment, and creates a sense of here and now, of being there. What characterizes Rieu's concerts as performed and lived events? The Schönbrunn palace concerts were not only challenging in logistical terms, but in a performative sense they were an almost absurd accumulation of complexity. As part of his famous *Le Carnival des Animaux* (1886), the French composer Camille Saint-Saëns wrote a cello solo that evokes the swimming of a swan over the rippling water. In Melbourne that piece of music was played by the cellist, Tanja Derwahl, against the background of the Schönbrunn façade, with figure skaters on both sides and dancing couples in a ballroom behind her. The video footage of all those individual events was shown on six huge screens, interspersed with shots of a listening and dancing audience. The images of this mega-event spread across the world through DVDs and video clips on YouTube. Rieu's concerts create a sense of liveness through the interplay between the reality of the orchestra on the stage and its digitally mediated performance on screen (Auslander 1999).

Rieu developed the repertoire, structure and staging of his concerts in the years of the salon orchestra and the Johann Strauss Orchestra in the 1980s and he emphasizes that not much has changed since then. His talks with the audience, the combination of different genres and styles, the way the stage is decorated: it changed in scale, but not in character. Although the numbers will be different on every programme, any Rieu-concert follows a format that is the same everywhere. At the beginning of every concert, Rieu and his musicians walk to the stage from the back of the hall, waving and smiling at the audience, always accompanied by the same music. The sequence of songs and talks to the audience is reminiscent of a roller coaster as the audience moves from one experience to another: the melodic beauty of the aria 'Nessun dorma' from Puccini's opera *Turandot*, the jokes Rieu makes about the audience ('You are the best choir in the world!'), the balloons that descend from the ceiling of the hall at the end of the concert, the seemingly endless series of encores. This standardized formula is followed all around the world.

Normally, the encores signal the moment when Rieu gives the stage to local music. During a concert in Istanbul, Turkey in November 2014, he jokingly gestured to the audience that it should leave the hall. 'You are tired!' Instead of ending the concert, Rieu asks four stagehands to carry four chairs and microphones on stage. He announces the next song: 'Give them an enormous applause, the best musicians from Istanbul!' The ensemble on stage is led by Nagme Yarkin, who plays a kemençe, a small three-stringed fiddle characteristic of Turkish folk music. The other three musicians play a ud, a lute with a short neck of Arab origin, a kanun, a kind of zither played with vingerplectra, and a tar or frame drum that can be found everywhere in the Arab world. The orchestra plays an accompaniment in triple time reminiscent of a waltz, but once the Turkish instruments come into play, the audience starts to sing. Everyone knows the classic song that is being played.

Seen from a performative perspective, Rieu's concerts have the predictability of a ritual. Whether he plays in Brazil, England or Turkey, the structure of the programme is the same everywhere. Performing the music is key to the concert event, but its success in turn rests on other performances, such as identities. Rieu plays a subtle game with distance and proximity, liveness and mediation. Both during the live concerts as well as on his CDs and DVDs, he uses of a wide range of cultural stereotypes – first and foremost, of course, in his music, condensed to adaptations that can be understood everywhere, but also in his references to countries and regions. The LED screens on the stage show archetypal images: mills from the Netherlands, a sunlit Italian town, minarets in Turkey, a bullring in Spain. His shows are like mirrors in which the audience can recognize itself. As a global artist, Rieu waltzes around the world to give his audience a sense of coming home (Bude and Dürrschmidt 2010).

Audiences

> One of the highlights of the concert in the SSE Arena in London is the final chorus of Beethoven's Ninth symphony. Three sopranos and three tenors sing the words 'Alle Menschen werden Brüder', the orchestra accompanies at full strength. The LED screen behind the stage shows the universe, slowly moving stars. The camera zooms in on the earth. It accelerates and descends to Europe, Britain, London, the SSE Arena. Exactly at the moment of the imposing final chord, held long by the soloists and the orchestra – Rieu with his violin in his left hand, directing with his right – the audience sees itself on the large LED screen. Live, applauding.
>
> At the beginning of the concert, Rieu tells his audience that he has many nationalities in his orchestra. Introducing himself: 'I come from Holland! And where did we all come together tonight?' A woman shouts: 'London!' The audience laughs. Rieu: 'Exactly at the centre of the universe! With the best audience of the whole world!' In London they understand the irony, as everywhere. For Rieu each and every audience is the best of the world.
>
> (Field notes)

One consequence of the concept of musicking is that it challenges the distinction between active musicians and passive listeners. This understanding of the division of labour between performers and audiences, where music is played for people who listen in attentive silence in order to appreciate its sounds and structures, goes back to the nineteenth century (Johnson 1994). Traditional concert halls like the Concertgebouw that opened in 1888 in Amsterdam, can be seen as architectural spaces dedicated to music as an autonomous art form, to be appropriated according to relatively stable conventions, and producing a practice of disciplined listening (Forsyth 1985; Dietz 2011). The size of these concert halls turns out to be intimately linked to the reverberation time that best suits the performance of nineteenth century symphonic repertoire: around two seconds (Cressman 2012). For André Rieu, to make the concerts of his traveling orchestra profitable, he has to perform in venues that have at least 6,000 seats. Whereas traditional concert halls have their own acoustical fingerprints, Rieu's music depends on acoustic mobility. This means that he has to renegotiate the relations between music, performance space, acoustics, and listening conventions that characterize the traditional classical concert.

On stage, Rieu conducts his orchestra as Johann Strauss did, as a *Steh-Geiger*, a violinist who stands in front of the orchestra. In that role he mediates between the orchestra and the audience. With his texts between the songs, he puts the audience in a state of mind that matches the next song. He listens to a vocal or instrumental solo and gives the public the opportunity to follow what is going on musically through his facial expressions. In his interpretation of the role of conductor, Rieu is not the untouchable maestro who from a position of omnipotence transfers his musical will to the orchestra. He even mocks the seriousness of the traditional conductor – even though he takes his music very seriously the raised eyebrow and the gesture of the slapstick are never far away.

The differences between the performance practice of Rieu and conventional classical musicking go beyond the role of the score, the use of adaptations, the improvisational way of playing by the musicians and the hybrid interpretation of the role of the conductor. During a Rieu concert, the audience plays an all-important role in co-producing the concert as an event. He aims not at the expert listener who is able to listen to a piece of music, and to analyse at the same time, as Adorno (1962/1973) has put it, but wants his listeners to be immersed in the spectacle he creates for and with them. He invites his audience to respond to his music, to stand up and dance during a waltz. Rieu makes his audience part of the event of the concert. He ridicules latecomers by addressing them directly from the stage, and he leaves no opportunity unused to mock the traditional concert ritual and the figure of Adorno's silent, expert listener. For him, listening to music is not an intellectual and aesthetic activity, but a total experience. The cloud of balloons swirling down from the ceiling is just as beautiful as the last dramatic notes in an aria sung by the three Platin Tenors.

Rieu's concerts eliminate the distance between stage and audience, between the composition as an autonomous artwork and an attentive listener who reflects on its aesthetic qualities. They are inclusive in many ways. This is true not only for the breadth of his repertoire, but also for the people he gets on stage. Several years ago the Maastricht music school celebrated its 125th anniversary. Asked if he wanted to contribute to the festivities, Rieu invited all of the string instrument pupils on the stage during his yearly concerts on the Vrijthof, the main square in Maastricht. In a more figurative sense, he could be said to give the stage to his audiences when he performs adaptations of local music. He presents their own music to his audience, as if it were a gift that he wraps in the universal and yet characteristic sound of his orchestra. In that sense his audiences are as important agents in the mobile music events that he organizes as the performers (Auslander 2004).

In London Rieu says goodbye, as usual with 'Adieu, mein kleiner Gardeoffizier', a hit by Robert Stolz. The orchestra waves to the audience. The audience knows the ritual and waves back. Then the concert ends with 'We'll meet again', the famous song by Vera Lynn. The orchestra plays the melody in a beautiful and modest Rieu arrangement, the audience sings the text. Seven thousand voices in unison.

(Field notes)

Conclusion

How does a musical event change its meaning when it becomes mobile? The case of Rieu's concert tours suggest that their performance depends on finding a balance between a standardized way of working and local improvisation, both on and offstage. As I have shown, his practice of musicking is intimately bound up with the fact that Rieu and his orchestra travel around the world: his music is performed in the act of travelling. Based on my ethnographic observations, I argue that the concerts of Rieu, being global yet situated events, have to be understood as a musical practice that revolves around aesthetics of adaptation.

First, Rieu has to adapt and arrange the music he plays in order to tailor it for his orchestra that has a fixed composition. Thanks to the experience of his musicians, Rieu is able to play basically any music in a style that is recognizable and agreeable to his audiences. The musical characteristics of this style – limited duration of the adaptations, a focus on high and low voices, reduced harmonic complexity – make it as it were 'transportable' between various musical cultures. Rieu's approach thus draws on music as a universal language.

Second, given the costs of organizing his concerts, Rieu needs venues that are able to host 6,000 people. The arenas and stadiums where Rieu plays, all look more or less the same. This also applies to the hotels where he and his musicians and staff stay, as well as the airports at which they call. The sound, theatre and lighting technologies Rieu uses meet standardized norms, as well as the contracts he signs with venues. In this world of seemingly frictionless mobilities, everything comes down to predictability and good planning. Rieu's music became a worldwide success because he succeeded in adapting the specificity of his concerts to this global infrastructure, the spaces of flows of mobile cultural events, while staying in control in an artistic sense.

Third, when performing standardized concert programmes in standardized locations all over the world, Rieu has to find ways that local audiences will relate to them. He has to adapt to local situations without changing the programme all the time. He does so by performing an experience of belonging or even homecoming during his concerts. More than any other global artist, Rieu presents himself as somebody who belongs somewhere. Everyone knows Maastricht is his hometown and in his videos the Vrijthof square in Maastricht is presented as embodying a unique sense of place. A sense of local identity can also be experienced by his audiences in his adaptations of the music of the country he visits. Hearing it in a Rieu arrangement makes it sound strange and familiar at the same time. Something similar can be said about the way Rieu includes his audience in the spectacle of his concerts, by reducing the distance between performers and listeners characteristic of traditional classical concerts. In other words, Rieu and his orchestra need to travel in order to give their audiences an experience of proximity – to the music, to the performers, and to themselves.

How does the case study on André Rieu and his Johann Strauss Orchestra contribute to an event mobilities framework? In the introduction to this volume, mobilities approaches to researching events have been discussed in four dimensions, namely 'interruptions', 'transitions', 'framings', and 'materialities'. In this chapter, I have explored and analysed the performativities and choreographies that characterize Rieu's concert tours as aesthetics of adaptation. Who would have thought that a giant concert is an immutable mobile, to put it in Bruno Latour's terms (Latour 1986)? In order to travel, these concerts have to remain stable as the predictable and standardized musical events that global audiences seek to experience, yet in order to move across various regions, both materially and imaginatively, they have to be flexible enough to engage with and adapt to local situations, communities and traditions. This research therefore suggests 'adaptations' as a fifth dimension of event mobilities.

Note

1. I would like to thank André and Marjorie Rieu, Frans Neus, and Frank Steijns as well as the musicians, technicians and office staff of the Johann Strauss Orchestra and André Rieu Productions for sharing their experiences and practices with me. Jac van den Boogaard, Darryl Cressman, Harro Maas, Maaike Meijer and Bernike Pasveer gave valuable comments on earlier versions of this chapter.

References

Adey, P., Bissell, D., Hannam, K., Merriman, P. and Sheller, M. (eds) (2014) *The Routledge Handbook of Mobilities*. London: Routledge.

Adorno, T. W. (1962/1973) Typen musikalischen Verhaltens. In *Einleitung in die Musiksoziologie*. Frankfurt Am Main: Suhrkamp Verlag, pp. 17–32.

Anderson, B., Morton, F., and Revill, G. (2005) Practices of music and sound: Editorial. *Social and Cultural Geography*, 6(5): 639–644.

Auslander, P. (1999) *Liveness*. London: Routledge.

Auslander, P. (2004) Performance analysis and popular music: A manifesto. *Contemporary Theatre Review*, 14(1): 1–13.

Bærenholdt, J. O., Haldrup, M., Larsen, J. and Urry, J. (eds) (2004) *Performing Tourist Places*. Aldershot: Ashgate.

Bærenholdt, J. O. and Haldrup, M. (2006) Mobile networks and place making in cultural tourism: Staging Viking ships and rock music in Roskilde. *European Urban and Regional Studies*, 13(3): 209–224.

Bærenholdt, J. O and Granås, B. (eds) (2008) *Mobility and Place: Enacting Northern European Peripheries*, Aldershot: Ashgate.

Bayley, A. (2010) *Recorded Music: Performance, Culture and Technology*, Cambridge: Cambridge University Press.

Becker, H. S. (2008) *Art Worlds*. Berkeley, CA: University of California Press.

Beer, D. (2010) Mobile music, coded objects and everyday spaces. *Mobilities*, 5(4): 469–484.

Born, G. (ed.) (2013) *Music, Sound and Space: Transformations of Public and Private Experience*. Cambridge: Cambridge University Press.

Bude, H. and Dürrschmidt, J. (2010) What's wrong with globalization? Contra 'flow speak' – towards an existential turn in the theory of globalization. *European Journal of Social Science*, 13(4): 481–500.

Bull, M. and Back, L. (2003) *The Auditory Culture Reader*. New York: Berg.

Büscher, M., Urry, J. and Witchger, K. (eds) (2011) *Mobile Methods*. London: Routledge.

Carney, G. O. (1990) Geography of music: Inventory and prospect. *Journal of Cultural Geography*, 10(2): 35–48.

Carney, G. O. (1998) Music geography. *Journal of Cultural Geography*, 18(1): 1–10.

Collins, H. (2001) 'What is tacit knowledge? In Schatzki, T.R., Knorr Cetina, K. and Von Savigny, E. (eds) *The Practice Turn in Contemporary Theory*. London: Routledge, pp. 115–128.

Connell, J. and Gibson, C. (2003) *Sound Tracks: Popular Music Identity and Place*. London: Routledge.

Crang, M. (2006) Circulation and emplacement: The hollowed out performance of Tourism. In Minca, C. and Oakes, T. (eds) *Travels in Paradox: Remapping Tourism*. Maryland: Rowman and Littlefield Publishers, Inc.

Cressman, D. (2012) *The Concert Hall as a Medium of Musical Culture*, PhD dissertation, Simon Fraser University.

DeNora, T. (2000) *Music in Everyday Life*. Cambridge: Cambridge University Press.

Dietz, B. (2011) Composing listening. *Performance Research*, 16(3): 56–61.

Edensor, T. (2001) Performing tourism, staging tourism: (Re)producing tourist space and Practice. *Tourist Studies* 1(1): 59–81.

Fischer-Lichte, E. (2008) *The Transformative Power of Performance*, London: Routledge.

Forsyth, M. (1985) *Buildings for Music: The Architect, the Musician, and the Listener from the Seventeenth Century to the Present Day*. Cambridge, MA: MIT Press.

Hannam, K., Sheller, M. and Urry, J. (2006) Mobilities, immobilities and moorings. *Mobilities*, (1)1: 1–22.

Horner, B. (1998) 'On the study of music as material social practice. *Journal of Musicology*, 16(2): 159–199.

Jóhannesson, G. T. (2005) Tourism translations: Actor-Network Theory and tourism research. *Tourist Studies*, 5(2): 133–150.

Johnson, J. H. (1994). *Listening in Paris: A Cultural History*. Oakland, CA: University of California Press.

Katz, M. (2004) *Capturing Sound: How Technology has Changed Music*, Los Angeles, CA: University of California Press.

Kwon, M. (2002) *One Place after Another: Site-specific Art and Locational Identity*. Cambridge, MA: MIT Press.

Latour, B. (1986). Visualization and cognition: Thinking with eyes and hands. *Knowledge and Society: Studies in the Sociology of Culture Past and Present*, 6, 1–40.

Leppert, R. and McClary, S. (eds) (1987) *Music and Society: The Politics of Composition, Performance and Reception*. Cambridge: Cambridge University Press.

Leyshon, A., Matless, D. and Revill, G. (eds) (1998) *The Place of Music*. New York: Guilford Press.

Martin, P. (1995) *Sound and Society: Themes in the Sociology of Music*. Manchester: Manchester University Press.

Merriman, P. and Webster, C. (2009) Travel projects: landscape, art, movement. *Cultural Geographies*, 16, 525–535.

Morton, F. (2005) Performing ethnography: Irish traditional music sessions and new methodological spaces. *Social and Cultural Geography*, 6(5): 661–616.

Nóvoa, A. (2012) Musicians on the move: Mobilities and identities of a band on the road. *Mobilities*, 7(3): 349–368.

Peters, P. F. (2012) Roadside wilderness: US national park design in the 1950s and 1960s. In Patin, T. (ed.) *Observation Points. The Visual Poetics of National Parks*. Minneapolis: University of Minnesota Press, pp. 55–76.

Peterson, M.F. and Kara, A. (2013) *Taking André Rieu Productions to Brazil?* Retrieved March 17, 2015, from https://www.iveycases.com/ProductView.aspx?id=57156.

Pinch, T. J. and Trocco, F. (2009) *Analog Days: The Invention and Impact of the Moog Synthesizer*. Harvard: Harvard University Press.

Rieu, M. (2013) *André Rieu. Mijn muziek, mijn leven*. Maastricht: André Rieu Publishing BV.

Rogers, A. (2012) Geographies of the performing arts: Landscapes, places and Cities. *Geography Compass*, 6(2), 60–75.

Saldanha, A. (2002) Music, space, identity: geographies of youth culture in Bangalore. *Cultural Studies*, 16: 337–350.

Salter, C. (2010) *Entangled. Technology and the Transformation of Performance*, Cambridge, MA: The MIT Press.

Sheller, M. and Urry, J. (eds) (2004) *Tourism Mobilities: Places to Play, Places in Play*. London: Routledge.

Small, C. (1998) *Musicking: The Meanings of Performing and Listening*. Middletown CT: Wesleyan University Press.

Sterne, J. (2012) *MP3: The Meaning of a Format*. Durham: Duke University Press.

Stokes, M. (ed.) (2000) *Ethnicity, Identity and Music: The Musical Construction of Place*. Oxford: Berg.

Thrift, N. (2007) *Non-representational Theory: Space, Politics, Affect*. London: Routledge.

Urry, J. (2006) Preface: Places and performances. In C. Minca and T. Oakes (eds) *Travels in Paradox: Remapping Tourism*. Maryland: Rowman and Littlefield Publishers.

Urry, J. (2007) *Mobilities*. Cambridge: Polity Press.

Walsh, N. and Tucker, H. (2009) 'Tourism 'things': The travelling performance of the backpack. *Tourist Studies*, 9(3): 223–239.

Wood, N., Duffy, M. and Smith, S. J. (2007) The art of doing (geographies of) music. *Environment and Planning D: Society and Space*, 25(5): 867–889.

4 Framing identities and mobilities in heavy metal music festival events

Karl Spracklen

> Getting ready to go to Bloodstock 2014, it's not just a question of dressing for the mud. Like any metal fan, I need to wear the right tee-shirts. So my Symbel tee-shirt goes in the bag first. A tiny black-metal band from a tiny label, maybe 50 people in the world have that tee-shirt. The next one is Opeth – everybody likes Opeth, they are the Iron Maiden of the extreme-metal community. Symbel guarantees admiration from fans who know it is an obscure band, because the tee-shirt follows the code of black metal: shadowy picture, man with corpse-paint, indecipherable, Satanic logo. But Opeth will start conversations.
>
> (Field notes)

In thinking about the decisions I was making over what tee-shirts to take with me to the festival, we can imagine the ways in which the idea of an event might start to be understood through the framework of leisure mobilities (Hannam et al. 2006; Hannam 2013; Hannam et al. 2014). In a world where individuals, ideas and material goods have speeded up their transition around the world, leisure practices and popular culture have become a key space for the representation of identity and community, not only as a way of resisting the mobile and transient, but also as a way of celebrating such mobilities. In choosing to wear a particular tee-shirt a heavy metal fan chooses to express resistance to the fluid, globalized world – but the festival, the band, the tee-shirt, are all objects subject to the forces of globalization, commodification and change identified in the mobilities framework (Urry 2007).

Alternative subcultures in pop music have been sites of performativity and spaces where community is constructed ever since pop music globalized and mobilized in the 1950s (Bennett 2000, 2001; Hebdige 1979; Spracklen 2014). Pop music is a force for globalization and is a part of the wider cultural industries identified and critiqued by Adorno and Horkheimer (1992). Recently, attention has been paid by scholars such as Keith Kahn-Harris and this author to the position of heavy metal as a genre that crosses the boundaries between the commercial mainstream and the counter-culture and counter-hegemonic politics of alternativeness (Kahn-Harris 2007; Spracklen 2014). Heavy metal is a form of rock music that came to be recognized by critics and fans as a genre of pop in the 1970s, though it had its origins in the 1960s. Heavy metal bands use distorted guitars and heavy drumming as a musical backdrop to songs about being rebellious, marginal or dangerous. As heavy metal has become popular and its top bands have crossed over into the gaze of the public sphere, it has re-invented itself through ever-complex sub-genres that claim to be underground, counter-culturally subversive and an expression of the true, authentic *metalness* of heavy metal: being an individual, and rejecting the mainstream (Weinstein 2000). Heavy metal is profoundly global, a Northern popular cultural form that has spread across the world an ideology of individualism and belonging that appeals to the middle class, urban secularists and liberals in the South. Yet heavy metal feels itself to be marginalized within local popular cultures, and for many heavy metal fans being a part of the heavy metal scene is a way of expressing distaste at modernity, commercialization and globalization (Spracklen 2006; Weinstein 2000).

In this chapter, I explore these themes through a case study of the pilgrimages and mobilities surrounding the Bloodstock Music Festival, a heavy metal festival attended by 10–15,000 heavy metal fans every year in the UK. I use reflections on my own pilgrimage to the festival in 2005 and 2014, along with a virtual ethnography. I also examine the ways in which fans discuss the Festival's line-up and other matters on the official festival forum as a way of contesting and negotiating the tensions between the local and the global, change and stasis, and mainstream and alternativeness (Spracklen 2014; Spracklen et al. 2013). Theoretically I draw upon the work of Baudrillard and Habermas to show that at stake is control of a communicative performativity, which in turn produces a hyper-reality. Before I turn to my case study it is necessary to situate this chapter in the literature on mobilities and music tourism and festivals, and the relevant theoretical frameworks of Habermas and Baudrillard.

Theorizing music festivals through an event mobilities framework

The globalization of heavy metal and its status as a form of popular music is evidence of the ways in which accelerated technological and cultural changes are occurring in this new century. As Urry (2007) has explained, such changes are a result of the condition of late modernity and global capitalism: people are forced to be on the move to find work, to find function and meaning. In this, tourists, pilgrims and workers become fellows on a quest for some existential search for identity and belonging in a world that makes such belonging impossible (Urry 1990). What is considered to be culturally authentic, or aesthetically and morally appropriate, has become side-lined by the growth of homogeneity in music and in society (Bauman 2000; Bryman 2004; Ritzer 2004). In this transformation music becomes part of the global entertainment industries, and performers and fans become global pilgrims, moving from space to space, festival to festival, in the pursuit of another pay-check or another experience (Rojek 2013).

The festivalization of popular culture and music is something explored by a number of researchers in tourism and leisure studies (Bennett et al. 2014;

Johansson and Kociatkiewicz 2011; Kanai 2014; Rojek 2013; Spracklen et al. 2013). Festivalization is the process in which the public spaces of popular culture are being turned into privatized festivals and events, a process driven by global capitalism. Music festivals have become part of everyday popular culture. Mega-festivals have become international brands and trans-national corporations (Rojek 2013). The number of tickets sold and the corporate sponsorship portfolios allow such festivals to dictate the market for artists, simultaneously offering huge amounts of money for headliners while making people lower down the bill pay to perform (Jones 2012; Rojek 2013). The mega-festivals are important earners for artists and labels that have merchandise to sell, and they are too often the only part of the industry that makes them any money – so bands and labels are reducing the amount of time they spend touring or promoting music, or even releasing new music. The business model of festivalization itself has crossed boundaries to become the standard way in which concerts and gigs are arranged and consumed around the world. Even small genres and scenes feel the need to follow the festivalization route, transforming their subcultural and counter-cultural practices into commodified spaces (Bryman 2004; Rojek 2013).

For fans of music, there is still the chance to be a pilgrim to a liminal space, where one encounters the sublime or the spectacular – where one feels *communitas* (Turner 1969; Urry 1990). There has been huge range of research on music tourism, from Robert Fry's work on Nashville (Fry 2014) to the competing narratives about the impact of the Beatles on Liverpool (Cohen 2005, 2007, 2012). There is an interest in both the policy and promotion of music tourism and the role of the music traveller, finding their own way to the spaces hallowed by their favourite artists. In heavy metal this might be seen in the way people visit the West Midlands to see the places where the key and formative band Black Sabbath used to play before they became famous. These individuals wish to use their agency and mobility to find identity and belonging in re-treading the places, and re-telling the stories, of the artists they like (Connell and Gibson 2003). On a more mundane level, music fans may be travellers by moving to see bands tour, or to attend festivals such as Bloodstock at which they can identify with their subculture. My own work on Whitby's Gothic Weekend shows how the authenticity of being a fan can still be at stake in among some people attending such a festival, even though there are many others enjoying the performativity of being alternative 'for the weekend' (Spracklen and Spracklen 2014).

Such agency and performativity might be understood as a form of communicative rationality and action. Habermas says that humans construct their lifeworld, their society and culture, through the process of communicative discourse (Habermas 1984, 1987, 1989, 1990). The people and groups we connect with in our leisure help us in that communicative action, and help us to maintain our freedom from the instrumentalities of late modernity, such as the power of global capitalism and nation-states (Spracklen 2009, 2011). Performativity can be a routine task, but all-to-often the ontological and epistemological meanings of the things that are the subject of the performance are themselves constructed. In helping me make sense of this notion in the rest of this paper, I use Baudrillard's ideas of hyper-reality and the *simulacrum* (Baudrillard 1988, 1994, 1995). Hyper-reality refers to how we live in a world so distorted by the process of mediation, the representation of the world in the mass media, that it is impossible to know anything 'real' other than through a symbol or a mediation of it. We can never know the authentic metal fan, only the ways in which metal fandom is mediated. But fans and musicians and others such as festival organizers will continue to try to make some meaning from that mediation, even if that meaning is partial. That is, hyper-reality becomes the reality, but a reality where identity and belonging depend on the construction of the simulation. Such mediation invariably creates something that is only ever a copy of the essential thin that remains un-revealed – this is the *simulacrum*.

Bloodstock Festival

Rock festivals have been the focus of alternative subcultural performances and identity since the 1960s (Bennett et al. 2014; Connell and Gibson 2003; Weinstein 2000). Heavy metal festivals emerged on the festival scene with the surge of interest in (and mainstreaming of) the genre in the 1970s. The most successful metal festivals in Europe were those such as Wacken in Germany, which catered for the true or traditional metal taste of the German rock scene (Walser 1993; Weinstein 2000). Heavy metal had a peak of interest by the late 1980s, but its popularity dipped through the 1990s. In this period, metal fandom shrank into sub-genres such as death metal, doom metal, black metal and power metal (Kahn-Harris 2007). The latter is a sub-genre that musically follows the style of early Iron Maiden, and other classic or traditional acts such Judas Priest and Manowar: typically bombastic songs about warriors and fantasy epics, sung in high-pitched voices. Power metal and other forms of traditional metal were and are incredibly popular in Germany, but at the turn of the century they were marginal in the UK metal scene.

Bloodstock was originally launched to promote power metal and traditional (or classic) heavy metal to its small number of dedicated fans in the United Kingdom. As the official history on the festival website claims, the festival was an attempt to re-kindle the excitement the founders had felt at the height of the 1980s' metal boom, a way to try to tap into nostalgic memories of the hugely successful Monsters of Rock festivals held in the UK in the 1980s:

> Born out of the desire to build a festival the like that had not been seen since the glory days of Donnington's Monsters of Rock, two individuals from totally different backgrounds came together to bring their fellow Metalheads the best Metal festival in the UK, BLOODSTOCK.
>
> (http://www.bloodstock.uk.com/events/history,
> accessed 1 February 2015)

Paul Gregory, a founder of the festival, was an artist who had been commissioned to paint covers for 1980s' UK classic metal band Saxon, so he used his contacts in the industry to get the first bands booked (including Saxon, who headlined) for the initial 2001 one-day indoor festival. The name is suitably and stupidly metal, a pun of course on the more famous 1960s Woodstock Festival of the counter-cultural movement in the United States. Gregory's co-founder Vince Bretheridge chose Derby as the home for Bloodstock, and the first festival was held there in the Assembly Rooms, with a capacity of 2,500. According to the official history, the first festival ran at a loss, though they had 700 fans. The following year they increased the number of fans to 1,500, partly as a result of booking Blind Guardian, a power metal band massive in Europe.

Over the next few years the festival gradually expanded within the Assembly Rooms with different stages, more bands and a multi-day programme. By 2005 the organizers bowed to the pressure from fans unable to get tickets and created an outdoor version of Bloodstock branded as Bloodstock Open Air (BOA). The first BOA was held at Catton Hall, which at the time was said to have a capacity of up to 10,000 (according to the Wikipedia site for the festival), though recent years has seen this increase up to 15,000. This year also saw the intervention or sponsorship of Wacken Open Air in Bloodstock. The exact arrangement is unclear, but Wacken clearly has some sort of stake in the business, assisting with marketing and aligning the Bloodstock brand to its own (Wacken Open Air: WOA) in terms of design. In 2005 and in 2006 both indoor and outdoor versions of the festival ran. But the huge success of the outdoor festival and perhaps the pressure of running two events in tandem led the organizers to abandon the Assembly Rooms altogether to focus on an enhanced three-day BOA in 2007.

Even though the festival always had a varied line-up, the early years were dominated by power metal and bands that made it big in the 1980s. Since the Assembly Room days, the festival has extended its remit to book bands far beyond power metal and traditional metal, bands that have graced more main-stream metal and rock festivals: the headliners in 2014 were the American band Down, who have a mainstream appeal through their singer's previous job with the world-renowned mainstream metal band Pantera; the Norwegian black-metal band Emperor, who had reformed just to headline metal festivals through Europe; and Megadeth, a popular but middle-of-the-road American thrash band known world-wide as the band formed by the guy who got thrown out of Metallica. The festival has also increased the number of bands and the number of days of perfor-mances, from three to four. At the same time, Bloodstock has supported emerg-ing, un-signed bands through replicating Wacken's community schemes, local events where bands can play against each other to win slots to play on the unsigned stage at BOA. The bands that make a strong impression on the unsigned stage can progress through to the other stages in the following years. In the last few years some bands I have followed as part of my black metal research have come through this route, such as Old Corpse Road and Northern Oak. In BOA, then, there is a combination of a desire to give something to the metal commu-nity, to perform metalness, while being a profit-making part of the festival indus-try. In the UK, it competes for business with other heavy metal festivals such as Download, rock festivals such as Leeds and Reading that have heavy metal bands in their line-ups, as well as smaller underground festivals such as Damnation aimed at extreme metal fans.

Ethnographic reflections on attending Bloodstock

I would not describe myself as a power metal fan, or a true or traditional metal fan. But I am a fan of heavy metal, especially extreme (black, doom, folk, Viking, death) metal,[1] and I have attended Bloodstock on two occasions. I have never felt the need to identify with metal or Bloodstock so much that I attend the festival every year, whatever the line-up or the weather. I do not like the horrendous conditions in the outdoor camp-sites so have always been reluctant to attend any outdoor music festival of any kind. What made me go to Bloodstock in 2005 was the quality of the line-up (the Swedish power metal band Hammerfall were there, along with Viking death metal band Amon Amarth and British doom metal band Cathedral) and the idea that it was all happening under one roof. I was disappointed that the festival abandoned the indoors and became an outdoor festival just like any other outdoor festival. I read stories of mud and sunburn and mud and sick and was glad I wasn't there, though sometimes I felt disappointed that the old Bloodstock had gone. But year-on-year we checked the line-up as bands were announced, and I had conversations with my wife about how many bands we needed to see on the line-up if we were to go. She had been camping to outdoor music festivals in the 1990s so she made fun of me for being too scared of the shared toilets and the drunkenness. What made me choose to get tickets for BOA in 2014 was a combination of the line-up (black-metal headliners Emperor, along with Rotting Christ and Orphaned Land) and my realization that the festival offered VIP camping with self-erected tents, a real-ale beer tent and quality toilets and showers.

In 2005 the transient lives of the bands and the pilgrim-paths of the fans were clearly delineated. For the bands this was just another festival booking, and the professional musicians in the headlining acts were ushered around by roadies and managers between sound-checks, signing events, press conferences and meeting and greeting VIPs. The festival was not completely commercialized and commodified, though. Because the venue had a small capacity and an open layout between various rooms, it was possible to see some of the musicians and the festival organizers mingling with the fans hanging around in the corridors. One of the myths held by the communicative discourse in heavy metal is the belief that there are no barriers between the fans and the musicians; that everybody in the scene is grounded, and as long as everybody can prove their belonging to metal through recognition of key bands then they are accepted into the imagined, imaginary community. For the fans, the festival was a culmination of year-long anticipation. In the main hall we watched Hammerfall play to a packed audience waving fake swords of various kinds. We watched Amon Amarth play to a sea of raised drinking horns, carried by people dressed as Vikings and mediaeval knights. But for the most part, the fans wore band tee-shirts and hoodies to distinguish themselves as belonging to a particular communicative space in the Habermasian lifeworld (Habermas 1984, 1989). For the men in particular, there was a competition to be seen wearing the coolest shirt, the most rare or obscure band, the most authentic performance of the hyper-real *simulacram* of metalness

(Baudrillard 1994). At this indoor festival the number of men greatly exceeded the number of women, but the presence of female-fronted gothic metal band Within Temptation had resulted in an influx of their fans, which were more evenly balanced across genders. This was also a predominantly white crowd with various British accents. The festival felt safely local, despite having the big headliners on the main stages. Old friends bumped into each other in the corridors, in the bar and outside on the street or in one of the real-ale pubs nearby – and despite the drinking, there was no violence or tense atmosphere as most of the drinkers were old hands who looked like they had had many pints in their lifetimes.

In 2014 we booked ourselves into the VIP camping through the official website, then found ourselves following the line of cars through the small country lanes near Catton Hall. We got in and found that the VIP camping site was already quite full. There were groups of people sitting around drinking heavily and singing metal standards badly. The toilets were already suffering from overuse, a problem that plagued the festival through the rest of our stay. I had started to realise that this is how festivals make their money, by cutting as many corners as possible, knowing that the fans will turn up anyway even though the conditions are not much better than something out of the middle ages (an irony for a music that dwells in that period in many of its sub-genres). We had security guards on the VIP gate and on patrol, but that did not stop people's stuff being stolen. We were savvy enough to not have any valuables other than our cash and a phone. As VIPs we had access to a real-ale tent, some fancy food stalls and entry to the main arena through a gate where the guards were friendly. Friends we knew who were staying in the main camping area told us tales of having to queue at the gates for minutes at a time as people had their bags searched and had their drinks confiscated. Our petty-bourgeois status spared us their treatment.

The grass in the festival arena was soon worn down to bare earth (and when it rained it turned into a dangerous kind of sludge). The arena had food stalls, a huge beer tent, a fairground and a market place of alternative shops. There are over ten thousand people here, and not enough facilities, not enough bars, not enough chairs in the tea shops. The tee-shirts people are wearing are more mainstream (metal, rock and pop) than those I saw in 2005, and worn by a younger crowd. There are more young women, too, which is a good sign of metal's growing diversity (albeit still a mainly white one); but some of the young women are performing to the crowd by wearing provocative clothing. Many of the fans remain friendly and welcoming, but there is an undercurrent of sullen animosity and drunken aggression in the arena and in the camp-sites. Some of the smaller band musicians were mixing with the crowd but the headliners were being ferried in and out of the festival arena. I met up with some musicians who told me they had been given free camping and entry to the festival, but no fee. This was for them a good result, as rumours were going around that some bands might be paying to play. Another band's members told me they had been given free tickets for their entourage, hotel and travel paid for – but no fee. This seems to be another way in which the logic of instrumental rationality makes festivals a success: driving down the cost of booking artists lower on the bill, saving the budget for the headliners. I felt sorry for the musicians I spoke to. They have to play festivals to raise their profile and show labels and the media that they are important, but the festival industry is reluctant to give them a fair share of the huge profits it makes. By Saturday night we have had enough of the aggressive drunks, the blocked toilets and the cost of the falafel wraps. I get to see Emperor headline the main stage in the rain, while people in corpse-paint sleep in their deck-chairs (too drunk or too old to stay awake to watch their heroes). The next morning we leave a day early, just as the arena and the camp site turn into a quagmire of mud.

Online Simulacrum

The official Bloodstock Community is a forum on the festival website where fans have an opportunity to talk about metal in general as well as BOA itself. The site has a popular sub-forum where news on gigs and concerts can be posted by any member of the forum. Some of these gigs are free events in pubs by unsigned bands, but the forum also allows news to be posted about bigger events, professional bands' tours, even rival metal and rock festivals. This is seen as an important service by fans who comment on such posts, often supporting or dismissing signed, professional acts they like and loathe in equal measure. The eclectic and open nature of what is posted is of course restricted only to metal, but the bands that are mentioned run across the entire genre. For the regular users of the forum, this gives them the chance to make critical judgements about the kinds of bands that might be touring, line-ups of festivals and events and the quality of support acts. For example, the Finnish band Sonata Arctica, a power metal fan-favourite at BOA and at the big European festivals such as Wacken, has faced strong criticism by some fans in advance of a gig in London in 2015, with one fan complaining that 'After the last three times I've seen them, they'd be lucky to get £3 out of me' (Darkweasel, 'Sonata Arctica & Freedom Call', posted 8 February 2015 at http://www.bloodstock.uk.com/community/viewtopic.php?f=6&t=81807& start=15, accessed 15 February 2015). For the unsigned bands that are able to post and add comments, the forum allows them to create a virtual fan-base, reminding users that they are still active, still playing gigs and releasing demos. This promotion, discussion and criticism is viewed as part of the communicative discourse that is a normal part of the metal scene, though knowing to do this relies itself on mediation and an awareness of the rules of the *simulacrum*.

The sub-forums about BOA provide fans with a space to exchange tips about the best place to eat, how to get cheap tents and camping gear, a space to complain about things going wrong at the festival, as well as a space to discuss line-ups and even recommend bands to the BOA organizers. After our own poor experience of the toilets and showers in the VIP camping and the unfriendliness of some of the people, I went onto the forum to see how the regular BOA attenders felt about these things. It became clear we were not the only people who felt the conditions in the VIP facilities were unacceptable, though users on the forum suggested this was just what festivals were like and one just had to put up with it.

On the issue of the unfriendliness of some of the festival-goers, the consensus on the forum was that the festival was attracting some people who were out to steal things, and the forum posters gave a number of examples where they had lost valuables. But again, the view was that this was just what happened at festivals, and people had to be careful and sensible.

On the part of the forum where fans discuss potential bands for the festival and the line-ups as they are announced, there is a strong sense of communicative rationality at work, and a consensus that BOA should have bands that are part of the underground, marginal or unfashionable sub-genres (even if these bands might still be professional bands being booked as headliners, such as Emperor or Blind Guardian). Bands mentioned on the various wish-lists for 2015, such as Opeth and Enslaved, have appeared on the bill for 2015, which suggests the bookers at BOA are aware of the tastes and desires of their committed, long-term punters. But there is discord among the forum users over the direction of travel the festival is going. There is a consensus emerging on the forum that the organizers are booking too many mainstream metal bands, which are described as Download or DL bands: bands that have played the more commercial mainstream Download metal festival. This fear is summed up in the following post in the thread 'Next Announcement' (Skippy, posted 3 February 2015 at http://www.bloodstock.uk.com/community/viewtopic.php?f=54&t=81137&start=1095, accessed 15 February 2015):

> If it was a case of them getting a few Download bands its not too bad. It's not though, the top six bands this year are bands that played Download last year, three of them one after another. However you splice it, that's a lack of ambition, especially when you're eating you're top slots to traditional BOA bands. They seem to be limiting the bigger bands they can get, as they seem to be thinking that only bands that will appeal to a mainstream audience can get those slots (or at least they seem to prefer it). They are slowly edging out most underground bands, and making it similar to the Download repeat system – they already seem to think the only power metal band they can book is Sabaton. It's totally the wrong move if you ask me – so far this year looks OK for me, but unless next year is a radical shift I can see me trying somewhere else soon.

Fans, then, are worried about the direction the festival is travelling, and whether there will still be space for them to perform their metalness in the way in which they have become accustomed.

Conclusion

Everyone associated with the festival, and everyone in heavy metal, uses their agency to affirm their place in metal, and their place in the world. The festival becomes a place of event mobilities (Hannam 2013; Hannam at al. 2014) at a time of lifestyle and work mobility (Urry 2007): a place of transitions, interruptions, framings and materialities. Musicians, festival organizers and fans try to use their Habermasian communicative rationality (Habermas 1984; Spracklen 2006, 2009, 2011, 2014) to construct a sense of belonging through a certain performativity: that of the true metaller. At the same time, there are conflicting instrumental rationalities at work around the festival (Habermas 1987; Ritzer 2004; Rojek 2013). Musicians become mobile, global citizens moving around the world to make money and survive as professionals (Urry 2007). Festival organizers become more concerned to stretch what counts as a true metal performance and true metal identity, as they try to maximize their profit margins. BOA becomes more and more like just another metal festival, or another music festival. In this shift, the festival organizers adopt the language and practices of global festivalization. Following Baudrillard (1988, 1994), we can see that the organizers are at work trying to mediate and control people's experiences, constructing a hyper-real metal subculture that fits BOA into the postmodern world of festival experiences and brands (Rojek 2013). This festivalization is clearly seen in my ethnographic reflections.

For the fans, this festivalization and mainstreaming creates an existential despair. They want the festival to be a simulation of a different hyper-reality, the hyper-reality of communicative metal fandom, where performativity defines belonging. They want the festival to be a place where they can resist the forces of transience and mobility (Urry 2007). They do not want the festival to go broke and disappear, but they are concerned that 'their' festival is changing, becoming no longer a place where their subcultural favourites perform and their interests are met. For the moment the fans online still care enough about the festival and their place in the festival to post suggestions about line-ups and make critical noises about the direction in which the festival is turning. That is, they still feel able to feel that the festival is more than just a capitalist venture, that it is an organization that cares about the music and its fans. How long the two different hyper-realities can continue to be constructed in the same space is questionable – the power of the instrumental rationality at work behind festivalization is a product of the mobilities at work in contemporary, global society (Hannam et al. 2006) and its form of hyper-reality suggests the concerned fans may already have lost the struggle over the communicative performativity of metalness. If that is the case, then the pilgrimage and travel will become tinged with nostalgia for a subculture that has become marginal, then the pilgrimage will stop altogether as the last extreme metallers give up, sell out or pass away.

Note

1. Extreme metal is extreme by sound and by its position in the independent, underground music industry. Extreme metal includes the sub-genres of doom (slow paced and sorrowful), death (fast and angry, with growls), and black (fast and even more angry than death, with elitist ideologies and/or Satanic themes). Folk and Viking metal use black metal combined with themes and sounds taken from folk music and/or historical themes.

References

Adorno, T. and Horkheimer, M. (1992) *Dialectic of Enlightenment*. London: Verso.

Baudrillard, J. (1988) *Selected Writings*. Cambridge: Polity.

Baudrillard, J. (1994) *Simulacra and Simulation*. Ann Arbor: University of Michigan Press.

Baudrillard, J. (1995) *The Gulf War Did Not Take Place*. Sydney: Power Publications.

Bauman, Z, (2000) *Liquid Modernity*. Cambridge: Polity.

Bennett, A. (2000) *Popular Music and Youth Culture: Music, Identity and Place*. London: Macmillan.

Bennett, A. (2001) *Cultures of Popular Music*. Buckingham: Open University Press.

Bennett, A., Taylor, J. and Woodward. I. (2014) *The Festivalization of Culture*. Farnham: Ashgate.

Bryman, A. (2004) *The Disneyization of Society*. London: Sage.

Cohen, S. (2005) Screaming at the Moptops: Convergences between tourism and popular music. In D. Crouch, R. Jackson and F. Thompson (eds) *The Media and the Tourist Imagination*. London: Routledge, pp. 76–91.

Cohen, S. (2007) *Decline, Renewal and the City in Popular Music Culture: Beyond the Beatles*. Aldershot: Ashgate.

Cohen, S. (2012) Urban musicscapes: Mapping music-making in Liverpool. In L. Roberts (ed.) *Mapping Cultures: Place, Practice, Performance*. Basingstoke: Palgrave Macmillan, pp. 123–143.

Connell, J. and Gibson, C. (2003) *Sound Tracks: Popular Music, Identity and Place*. London: Routledge.

Fry, R. W. (2014) Becoming a 'true blues fan': Blues tourism and performances of the King Biscuit Blues Festival. *Tourist Studies*, 14(1): 66–85.

Habermas, J. (1984) *The Theory of Communicative Action, Volume One: Reason and the Rationalization of Society*. Cambridge: Polity.

Habermas, J. (1987) *The Theory of Communicative Action, Volume Two: The Critique of Functionalist Reason*. Cambridge: Polity.

Habermas, J. (1989) *The Structural Transformation of the Public Sphere*. Cambridge: Polity.

Habermas, J. (1990) *The Philosophical Discourse of Modernity*. Cambridge: Polity.

Hannam, K. (2013) 'Shangri-La' and the new 'great game': Exploring tourism geopolitics between China and India. *Tourism, Planning and Development*, 10(2): 178–186.

Hannam, K., Butler, G., and Paris, C. (2014) Developments and key concepts in tourism mobilities. *Annals of Tourism Research*, 44(1): 171–185.

Hannam, K., Sheller, M. and Urry, J. (2006) Mobilities, immobilities and moorings. *Mobilities*, 1(1): 1–22.

Hebdige, D. (1979) *Subcultures: The Meaning of Style*. London: Routledge.

Johansson, M. and Kociatkiewicz, J. (2011) City festivals: Creativity and control in staged urban experiences. *European Urban and Regional Studies*, 18(4): 392–405.

Jones, C. (2012) Events and festivals: Fit for the future? *Event Management*, 16(2): 107–118.

Kahn-Harris, K. (2007) *Extreme Metal*. Oxford: Berg.

Kanai, M. (2014) Buenos Aires, capital of Tango: Tourism, redevelopment and the cultural politics of neoliberal urbanism. *Urban Geography*, 35(8): 1111–1117.

Ritzer, G. (2004) *The McDonaldization of Society*. Pine Oaks: Sage.

Rojek, C. (2013) *Event Power*. London: Sage.

Spracklen, K. (2006) Leisure, consumption and a blaze in the Northern sky: Developing an understanding of leisure at the end of modernity through the Habermasian framework of communicative and instrumental rationality. *World Leisure Journal*, 48(3): 33–44.

Spracklen, K. (2009) *The Meaning and Purpose of Leisure*. Basingstoke: Palgrave.

Spracklen, K. (2011) *Constructing Leisure*. Basingstoke: Palgrave.

Spracklen, K. (2014) 'There is (almost) no alternative: The slow 'heat death' of music subcultures and the instrumentalization of contemporary leisure. *Annals of Leisure Research*, 17(3): 252–266.

Spracklen, K. and Spracklen, B. (2014) The strange and spooky battle over bats and black dresses: The commodification of Whitby Goth Weekend and the loss of a subculture. *Tourist Studies*, 14(1): 86–102.

Spracklen, K., Richter, A. and Spracklen, B. (2013) The eventization of leisure and the strange death of alternative Leeds. *City*, 17(2): 164–178.

Turner, V. (1969) *The Ritual Process: Structure and Anti-structure*. Ithaca: Cornell University Press.

Urry. J. (1990) *The Tourist Gaze*. London: Sage.

Urry, J. (2007) *Mobilities*. Cambridge: Polity.

Walser, R. (1993) *Running with Devil: Power, Gender and Madness in Heavy Metal Music*. Hanover: Wesleyan University Press.

Weinstein, D. (2000) *Heavy Metal: The Music and its Culture*. New York: Dacapo Press.

5 *Game of Thrones* to game of sites/sights

Framing events through cinematic transformations in Northern Ireland

Rodanthi Tzanelli

The invitation of Viator, a TripAdvisor online engine, to consider how the *Game of Thrones* (henceforth *GoT*, 2011–ongoing), HBO's epic medieval drama 'has more than just plot twists and CGI wizardry up its sleeve' pre-empted the touristification of various filmed natural landscapes (especially, but not exclusively, in Europe). As early as 2010 and 'while the on-screen War of the Five Kings [was] rag[ing] on', the TV series' fans were advised 'to play out their own adventures in the real-life filming locations' (Viator, April 2015). The online 'rundown' of filmed locations on this webpage was soon to be replicated by holiday operators, who sought to integrate the *GoT*'s grand mythistorical backdrop into the mundane exceptionalism of multiple tourist performances of its plot, its landscapes and values. This combination of representations of realist fiction (a plot of murder, sex and betrayal) with non-representational (embodied) tourist practices in such digital business spaces stands at the crossroads of events mobilities as products of digital-cinematic markets and their individualized interpretation. By operating as an assemblage of film fans/tourists, digital and cinematic technologies, and natural landscapes, *GoT* events mobilities (the story, the filmed landscapes' staged tourisms and the fans' actual pilgrimages to them) are prone to multiple interpretations. Even when they are not bound by memories enclosed in specific physical sites, such cinematic-cum-tourist productions of meaning retain a rudimentary connection to one or more social contexts (Büscher and Urry 2009; Büscher et.al. 2011) – at least, this is what Baudrillard's (1973, 2006) thoughts on simulation suggest in a postmodern fashion. Giddens' conception of 'double hermeneutics' (1987) which suggests that most human communications emerge within a social structure (provided in our case by the *GoT* tourist services and their connection, as we will see below, to national identity myths and institutions), acknowledges how mundane and epic mobilities are not disconnected but part of global cultural and political complexities. The interplay between these two mobility modes (one slow and mythical, the other fast and everyday) defines the motion of events as 'a change of the very frame through which we perceive the world and engage in it (Žižek 2014: 10; see also introduction to this book). The potency of such hermeneutic work is certainly more evident, where it guides collective action – as is of course the case with the layers of meaning-making we will explore in the *GoT* digital-cinematic tourist industry, which maintains interpretative flows through sets of texts, images, embodied or even virtual practices. More precisely, this study focuses on a notable convergence of slow and fast 'events' within the *GoT*'s media-tourism-tourist assemblages that opened up new developmental opportunities in Northern Ireland and more recently enabled the simulation of human socialities. My focus is the adaptation of George R. R. Martin's popular fantasy novels, *A Song of Ice and Fire* (1996–ongoing) into a TV series under the title *A Game of Thrones* and the subsequent advertising of filmed locales in Northern Ireland as tourist destinations.

Showcasing Northern Ireland as the fictional home of some of Martin's fantastic regions already encloses a hermeneutic move by certain Irish and British stakeholders, so we could consider it as part of a marketing enterprise. We need a large dose of critical realism here to assess this: filmed in multiple sites – including a Belfast studio and on location elsewhere in Northern Ireland, Malta, Scotland, Croatia, Iceland, the United States, Spain and Morocco – and rolled over to six successful seasons by HBO, the *GoT* developed into a popular culture in its own right. *Realpolitik* enters our tale further down the line, when the filmed locations became enmeshed into reconfigurations of space as (home)land, now ever more spectacularized with the help of old and new media technologies (Shields 1991). The transnational nature of *GoT*'s filmed locations and the 'Oriental' feel of its mesmerizing music (composer: Ramin Djawadi) transposed the series' fantastic plot of family intrigue and power games onto real territorial contexts of tourist policy-making. I illuminate the Northern Irish political-cultural context of cinematic tourism to consider how the series' hyper-real plot (of kings, royal families, dragons and witches) has informed territorialized claims over tourist flows in the province's filmed locations. Defined by folk legends and gifted with natural riches, these Northern Irish sites are implicated both in World Heritage complexities and the ethno-national sensibilities of the island's 'troubled' events. I contend that the fictional plot feeds into the filmed Northern Irish territories' political, cultural and natural histories and vice versa, producing profitable 'hermeneutic cycles' (Tzanelli 2007: 14) that, despite their 'apparent' circularity, actually enable Northern Ireland to build its cultural future as a tourist destination both within Europe and globally.

All mobilities produce geographies of power (Cresswell 2006); they maintain a socio-cultural kinetics that impinges on physical borders and virtual/imaginary boundaries. Indeed, the novels' cinematic adaptation produced a 'constellation of mobilities' that brought together practices of technological movement (filmmaking), professional migration (successive relocations of artistic and technical communities to filmed sites), virtual travel (setting up *GoT* Internet sites) and embodied (film-induced) tourism. My consideration of these phenomena as aspects of a singular 'cinematic tourism', following the moves enacted from within and around films (Tzanelli 2007, 2013), dovetails with Cresswell's (2006) emphasis on 'mobility constellations'. I examine how the series' disparate filmed sites (its territorially existing 'node' that spreads across countries, mostly located within Europe) are currently being filtered through its plot and 'reconfigured' (interpreted) as Irish cultural capital (a 'heritage node') online, in sites regulated by transnational, Northern Irish and Irish tourism and event providers. Although I do not examine tourist interpretations of this marketing, I maintain that industries mobilized particular aspects of human intimacies so as to appeal to their projected clientele (ideal tourist types). Of paramount importance in this process is the uses of Northern Irish 'dark tourism' or 'thanatourism', by which I refer to the embodied, emotional and now virtual/digital visits to physical sites and landscapes marked by death and suffering – in particular, terrorism, massacres and civil conflict (Slade 2003; Korstanje and Tarlow 2012). On this, it is worth recalling once more, the way Žižek (2014) clusters both brutal political changes, natural disasters, intense experiences of works of art and intimate decisions under the same definitional rubric of 'events'. The marketing of filmed Northern Irish sites draws on combinations of Northern Ireland's thanatic heritage matrix (its dark history of civil strife and terror). This matrix only apparently clashes with the province's natural beauty (its legends, fantastic-literary and real-natural imagery), and the TV series' synaesthetic (multi-sensory) content, thus facilitating synergies between capitalism and nationalism. This synergy favours capitalist necessity, which dictates historical oblivion (Northern Ireland minus its terror) as a way to deal with collective trauma.

I proceed to explain how such flows produce highly politicized mobilities. These mobilities' synaesthetic digitality – otherwise put, their online representation of combined (*syn*) sensory (*aesthesis*) tourist performances – enhances especially, but not exclusively, Irish identity's ocular properties. As is the case with other post-colonial nations that reside in the political and geographical margins (of Europe), the role of image has been pivotal in the twin Ireland's battle for legitimate self-presentation to the world, first as a solidary community, and later as an exotic tourist destination (Delanty and O'Mahony 2002; Bolan and O'Connor 2008). Northern Ireland's *GoT* mobilities market tourism's quotidian events while also reiterating the 'nation's' sacred time and essentialized existence – in global spaces of flows (Castells 2004; Jensen 2010, 2013, 2014; Jensen and Richardson 2004) and for purposes extending beyond those supporting the traditional nationalist logic, which dwindles alongside Irish separatism. The following two sections examine allegorical associations between the literary-cinematic plot and real socio-political developments in the region. The fourth section addresses the mobilization of such national-cum-global complexities (e.g. Urry 2003) in the digital advertising of Northern Irish sites, which replaces historical trauma with fantastic scenarios more palatable to tourists.

GoT's dark potential and Northern Irish memory flows

The novels' fictional characters and the selection of actors and filmed sites were not random but constitutive of the literary plot's dark character as well as its association with blends of ethno-national habitus (e.g. a 'propensity to conflict and feud'). At the same time, this association did not turn the literary-cum-cinematic narrative from a simulation to straightforward representation of 'real events'. It is better to consider the *GoT* as an allegory from which regions in need of economic bolstering benefit. Frederic Jameson's original claim that 'all [third-world] cultural productions ... are necessarily allegorical, and in a very specific way: they are to be read as ... national allegories, even when...their forms develop out of predominantly Western machineries of representation' (Jameson 1986: 67) needs to be tailored to Martin's and the *GoT* screenwriters' (D. Benioff, D. B. Weiss, J. R. R. Martin) historical and fictional hybridizations. Such hybridizations are an offshoot of new global complexities (Urry 2003) in that they disseminate ethnically rooted narratives outside (*alloú*) their cradle, in global market networks (*agorá*: the ancient market also space of public exchange). Such neo-liberalization processes should not be projected onto artistic creativity uncritically, but placed among successive hermeneutic chains by different agents in a disorganized socio-economic map, where different mobilities are designed and staged (Lash and Urry 1987; Jensen 2013, 2014). Following Lash and Urry (1994) we may argue that, in the case of Northern Ireland, a potential hermeneutic chaos – potentially prompted by the coexistence of competing interpretations of the same tourist signs, landscapes, histories and products at the expense of their coherent marketing – was stabilized due to the global recession, which called for a reliable and unchallenged version of (their) meaning. I return to this below.

Martin's novels, which follow the violent dynastic struggles among the families of the Seven Kingdoms of Westeros to control the Iron Throne, certainly resemble conventional family friction. However, their inception from fusions of true events and characters from European history (Holland, 2013) (including the English War of Roses (1455–85), the adventures of Isabella of France's (1295–1358) family or the uses of the Byzantine 'Greek Fire' in anti-Islamic warfare) produced an artistic displacement of times – a *heterotopia*. Michel Foucault's (1986) term was used to describe places and spaces functioning in non-hegemonic conditions and thus hosting forms of otherness in safe states of in-betweenness and indeterminacy. Without discarding this definition, I prioritize the role of time in communal narratives of otherness, as well as its marketing in tourist industries today. In other words, instead of inducing hermeneutic and emotional chaos, historical traumas and dissonant events (e.g. Žižek's (2014: 1) ruptures) can inhabit a contrived (by the state and/or tourist/digital industries) *heterotopia* as a safe mental and geographical 'space'. This temporal displacement is accompanied by a spatial one to endorse neoliberal strategization in movie tourism: for example, it informs a common practice in location-hunting for films with no real or accessible sites (Bolan 2010) that is endorsed by the deterritorialized Internet, where relevant cinematic holidays are sold. For the first season exterior scenes were shot at Sandy Brae in the Mourne Mountains (the 'Oriental' Vaes Dothrak), Castle Ward (Winterfell), Cairncastle (Lord Stark's execution site), Magheramorne quarry (Castle Black) and Shane's Castle (tourney grounds) (Josh 2012): all in Northern Ireland; Doune Castle near Stirling in Scotland (exterior Winterfell scenes) – already 'a place of pilgrimage for movie fans after it featured as Castle Anthrax in the 1975 film Monty Python and the Holy Grail' (BBC 2009); finally, Malta and Morocco (the southern scenes). The second season moved the southern setting from Malta to Croatia (Dubrovnik), whereas 'Frostfangs' and the 'Fist of

First Men' were filmed in Iceland. The third season returned to Morocco to film the scenes of the city of Essaouira and Daenery's (the exotic Dothraki Queen) Essos stay (Phelan 2014).

The overt association of Northern Ireland with ancestral origins is matched in this place-assortment with sites standing symbolically or physically at the margins of European 'civilization', as a, by now antiquated, but still potent 'Orientalist' discourse would purport (Said 1978). Hence, the *GoT*'s narrative node is based on a peculiar Oriental-European cultural fusion of violence, exoticism and natural beauty. Indeed, Martin's and his cinematic companions' critical take is based on a discursive *bricolage* of realist approaches to violence – what with Morocco's crypto-Islamic identity, or Irish associations with a crippling civil war in the British post-colonial context. Conflict is explicitly relocated in the exotic domain of mystical pasts, castles, rock formations, deserts and nomadic people who happen to marry exiled princesses, determined to claim back their place in civilized parts of the world. The play on cultural as 'structural hybridization' based on imaginary civilizational borders and crossings (Nederveen Pieterse 1997) finds a synaesthetic extension in composer Djawadi's use of decidedly non-medieval renditions of songs from the series source novels by noted Indie bands. German-Iranian Djawadi claimed that he was inspired to write the main title music by an early version of the series' computer-animated title sequence, but the music's use in key moments of the main characters' lives certainly turned it into part of the series' central scenario of adventure, scheming, murder and horror (Savas 2012). Its contrapuntal theme can be likened to Said's contrapuntal epistemology (Chowdry 2007) which sets different worldviews side by side to highlight meeting points (of cultures and world civilizations). Such artistic hermeneutics were complemented by the maintenance of regional, especially Northern and Southern English, accents in cinematic dialogue, to denote spatialized difference as a form of ethic habitus (Tzanelli 2007).

The selection of Northern Ireland as a sort of *heterotopic* area in the form of landscape markers signifies borderland European civility. Cinematically or technologically the province encloses both Eastern and Western influences (music, accents, aristocratic nomadic characters) and produces a mobility vortex (e.g. Hannam et al. 2006; Sheller and Urry 2006; Tzanelli 2013) into which artistic technology sucks numerous histories about the actual filmed places. At the level of literary-cinematic narrative, Northern Ireland fits a centuries-old 'political bill', whereby first Celtic flows produced ancestral traces of Northern *British* heritage. Subsequently, these became enmeshed into regional anti-colonial struggles that past medieval and early modern times would solidify as a religious-nationalist split between pro-British Protestants and anti-colonial separatist Catholics. The infamous 'Troubles' that intensified the conflict between Unionists and Loyalists over the constitutional status of Northern Ireland lasted between the late 1960s and the 1998 'Good Friday Agreement', further sinking the island into blood and pushing Irish populations to (self-) exile (McKittrick et al. 2007).

Such coerced mobilities produced global representations of Irishness – of relevance in this study as fragile moments that contemporary cultural industries (media and tourism) transform into mundane consumption rituals (e.g. visiting and photographing sites, monuments, nature and histories). Historical research has highlighted that especially the colonial era and periods of transatlantic Irish migration, consolidated the image of the mobile Irish subject/vagabond as non-European, 'black' (Curtis 1971) – a nominalization the Irish Protestant elites projected onto Catholic populations to maintain their superiority and participation in British post-colonial nation-building. Interestingly, this 'bill' is nicely matched in the *GoT*'s instance by the selection of Balkan sites for filming, which were also implicated in genocidal processes of ethnogenesis, first with the collapse of the Ottoman Empire (early 1900s) and then with the demise of communist influence (1990s). The ubiquitous use of 'Balkanization' in global politics as byword for unresolved civil conflict is firmly connected to the region: the Balkans have been repeatedly discussed as indicative of Orientalist tendencies and alleged civilizational clashes with 'Europe proper' (Todorova 1997). The addition of Maltese locations does not deviate from this theme, as the island is geographically distant from well-known European cultural centres and politically connected to histories of British colonization: its rugged landscape, medieval ruins and Mediterranean climate make it picturesque in a dark and natural fashion.

As a highly complex case, these events in historical and mythical provenances, change meaning and function. The extraordinary (*GoT*'s magic, political intrigue and illicit love scenarios) is reconfigured into the everyday and back again into the political realm – for, globally Northern Irish sites are overdetermined by the island's dark histories. Perhaps currently the *GoT* informs 'geographically specific formations of … narratives about mobility and mobile practices' (Cresswell 2010: 17) from a fictional stance. Yet, Ireland is the site of ethno-nationalist memories; even mythical narratives of national formation survive primarily in realist contexts – for, 'it is always through [a] process of interpretation' that cultures 'are kept alive' (Kearney 1984: 38; Bleicher 1980: 225). We should consider the *GoT*'s fictional *lieux* as clever modifications of Northern Irish histories of conflict – an abstraction of real *milieux de memoire* (Nora 1989) in the province. Northern Ireland may be unrecognizable from the outside as Ned Stark's ancestral home, but the popular knowledge that it mythically served as the site in which a 'fictional family' met its end is vital. Its exchange with Croatian locations in the second season ('King's Landing might be the single most important location in the entire show, and it has to look right', explained Co-Executive Producer David Benioff (Josh 2012)) turns an assortment of locations from Europe's geographical margins into a single mythical site of disaster. By audio-visual means, the Northern Irish locations partake in the *GoT*'s 'mediated centre' – the filmed places that the process of spectacularization turns into a 'sacred' popular domain (Couldry 2003a, 2003b). The plot's sorcery background suggests that there is darkness in family feuds – a perfect accompaniment to the tourist staples that the Northern Irish Tourist Board wishes to offer to global cinematic tourist clientele. But in this effort, hard core politics dies hard.

Network capital and memory: politicizing, touristifying, modifying

We note then that the *GoT* evolving multi-industry is an example of how clusters of past and contemporary events are framed by global media-tourist systems – what I proceed to explore as the role of memory in the production and mainte-nance of 'network capital'. The implication of politics in the show has found some world-wide uses that are worth a mention here – for not only do they belong to the *GoT*'s mobile hermeneutic matrix, they are decisively embedded into its tourist flows. First, global popular culture found a new term in 'sexposition' (exposition of secrets during sex, in brothels). This was originally coined by the US blogger and critic Myles McNutt to describe the many scenes in the HBO fantasy series that play out against a backdrop of sex and nudity (Hann 2012). Second, the Supreme Court battles of the US healthcare legislation figured in media platforms after the HBO series as a 'Game of Robes' to highlight the legis-lation's dramatic and conflictual nature (Brescia 2012). The figurative use of the series' title in situations of intense conflict and deceit also connected to the Syrian conflict – in particular, Bashar Al Assad's 'killing rampage' in order to stay on his throne (Varsavsky 2012) – and the power games within the Chinese Government (Garnaut 2012). Among the series' self-confessed fans are US President Barack Obama, former Australian Prime Minister Julia Gillard and Dutch Foreign Minister Frans Trimmermans, whose 2013 speech discussed European politics with quotes from Martins' novels (Kirkup 2013).

It is small wonder then, that with an eye to gaining ground next to New Zealand's J. R. R. Tolkien – Peter Jackson's literary-cinematic success (e.g. *The Lord of the Rings* cinematic trilogy (2000–2003)) – Invest Northern Ireland and the Tourist Board launched a concerted campaign to turn the filmed North Irish sites into a primary destination for cinematic tourist fans. Notably, the series receives funding from Northern Ireland Screen, a government agency financed by Invest Northern Ireland and the European Regional Development Fund (Northern Ireland Screen 2012). As of April 2013, Northern Ireland Screen awarded the show £9.25 million and according to government estimates, benefited the Northern Ireland economy by £65 million (Bradley 2013). The series had already embraced real politics long before the announcement of Northern Ireland MLA and current Minister for Enterprise, Trade and Investment Ariene Foster that 'the Tourism Ireland adverts are especially designed to bridge the fantasy of Game of Thrones with the reality of Northern Ireland' (Tourism Ireland 2014). Her complementary comment in an Assembly answer that 'throughout its lifespan it is likely that Game of Thrones will deliver the widest media exposure Northern Ireland has ever achieved outside of politics and the Troubles' (McAdam 2012) certainly falls back to the political interpretations the series found elsewhere in the world. Her attempt to read the fantastic through a series of traumatic events in Irish history wilfully uses the province's most damaging 'traumascape' (Kaelber 2007) – one of twentieth-century's civil conflicts that recycled the necessity for Irish partition in the post-colonial era. Based on a homology or likening rationale (just like *GoT*'s family intrigues, so the Irish civil conflict), Foster's hermeneutics reproduces a communitarian logic to streamline Irish troubles into tourism mobilities.

Out of all potential interpretations of the *GoT*'s central scenario or 'archplot' (McKee 1999), the one that stresses the demise of 'family utopia' persists across countries and cultures. Its association with variations of the trauma of European modernity (civil war, genocide) is what marketing imperatives seek to ameliorate or repress (according to Foster, 'outside politics', Northern Ireland shines). The *GoT*'s mythical context bears the potential to aestheticize some of Ireland's multiple realities (Dean 2007), to reconstruct an 'image' of the Irish imagined community as an Edenic place – a perfect *heterotopian* strategy in the management of events of rupture. The *GoT*'s politicization is, in short, a 'game of sites', in which Northern Ireland stands for a collection of aestheticized image-places in global consumption domains, not bloody *milieux de memoire*. My focus on this oscillation between real-political and utopian discourse borrows from Schütz's systematic examination of stratifications of the 'lifeworld' as 'multiple realities', finite provinces of meaning or 'sub-universes' (Henning 2002: 170). Foster's or Obama's objectives (their realities) differ from Martin's more generic pursuits, which are closer to Tolkien's literary allegory on social 'disenchantment' in *The Lord of the Rings* – mirrored in the end of Hobbit and Elfish eras due to the rise of warfare that destroys natural resources to provide 'compensation on the symbolic level for the political and economic processes that have destroyed the traditional fabric of … societies' (Spurr 1993: 132; White 1978: 153; Smith 2008: 174). So, we evidently deal with the political management of meaning of a fictional plot with the aim to engender and sustain global social relations and to generate 'emotional, financial and practical benefit' (Larsen and Urry 2008: 93) for Northern Ireland in the tourist trade.

Hence, Northern Ireland's 'network capital', its tourist 'currency' in Europe and beyond, is currently managed for the market as much as it aspires to be a 'government *of* the market' (Foucault 2009: 146 in Bærenholdt 2013: 26). Tourist mobilities figure here as governing principles, incorporated social practices of control through the movement of information – in our case, also the modification of a British-Irish province's thanatic memory flows of conflict and war. As histories of civil war transform into auxiliary media-tourist staple, the memories of death and suffering become less harmful and more marketable. Normatively, Bauman's (2007) argument that any attempt to sacralise dying as a spectacle is the prelude of the represented tragedy's neglect, fits Northern Ireland's tourist 'sexposition': much like the medieval custom of the representation of the ailing King, who could not make a public appearance, through a mask, a picture or a surrogate body (Belting 2007; Korstanje 2008), Northern Ireland's non-sovereign trajectory would better be represented through a TV series, a harmless spectacle. Given the strong ocular properties of both tourist advertising and nationalist discourse (Urry and Larsen 2011; Tzanelli 2013: Chapter 2) the selection of one over the other for the production of network capital conforms to political imperatives.

As is the case with any sociological analysis, the analytical subsumes the normative discourse, but in this chapter I prioritize the former: due to the global prevalence of e-tourist initiatives, Northern Ireland's *GoT* tourist governmobilities work through technological and institutional forms of self-government, through objects and digitized relations (Bærenholdt 2013: 29; Urry 2007). Perhaps Northern Ireland has been globally earmarked as a dark site of terrorism and strife, but its new mythical acquisitions can help it claim back its stolen prestige in another 'meaning province', so to speak (Graml 2004: 149; Tzanelli 2013: 57). The 'nature' and 'character' of a place can be modified with the help of new technologies of governance/mobility, in other words. To this end, the following section explores the persistence of darkness as part of the filmed places' aesthetic branding and design in the cyberspace.

Digital governmobilities: mastering Northern Irish 'nature'

The gap between digitization of cinematic narratives, real filmed landscapes in the *GoT* and the political discourse of Northern Ireland as an image-place are principally mastered in the cyberspace, where Irish *GoT* filmed locations are advertised by disparate stakeholders, regional-national and international. There, the series' musical background disappears and, save vision, all other human senses find little use. We need to bear in mind that landscapes have always been (re-) produced at the intersection of tourism with (visual and informational-communicational) technologies of mobility – a phenomenon more systematized in the current context of e-tourism or 'smart tourism' (Germann Molz 2012: 39). In any case, the *GoT*'s 'dark family narrative node' and the global financial profile of its cinematic networks, terminates, so to speak, in a Belfast studio and the province's e-tourist providers. This phenomenon is part of global mobility channels that connect locative media to international phantasmagoric communication centres, such as Hollywood and LA's city of bits (de Souza e Silva and Frith 2011; de Souza e Silva and Sheller 2014). In this section I explore the interpretative power of these locative apparatuses, bearing in mind that they too obey to more powerful global governmobilities that promise regional regeneration.

What we receive visually in *GoT* tourist websites is a series of landscapes as naturalized signs, ready to be granted meaning by web designers who are interested in generating profit more than preserving history. Urry's discussion of 'places that die' (2004: 208) to explain the shift from land (material forms of homeland) to landscape (its transformation into an ideal based on novel technologies of the eye) applies in this e-tourist context. This shift suggests that representations as such matter less than the ways they are produced, conserved or modified (Mitchell 1994). Controlled by national centres, such hermeneutics of place valorise culture in the technological spaces of late modernity, where imagined communities circulate ideas and customs for global consumption. But when we deal with both external advertising pressures (to enhance Northern Ireland's network capital) and international business collaborations, the death of place (the obliteration of its histories and cosmological moorings) can also give birth to (apropos Cosgrove 1998: 2) 'landscape ideas-as-ideals'. This does not merely denote a way of seeing-as-inhabiting material environments with the assistance of technologies of mobility but also encloses the utopian possibility to produce new memories of place as culture. Utopias are born out of *heterotopian* relocations of memory.

Lest we uncritically endorse neoliberal profiteering, it must be noted that the digital modifications of *GoT* actually filmed environments obey to the Western European principles of the picturesque, according to which landscapes matter principally as forms. Yet, by returning to the original sources of the series' visual inspiration (i.e. the 'real landscapes' of individual *GoT* episodes), especially Northern Irish e-tourist providers also capitalize on the alleged 'essence' of these places. Among them, the *GoT*'s Dragonstone (Downhill Beach, Londonderry), is discussed in Discover Northern Ireland.com (2014) as 'one of the most iconic locations … on the Causeway Coast … home to Mussenden – a tiny temple perched dramatically on a 120ft cliff top, high above the Atlantic Ocean'. The spot is close to a conservation area and is also advertised as ideal for a 'family day out'. Connected to scenes of revenge and vendetta, Carrick-a-Rede, Larrybane and Antrim are also officially advertised for their 'special Scientific Interest: unique geology, flora and fauna'. This is especially significant for Carrick-a-Rede, which is located near Giant's Causeway, Antrim – a geological formation that resulted from a volcanic eruption 60 million years ago. The filmed site is discussed as 'focal point of a designated Area of Outstanding Natural Beauty [that] has attracted visitors for centuries' (Discover Northern Ireland.com 2014). It must be noted that a great part of the Giant's Causeway and Causeway Coast World Heritage Site is today owned and managed by the National Trust. However, the recognition of the Coast as a World Heritage Site in 1986; as a national nature reserve in 1987 by the Department of the Environment for Northern Ireland; and as the fourth greatest natural wonder in the United Kingdom (Northern Ireland Tourist Board 2008) form a peculiar couple with the area's recent cinematic glamour. One wonders whose 'community heritage' is advertised – and to what ends?

Such unresolved questions are constitutive of the *GoT*'s digital governmobilities, which promote analogical classification of ideals: nature and landscaped 'physiognomies' (e.g. unusual geological formations) behave *like* natural human bonds we find in families. Their eco-systemic management conforms and reproduces the biopolitics (Foucault 1997) of the nation-state (the management of its populations), while simultaneously turning this into the maiden of governmobilities (the global management of naturalized ethnic character). There is no mention of the Troubles online, only of the archaic legends of these sites, scientific information on geographical formations and even their management, in some cases, by proper scientific institutions (Giddens 2009; Urry 2011). The 'scientization' of such Northern Irish landscapes transcends the imperatives of nationalism, as it responds to international-institutional calls. But such calls also enable the restoration of nature in the cybersphere's meaning province, where the *GoT*'s cinematic reality matters less than its recuperation as a Northern Irish ecosystem. At the same time, such 'recuperation' assists with historical healing. A narrative identical to Discover Northern Ireland's figures on Tourism Ireland's (2014) website, where it is stated that 'of course, aside from the fantasy landscapes, there's a good reason why Northern Ireland was picked by *GoT* location scouts. There are castles everywhere; incredible structures that catapult you right to the heart of the mythical land of Westeros', confirming the province's 'breath-taking natural beauty'. Note that Tourism Ireland was established under the framework of the Belfast Agreement of 'Good Friday' on April 1998, to increase tourism to Ireland as a whole. The institution has worked closely 'with its sister agencies on the island of Ireland, particularly in the development of this website, Fáilte Ireland, the national tourism development authority of the Republic of Ireland, and the Northern Ireland Tourist Board' (ibid.). The harmonization of the website's discourse on the *GoT* locations with that of Discover Northern Ireland is also in agreement with post-colonial and post-nationalist tourism policies. Agreement is achieved digitally by forgetting political disagreements in order to enable global tourist mobilities.

Therefore, it is more accurate to argue that the governmobile ethos of such websites is geared towards the mastery, packaging and international promotion of Northern Irish landscapes as the only part of 'Irish character', habitus and history worthy of salvation from oblivion. Although clearly implicated in Northern Irish political intrigues, this move is constitutive of post-industrial ecological movements that haunted Western (post-) modernity with the condemnation of humans to rootlessness and eternal mobility (Urry 2007; Cresswell 2010). The occulocentric techniques of these websites enable potential film tourists to accept death as a spectacle that stands outside their own experiences – to speculate the mask or image of the King from afar, as distant cosmopolitans (Szerszynski and Urry 2006), with little affective engagement with local 'troubles'. This aesthetic emphasis on the distant picturesque corresponds to the American poet William Cullen Bryant's (1817) coining of 'thanatopsis' to denote the speculation of one's own death through the eyes of others, while entertaining relief for avoiding it, at least temporarily. Thus, instead of considering thanatopsis as part of the dark tourist's fascination with other people's death, we may view it as the mechanism with which new technologies use consumerist prerogatives to enable prospective clientele to enjoy the gift of life. The promise of this gift is actualized through visual representations of tourism in filmed sites – as is the case with independent Belfast company 'Game of Thrones Tours' (2014), which warns prospective cinematic tourists that 'in Ireland, Winter is never far away. Winter is always coming, almost every day'. The likeness of rugged Irish climate-landscape to Martin's mythical domains allows for the transformation of thanatourist simulation into embodied performance for those who are not 'faint-hearted' (ibid.) and not interested in history's troubled events. Needless to add that such independent websites, which link the technologized phantasmagoric city (of Belfast and Dublin) to the 'dark' countryside (e.g. Williams 1974) still work in harmony with nationalist interests that wish to obliterate non-profitable traumatic 'events'.

Conclusion: *GoT* to game of sights/sites

In terms of theory, this chapter deliberated on conceptions of 'events' as both materializations of histories and collective memories and also places of imagination and literary fiction re-framed by contemporary industries (film and tourism) into consumable products for collective (film, internet and tourist) gazes and ears (Reijnders 2011). It did so via exposition of the ways a cinematically mediated *heterotopia* (of Irish dark and bloody histories) allowed for protective marketing of post-colonial violence as natural tourist spaces and visitor performances. Contextually, it analysed how the *GoT* TV series has been placed at the centre of tourism policy-making in Northern Ireland and locative media sectors, not in spite, but because of its potential to hybridize Ireland's traumatic memories of civil war. Its developmental potential in film and tourism industries (its 'financial node') in the current global recession is supported by its narrative node (the demise of family utopia from feuds). Its new e-tourist industry is constituted by various regional (e.g. locative tourism media in Northern Ireland) and independent agents that currently market regional landscapes online.

The rationale of such *GoT*-inspired websites, according to which filmed Northern Irish image-places are beautiful sites for mobile viewing subjects (Larsen 2001: 88), conforms to conceptions of the Western European 'beautiful' world-image, picturesque renditions of Northern Irish cultural nature as a way of disinterested 'world-making' (Duncan 1999: 153; Dann 2002: 6; Budd 2003; Hollingshead 2007). This is achieved in practice through digital transformations of true Irish 'family' feuds – the original thanatic inspiration of *GoT* location selection – into potential family tourist destinations, global film-tourist pilgrimages, or mere ecotourist spots (Couldry 2003a; Beeton 2006; Tzanelli 2013). These blends are constitutive of the *GoT*'s digital governmobilities, which promote analogical classification of ideals: nature and landscaped 'physiognomies' (e.g. unusual geological formations) are like naturalized human bonds supporting family socialities (Herzfeld 2001). Both can be scrutinized and understood by common mobile folk (tourists) only by visual means, if not purchased as tourism holidays. The cultural and political complexity of their *nature* is intrinsically connected to Northern Irish habitus, which can now travel the world in the form of images. The original nature of Northern Irish dark tourism as a means by which the living establish a relationship with death and the dead collectively (as a nation) or individually (as mourning family members) (Walter 2009) is now replaced with dispassionate tourist engaging with dead landscapes (Urry 2004) that allows Northern Ireland to build a mobile future on oblivion.

References

Bærenholdt, J. O. (2013) Governmobility: The powers of mobility. *Mobilities*, 8(1): 20–34.

Baudrillard, J. (1973) *Toward a Critique of the Political Economy of the Sign*. St Louis, MO: Telos.

Baudrillard, J. (2006) Virtuality and events: The hell of power. *Baudrillard Studies*, 3(2): unpaginated, translated by C. Turner. Available from http://www.ubishops.ca/ BaudrillardStudies/ (accessed 26 November 2014).

Bauman, Z. (2007) *Consuming Life*. Cambridge: Polity Press.

BBC News (2009) 'Medieval Keep Becomes Film Set'. 23 October. Available from http://news.bbc.co.uk/1/hi/scotland/tayside_and_central/8322843.stm (accessed 28 November 2014).

Beeton, S. (2006) Understanding Film-Induced Tourism. *Tourism Analysis*, 11: 181–188.

Belting, H. (2007) *Antropología de la Imagen*. Madrid: Editorial Katz.

Bleicher J. (1980) *Contemporary Hermeneutics: Hermeneutics as Method, Philosophy and Critique*. London and New York: Routledge.

Bolan, P. (2010) Film-induced tourism: Motivation, authenticity and displacement. PhD Thesis, Business School: University of Ulster.

Bolan, P. and O'Connor, N. (2008) Creating a sustainable brand for Northern Ireland through film induced tourism. *Tourism, Culture and Communication*, 8 (3): 147–158.

Bradley, U. (2013) The 'Game of Thrones' tourists: How much is the hit HBO fantasy series worth to its *Home*, Northern Ireland? 12 April. *The Irish Times*. Available from http://www.irishtimes.com/premium/loginpage?destination=http://www.irishtimes.com/culture/media/the-game-of-thrones-tourists-1.1357475 (accessed 29 November 2014).

Brescia, R. (2012) Game of robes: Why conservatives may ultimately praise the Roberts switch on health care reform. 6 July. *Huffington Post*. Available from http://www.huffingtonpost.com/ray-brescia/game-of-robes-why-conserv_b_1647678.html (accessed 29 November 2014).

Bryant, W. C. (1817) Thanatopsis. *North American Review*, 5(15): 338–341.

Budd, M. (2003) *Aesthetic Appreciation of Nature: Essays on the Aesthetics of Nature*. Oxford: Clarendon Press.

Büscher, M. and Urry, J. (2009) Mobile methods and the empirical. *European Journal of Social Theory*, 12: 99–116.

Büscher, M., Urry, J. and Witchger, K. (2011) *Mobile Methods*. London: Routledge.

Castells, M. (2004) Informationalism, networks and the network society: A theoretical blueprint. In M. Castells (ed.) *The Network Society*, Cheltenham: Edward Elgar, pp. 3–45.

Chowdry, G. (2007) Edward Said and contrapuntal reading: Implications for critical interventions in international relations. *Millennium*, 36(1): 101–116.

Cosgrove, D. (1998) *Social Formation and Symbolic Landscape*. Madison, WI: University of Wisconsin Press.

Couldry, N. (2003a) Media meta-capital: Extending the range of Bourdieu's field theory. *Theory and Society*, 32(5/6): 653–677.

Couldry, N. (2003b) *Media Rituals*. New York: Routledge.

Cresswell, T. (2006) *On the Move: Mobility in the Modern Western World*. London: Routledge.

Cresswell, T. (2010) Towards a politics of mobility. *Environment and Planning D*, 28(1): 17–31.

Curtis, L. P. (1971) *Apes and Angels: The Irishman in Victorian Caricature*. New York: Smithsonian Institution Press.

Dann, G. M. S. (2002) The tourist as a metaphor of the social world. In G.M.S. Dann (ed.) *The Tourist as a Metaphor of the Social World*, Wallingford: CABI, pp.1–18.

De Souza e Silva, A. and Frith, J. (2011) *Net-Locality: Why Location Matters in a Networked World*. Malden, MA and Oxford: Wiley-Blackwell.

De Souza e Silva, A. and Sheller, M. (eds) (2014) *Mobility and Locative Media: Mobile Communication in Hybrid Spaces*. London: Routledge.

Dean, J. (2007) The net and multiple realities. In S. During (ed.) *The Cultural Studies Reader*, third edition. London: Routledge, pp.520–534.

Delanty G. and O'Mahony, P. (2002) *Nationalism and Social Theory*. London: Sage.

Discover Northern Ireland.com (2014) Game of Thrones Tours. Available from http://www.discovernorthernireland.com/gameofthrones/ (accessed 08 December 2014).

Duncan, J. (1999) Dis-orientation: On the shock of the familiar in a far-away place. In J. Duncan and D. Gregory (eds) *Writes of Passage: Reading Travel Writing*. London: Routledge, pp.161–179.

Foucault, M. (1986) Of other spaces. *Diacritics*, 16(1): 22–27.

Foucault, M. (1997) The birth of biopolitics. In P. Rabinow (ed.) *Michel Foucault: Ethics*. New York: New Press.

Foucault, M. 2009 [2004]. Biopolitikkens Fødsel: Forelæsninger på Collège de France 1978–79 ([Danish transition from: Naissance de la biopolitique: Cours au Collège de France 1978–79]). Copenhagen: Gyldendals Bogklubber.

Gabriel, B. (2004) The unbearable strangeness of being. in B. Gabriel and S. Ilcan (eds) *Postmodernism and the Ethical Subject*, Montreal: McGill-Queen's University Press.

Game of Thrones Tours (2014) Available from http://www.gameofthronestours.com/ (accessed 10 December 2014).

Garnaut, J. (2012) Strongmen of China playing a risky Game of Thrones. 1 July. *The Age*. Available from http://www.theage.com.au/world/strongmen-of-china-playing-a-risky-game-of-thrones-20120630-219km.html (accessed 29 November 2014).

Germann Molz, J. (2012) *Travel Connections*. London: Routledge.

Giddens, A. (1987) *Social Theory and Modern Sociology*. Cambridge: Polity Press.

Giddens, A. (2009) *The Politics of Climate Change*. Cambridge: Polity.

Hann, M. (2012) How 'sexposition' fleshes out the story. 11 March. *The Guardian*. Available from http://www.theguardian.com/tv-and-radio/2012/mar/11/sexposition-story-tv-drama?newsfeed=true (accessed 29 November 2014).

Hannam, K. (2008) The end of tourism? Nomadology and the mobilities paradigm. In J. Tribe (ed.) *Philosophical Issues in Tourism*. Bristol and Toronto: Channel View Publications, pp.101–116.

Hannam, K., Sheller, M. and Urry, J. (2006) Editorial: Mobilities, immobilites and moorings. *Mobilities*, 1(1): 1–22.

Henning, C. (2002) Tourism: Enacting modern myths. In G.M.S. Dann (ed.) *The Tourist as a Metaphor of the Social World*, Wallingford: CABI, pp.169–188.

Herzfeld, M. (2001) *Anthropology: Theoretical Practice in Culture and Society*, Oxford: Blackwell/UNESCO.

Holland, T. (2013) 'Game of Thrones is more brutally realistic than most historical novels. 24 March. *Guardian*. Available from http://www.theguardian.com/tv-and-radio/2013/mar/24/game-of-thrones-realistic-history (accessed 28 November 2014).

Hollingshead, K. (2007) 'Worldmaking' and the transformation of place and culture. In Ateljevic, I., Pritchord, A. and Morgan, N. (eds) *The Critical Turn in Tourism Studies: Innovative Research Methodologies*. Oxford: Elsevier, 165–193.

Jameson, F. (1986) Third-world literature in the era of multinational capitalism. *Social Text*, 15: 65–88.

Jensen, O. B. (2010) Negotiation in motion: Unpacking a geography of mobility. *Space and Culture*, 13(4): 389–402.

Jensen, O. B. (2013) *Staging Mobilities*. London: Routledge.

Jensen, O. B. (2014) *Designing Mobilities*. London: Routledge.

Jensen, O. B. and Richardson, T. D. (2004) *Making European Space: Mobility, Power and territorial Identity*. London: Routledge.

Josh, R. (2012) Where HBO's hit Game of Thrones was filmed. 1 April. *USA Today*. Available from http://travel.usatoday.com/destinations/story/2012-04-01/Where-the-HBO-hit-Game-of-Thrones-was-filmed/53876876/1 (accessed 28 November 2014).

Kaelber, L. (2007) A memorial as virtual traumascape: Darkest tourism in 3D and cyber-space to the gas chambers of Auschwitz. *E-Review of Tourism Research*, 5 (2): 24–33.

Kearney, R. (ed.) (1984) *The Irish Mind*. Dublin: The Wolfhound Press.

Kirkup, J. (2013) Winter is coming: Politics and Game of Thrones. 30 May. *The Daily Telegraph*. Available from http://blogs.telegraph.co.uk/news/jameskirkup/100219397/winter-is-coming-politics-and-game-of-thrones/ (accessed 29 November 2014).

Korstanje, M. (2008) La Anthropología de la Imagen en Hans Belting. *Revista Digital Universitaria*, 9(7): 3–10.

Korstanje, M. and Tarlow, P. (2012) Being lost: Tourism, risk and vulnerability in the post-'9/11' entertainment industry. *Journal of Tourism and Cultural Change*, 10(1): 22–33.

Larsen, J. (2001) Tourism mobilities and the travel glance: Experiences of being on the move. *Scandinavian Journal of Hospitality and Tourism*, 1(2): 80–98.

Larsen, J. and Urry, J. (2008) Networking in mobile societies. In Bærenholdt, J. O and Granås, B. (eds). *Mobility and place: enacting Northern European peripheries*, Aldershot: Ashgate, pp. 89–101.

Lash, S. and Urry, J. (1987) *The End of Organized Capitalism*. Madison WI: University of Wisconsin Press.

Lash, S. and Urry, J. (1994) *Economies of Signs and Space*. London: Sage.

McAdam, N. (2012) Game of Thrones pumped £43m into Northern Ireland's economy, and more could be on the way. 16 May. *Belfast Telegraph*. Available from http://www.belfasttelegraph.co.uk/entertainment/film-tv/news/game-of-thrones-pumped-43m-into-northern-irelands-economy-and-more-could-be-on-the-way-28749710.html (accessed 29 November 2014).

McKee, R. (1999) *Story*. London: Methuen.

McKittrick, D. et al. (2007) *Lost Lives: The Stories of the Men, Women and Children who Died as a Result of the Northern Ireland Troubles*. Edinburgh: Mainstream.

Mitchell, W. J. T. (1994) *Landscape and Power*. Chicago: University of Chicago Press.

Nederveen Pieterse, J. (1997) Globalization as hybridization. In M. Featherstone, S. Lash, and R. Robertson (eds) *Global Modernities*. London: Sage.

Nora, P. (1989) Between memory and history: *Les lieux de memoire*. *Representations*, 26(2): 7–25.

Northern Ireland Screen (2012) Game of Thrones season 3 to film in Northern Ireland. 12 April. Available from http://northernirelandscreen.co.uk/news/2919/game-of-thrones-season-3-to-film-in-northern-ireland.aspx (accessed 29 November 2014).

Northern Ireland Tourist Board (2008) Giant's Causeway remains Northern Ireland's top attraction. 18 August. Available from http://www.nitb.com/ (accessed 10 December 2014).

Phelan, J. (2014) The 7 Kingdoms in 'Game of Thrones' are actually these 5 real-world places. 29 April. *Global Post*. Available from http://www.salon.com/2014/04/29/the_7_kingdoms_in_game_of_thrones_are_actually_these_5_real_world_places_partner/ (accessed 28 November 2014).

Reijnders, S. (2011) *Places of the Imagination*. Burlington, VT: Ashgate.

Said, E. (1978) *Orientalism*. Harmondsworth: Penguin.

Savas, K. (2012) Composer Interview: Ramin Djawadi. 22 December. *F.F.M.* Available from http://www.filmmusicmedia.com/interviews/composerinterviewramindjawadi-1 (accessed 28 November 2014).

Sheller, M. and Urry, J. (2006) The new mobilities paradigm. *Environment and Planning A*, 38(2): 207–226.

Shields, R. (1991) *Places on the Margin: Alternative Geographies of Modernity*. London: Routledge.

Slade, P. (2003) Gallipoli thanatourism: The meaning of ANZAC. *Annals of Tourism Research*, 30(4): 779–794.

Smith, P. (2008) The Balinese cockfight decoded: Reflections on Geertz, the strong programme and structuralism. *Cultural Sociology*, 2(2): 169–186.

Spurr, D. (1993) *The Rhetoric of Empire*. Durham, NC: Duke University Press.

Szerszynski, B. and Urry, J. (2006) Visuality, mobility and the cosmopolitan: Inhabiting the world from afar. *The British Journal of Sociology*, 57(1): 113–131.

Todorova, M. (1997) *Imagining the Balkans*. New York and Oxford: Oxford University Press.

Tourism Ireland (2014) Game of Thrones to promote Northern Ireland overseas: Foster. 2 April. Available from http://www.tourismireland.com/Home!/About-Us/Press-Releases/2014/Game-of-Thrones-to-Promote-Northern-Ireland-Overse.aspx (accessed 29 November 2014).

Tourism Ireland (2014) Fantasy blockbuster Game of Thrones chose Northern Ireland as one of its primary filming locations. Why? Find out .... Available from http://www.ireland.com/en-gb/articles/game-of-thrones/ (accessed 10 December 2014).

Tzanelli, R. (2007) *The Cinematic Tourist: Explorations in Globalization, Culture and Resistance*. London: Routledge.

Tzanelli, R. (2013) *Heritage in the Digital Era: Cinematic Tourism and the Activist Cause*. London: Routledge.

Urry, J. (2003) *Global Complexity*. Cambridge: Polity.

Urry, J. (2004) Death in Venice. In M. Sheller and J. Urry (eds) *Tourism Mobilities: Places to Play, Places in Play*, London and New York: Routledge, pp. 205–215.

Urry, J. (2007) *Mobilities*. Cambridge: Polity.

Urry, J. (2011) *Climate Change and Society*. Cambridge: Polity.

Urry, J. and J. Larsen (2011) *The Tourist Gaze 3.0*, third edition. London: Sage.

Varsavsky, M. (4 July 2012) 'The Game of Thrones around us', *The Huffington Post*. Available from http://www.huffingtonpost.com/martin-varsavsky/there-is-still-a-lot-of-g_b_1649089.html (accessed 29 November 2014).

Viator (April 2015) Game of Thrones sites in Europe. Available from http://www.viator.com/Europe-tourism/Game-of-Thrones-Sites-in-Europe/d6-t10684 (accessed 16 June 2015).

Walter, T. (2009) Dark tourism: Mediating between the dead and the living. In *The Darker Side of Travel: The Theory and Practice of Dark Tourism*, Bristol: Channel View Publications, pp.39–55.

White, H. (1978) *Tropics of Discourse*. Baltimore: Johns Hopkins University Press.

Williams, R. (1974) *The Country and the City*. New York: Oxford University Press.

Žižek, S. (2014) *Event: Philosophy in Transit*. Harmondsworth: Penguin.

6 Making home 'Under the Big Top'

Materialities of moving a small town every day and wintering in place

Rebecca Sheehan

For those vagabonds of heart, the phrase, 'running away from home to join the circus', suggests living a life devoid of home place – a life without connections to place. Reading the oral histories of circus people from three circuses that winter in Hugo, Oklahoma, USA, however, suggests otherwise. In their stories, complex geographies of home emerge that depart from traditional ideas of 'home'. I argue that for these circus people, home is created *through* points of arrival, departure, and connection *in* route and *in* Hugo. In what follows, I first review literature concerning home and mobilities to situate my study. Next, I explain the typical workings of the Carson & Barnes, Kelly-Miller, and Culpepper Merryweather circuses over a year, including a typical day during circus season. I then explore two activities: schooling and funerary activities for circus people. By examining the practices and materiality of movement and moorings at a variety of scales both geographically and temporally, I show how dynamic networks create home not as the road and Hugo but rather as their enfolding. My analysis is based upon 20 oral histories of long-time circus people who winter or who (now) live in Hugo.[1] All participants were white, including men and women (born between 1927 and 1977), who held an assortment of positions, including circus owner, performer, animal trainer, and booking agent. Most participants had held a variety of such positions – many came from circus families.

Home and mobilities

Traditionally, the concept of 'home' necessitates a sense of belonging situated over time in *a* place (Relph 1976; Tuan 1977; see also Blunt and Dowling 2006). Place then serves as the repository of home, constructed through reiterated moored material and social practices. Accordingly, home and a sense of self weave together, as according to Casey (2001: 406) 'there is no self without [home] place'. Ideally then, home is where a positive development of self-validation, self-assurance, and stability occurs, but scholars have shown that relationships with home are more complex than the nostalgic slogan, 'There's no place like home' suggests. Drawing from Clifford (1997) and Gilroy (1993), for example, Gustafson shows that roots and routes are not always in conflict in processes of making home; yet, he clearly situates security, continuity, and community in place and mobility with 'transcending one's "own" (home) place' (2001: 672).

Additionally, home may be a place of violence, disconnection, exclusion, and insecurity, especially among transient and homeless populations, which, obviously, negatively affects a sense of self. In order to experience home benefits – positive processes in the ongoing becoming of self – ideas of home may necessarily expand, where the prominence of a place is re-placed with multiple places, structures, and networks of connections (May 2000; Robertson 2007; Robinson 2002, 2011; Ursin 2011). Robinson (2002: 35) argues that for those experiencing homelessness, home is a 'network of connections which do not rest in one place or self alone'. Drawing from Bammer (1992), she explains that 'enacted space', rather than any particular place, is where persons experiencing homelessness often can feel belonging and autonomy – where one can be-at-home (Robinson 2002: 6). And in our hyper-mobile world today, it follows that the mutability of 'home' may be found in a variety of groups and contexts.

For example, other scholars have further complicated Gustafson's (2001) ideas of roots and routes to consider more amorphic and flexible concepts and practices of home in migrant and second-home geographies (Nowicka 2007; Datta 2008; Molz 2008; Ralph and Staeheli 2011; Paris 2011; Teo 2011; Chen 2012; Halfacree 2012; Lagerqvist 2013; Ellingsen and Hidle 2013). This scholarship draws from and builds upon mobilities literature, which explicitly considers movement and stillness at multiple scales. Drawing from actor-network theory, Nowicka illustrates that through social and technical networks, transnational professionals' understandings of home have permeable boundaries. In fact, she argues that home is 'a turning, and not the exit, point of movement' (2007: 72). Here, turning points are temporary focal points composed of routines of people, objects, and relationships. Similarly, Ralph and Staeheli argue that for migrants 'home' is 'accordion-like, in that it stretches to expand migrants outwards to distant and remote places, while also squeezing to *embed* them in their proximate and immediate locales' (2011: 518, emphasis added). In this, as other scholars argue, home is simultaneously mobile and in place. Similarly, research concerning second homes emphasizes the 'hetero*local*' qualities of home as multi-centred (Halfacree 2012, emphasis added), often showing how facets in rural and urban places are complementary in fulfilling a sense of home (Paris 2011; Lagerqvist 2013). Both migrant and second-home research recognizes movement in stillness – and stillness in movement that mobility scholars theorize (see, for example, Adey 2006; Hannam et al. 2006; Cresswell 2010, 2012) – analysing, for example, how a highly mobile life enables the purchase of a traditional cottage as a second home, which represents as well as provides a sense of rootedness (Lagerqvist 2013). This work explicates that the intertwining of movement and stillness produces complex, sometimes hierarchical, meanings of and within the multi-centred home, (Datta 2008; Ellingsen and Hidle 2013; Lagerqvist 2013). In such practices, home is often associated with (time) travels, relocation of possessions, and remittances that connect one home place to another (Cassiman 2008; Chen 2012; Lagerqvist 2013).

Yet, while the above research shows that such movements certainly shape home as lived and home as imagined, the travel itself is rarely examined as a constituent of home. Molz (2008) and Ellingsen and Hidle (2013) are exceptions. Examining round-the-world travellers, who have relatively affluent status (i.e. power), Molz argues that these travellers employing similar means as those above (social and technological networks, rituals, familiar objects), feel they belong anywhere. However, she argues that while these travellers feel they belong anywhere, home is actually the road itself, highlighting that 'home is evoked through the interplay between movement and stasis' (Molz 2008: 331). Ellingsen and Hidle draw more explicitly from Latour's (2005) idea of heterogeneous networks, showing that 'technology, infrastructure, landscape, and people' of the repeated journey to and from a second home contributes to a sense of belonging (2013: 262). Here 'the road', that is, the route, is part of an expanded concept of what home is and does. This can be related to Cresswell's (2010) ideas associated with constellations of mobilities where entanglements of movement, representation, and practice form home (see also Vannini 2011a), or rather enact home (Robinson 2002).

Indeed, Cresswell (2011: 717) calls for researchers to 'reflect on the productive tensions between the worlds of logistical flows' – the routes that connect places, including movements and moments of fixity. While he is referring to the complex systems associated with goods and services, examining the logistics associated with movement and stillness has merit in understanding expanded concepts of home. For instance, scholars examining nomadism and/or homelessness show that different groups and cultures may have varied interactions and relationships with place concerning the making of home. Here, home develops not *in a* place but rather in the *moving through* places to develop a sense of rootedness and connectedness (Somerville 1992; Hay 1998; Veness 1993; Andrews 2004). Christensen (2013) examines the socio-cultural dimensions of homelessness in now settled indigenous groups by considering how home is multi-scalar both spatially and temporally as well as individual and social.[2] In part, she shows that denying nomadism has had profound effects on the constitution of indigenous home place because their way of life has fundamentally changed. In this change, positive contributions of home concerning belonging and identity associated with the heritage of indigenous ethnicity are lost. To be sure, movement and networks may be incorporated into ideas of home, relying upon, for example, a feeling of being-at-home and belonging based upon *dynamic* lived experiences. I now turn to these facets of home for people from three specific circuses that winter in Hugo, Oklahoma, USA.

Routes

The Carson & Barnes, Kelly-Miller, and Culpepper Merryweather are all one-ring circuses. Typically performing in small towns, they each have between 40 to 70 employees and 20 to 30 vehicles. From approximately February to mid-October, each circus takes a different route, traveling through at least five states.

They perform two shows and spend one night at each town. Travelling ten to twelve thousand miles a season for 200 venues, circuses drive about an hour every day between towns. In the towns where they perform, circuses purchase supplies such as groceries, hay, and fuel and go to laundromats, movie theatres, and restaurants. Circuses return to these towns, but allow two to five years between visits. For the next season, circuses start booking shows in the late summer. Often circuses partner with 'fork and knife clubs' such as the Lions and Kiwanis or other community organizations, for a share of the profits. They do this by way of having a person from the club or organization designated as the 'circus chairperson' to be in charge of helping to advertise as well as to gain appropriate permitting.

Two weeks before the scheduled show day, the circus press agent arrives in the town to see how the sponsor is doing. The press agent also works with businesses in advertising the circus as well the business's product (such as Ford). Then a '24-hour person' from the circus reaches the town a day before the circus. This person makes sure that water and electric, for example, are available and ready on the site for the circus. The 24-hour person also meets with the fire marshal and health department official and ensures that food for the animals is delivered to each town. Until recent GPS devices, this person also placed arrows along the route to the next town, to supplement maps and written routes given to each driver.

On a typical circus day, the owner rises at about 5 a.m. and makes sure that his or her key staff are up. Then he or she leaves, heading to the next town to meet with the 24-hour person. The first trucks arrive in the next town 15–30 minutes after the owner. Meanwhile all other staff rise, have breakfast, and depart by 6:30 a.m., arriving in that next town by 7:30 a.m. By 9 a.m. some of the public arrives on the circus site to watch the circus tent go up and to see the animals; in addition, the circus may provide a tour and answer questions. Lunch is served for the circus people at the commissary around 11 a.m. At 2:30 p.m. performers begin to prepare for the first performance, with the midway call following at 3:30 p.m. Shows are at 4:30 p.m. and 7:30 p.m., running about two hours each. After the last show (9:30 p.m.), circus workers do the 'tear down' of the tent, taking approximately 45–70 minutes, and animals are secured and tended. Meanwhile other circus people usually gather at one trailer to wind down, eventually returning to their trailers to go to bed between midnight and 2:00 a.m.

The next day, the circus begins the routine all over, with circus owners waking their key staff again. One former circus owner did so by yelling out to staff trailers, 'Such-and-such you're in the wrong town!' Certainly, the short-lived stays on lots in towns can be disorienting. For instance, when two interviewees, a mother and daughter, were asked if they had a favourite town, they provided the following exchange,

Mother: Well, a lot of people would say, 'Where were you yesterday?' I don't know. (laughter)

Daughter: 'Where are you going tomorrow?' I don't know. (laughs)

Mother: You forget it so quick, it's amazing.
Daughter: Yes.
Mother: Because you do so many towns.

These sentiments reflect the pace of movement and the fleeting moorings associated with each town. As another interviewee explained, 'I mean, you just travel around. It's just like a wonderland, really ... [It's] like a sightseeing ship', suggesting a particular social distance between the towns and the circus people. The pace of the daily and monthly routines of brief, albeit repeated interactions, marks a lack of emotional connection between circus people and the towns where they perform.

In fact, when circus people discussed the towns where they perform, they referenced friendly business relationships rather than a sense of belonging to any place. Accordingly, while some circus people described how some places wanted and appreciated them more than other places, most discussed logistical workings and to a lesser extent entertainment, sightseeing, and educational opportunities. As another interviewee elaborated,

> Usually every town in the country has a feed store, and you can go in and buy your sweet feed and whatever you want. Then they would call the feed store and find out who has hay, locally, and you buy local hay, if you need the hay. Or find somebody that delivers and they'll deliver it to the circus grounds ... And the best feed for me, when I'm traveling, I like the Amish country because they have good, good feed. Their feed stores are really good. You buy them and they still come in that—instead of paper and stuff, they still come in burlap sacks, big burlap sacks ... on Sundays, [a bus] would make several trips back and forth to the circus and to town. They would have a list of everything that was in town, McDonald's, Arby's, China King, whatever. And then they would have a list of the movies, the bowling alley ...

The repeated ephemeral moorings (Vannini 2011b) are part of the circuses' constellations of mobilities but are not associated with belonging in or to places on the road. As Adey (2006) explains we need to pay careful attention to realize the relations and differences between movements. So while circuses have repeated moorings in towns, these moorings nevertheless do not create attachments in place as home or even as homes away from home.

Instead, circus people again and again described home-making through material and social practices within spaces of the circus caravan. For example, one interviewee explained,

> [We] didn't mingle in town [where we performed] ... I can't imagine anything else. I mean, because all these people, these show people and these shows that are on, is like a huge family, and I don't always find that in town ... [and] if you had quite a bit of family in the back yard, they would have a little private thing. I know one of the things I always liked so much about

Herb's show is after the show at night, the people would gather, they'd take turns, the women, serving a little lunch or some coffee or something like that in the back yard and everybody'd go to that trailer. The next time, it would be another trailer's turn to do it. Yes, when the show was over, you couldn't stay too long, because you had to get up and go to work the next morning, but if you had a two-day stand, boy, that was a plus. You really got to sit up and have a sandwich and just chew the rag and talk about old times and so on.

The back yard here is the area behind the big top at each town, where trailers for living quarters and other circus vehicles park. In the stillness of the back yard, time away from circus work and driving, that punctuates the flow of the circus (Bissell and Fuller 2011), we see one way in which home emerges for circus people. Thus, home-making practices rely more upon the space created by circus people where private interactions facilitated a sense of belonging rather than any particular place. These practices were habitual as was the movement, so that in moments of stillness (above) and the rhythm of movement of the circus *together*, home is enacted. As an interviewee made clear,

> Every day is so routine ... you get up in the morning, you drive to the next town, you get to the town, you set your trailer back up because before you leave you have to set ... all your little knickknacks ... all your little things down ... you stick them down so they don't fall ... always do your dishes the night before ... little things like that. I'd have a geranium I'd set out on my little stool in front of my trailer. That's my home. I'd bring it in at night and set it in my shower section ... You'd get to the lot, you'd set your house back up, run through, takes—shoot, you could clean a whole trailer from top to bottom in less than an hour. My job on Kelly Miller was to go to the cookhouse, get the grocery list, head to the store and buy the groceries and come back ...

As the passages above suggest, the routine encompasses more than work. Circus people made remarks such as, 'it takes a village to run a circus', and 'the circus is like a little town', indicating that the circus is in many ways its own place that travels through places, and that that movement is fundamental to the village or town. For example, when a retired circus person was asked about what she missed most about being on the road, she replied, 'I guess the moving ...' In that moving, place is created. Indeed, several circus people actually referred to the circus as 'place'. As one interviewee asserted,

> The circus is, maybe some people wouldn't think so, but the circus is a wonderful place to raise a child. It's a really protective community, and every-one's always watching out for the kids, but yet you have this freedom to run across the lot ... it's living life on the road in the centre ring, but there's still all the problems of living life that go along with it. You're not immune to any of the problems that you would have in Stillwater or wherever you live.

A sense of belonging and rootedness emerges in the logistics and routes of circuses that are repetitive, regular, and cyclical in nature across multiple temporal and spatial scales (Cresswell 2010; Ellingsen and Hidle 2013). Whereas scholars show how lives are grounded in multiple locations to construct home, in the circuses above, lives are grounded in the route (Ralph and Staeheli 2011; Halfacree 2012; Ellingsen and Hidle 2013; Lageqvist 2013). As Ursin (2011: 223) argues,

> Home is located cognitively in memories and narrations, and in everyday social interaction. The contemporary notion of 'home' as mobile does not indicate that one is home everywhere but rather that one may feel at home anywhere, depending on the circumstances.

Therefore, one may conclude that 'anywhere' for these circuses is the road, and that Hugo is merely a longer wayfaring station, similar to the towns where they perform. However, this interpretation belies the complexity concerning how circus people who winter in Hugo construct home. To explore this complexity, I want to unpack more this idea that one may feel 'at home anywhere'.

Hugo

The circuses begin to return to Hugo in mid-October. Their animals winter there as do many circus people, though some circus people intermittently leave to perform and work in other venues. Back in Hugo, circuses finish planning their routes for the next season. Additionally, other logistical and regular maintenance concerns for the road are addressed. For example, a former circus owner explained,

> Now, you have to begin from scratch to redo your route. Typically, it's already started. Usually, we started booking the next season at least by September 1. So you already know where you are going for the year, but logistically you have to, 'Okay, what equipment needs to be refurbished? What equipment needs to be replaced? Do I need a new tent? Am I losing people, serious staff that I'm going to have to replace? How soon do I need to start? The elephant truck needs a new floor and a paint job. We are going to have to redo the inside of the interior of the elephant truck.' So that's on your mind. You schedule that. 'How much time is it going to take to redo the truck? It'll tie up the barn for so many days ...'

Here, material practices in place prepare circuses for the show season, making home an enfolding of the road and Hugo. However, this logistical intertwining of the road and home includes a variety of other activities that go beyond 'work'. Due to space limitations, below I examine just two examples, schooling and funerary activities, to demonstrate how the road and Hugo come *together* as home through intertwining mutual material and social practices.

Schooling

Beginning in the 1940s, the Hugo school system worked with the circuses by allowing students in the circus to take their books with them on the road. A circus adult would then teach school five days a week, having students do the same lessons as those in the Hugo schools. Then, that teacher would take the lessons to the post office and mail them back to the Hugo schools. When the circus returned to Hugo, the circus children would be placed in the appropriate grade for two weeks. If they did well, they stayed; if they did poorly they had to go back a grade. However, as one of the oldest interviewees pointed out, 'They always made the next grade'. This goodwill between circus people and Hugo schools has been perpetuated in a variety of nuanced geographies.

Sometimes circus children, especially when they reach(ed) middle or high school, stay(ed) with a family member, friend, or boarding house while their parents travel(led) with the circus. As one interviewee explained,

> I got to travel on the circus with my family for the majority of the time. I wasn't actually in Hugo full-time until I started middle school. That's when mother stayed home with us, and we went to school for the full school season and only travelled on the circus during the summer months.

Despite the discontinuous relationship with Hugo schools, circus children and non-circus children typically integrate socially at school. As another circus person said,

> There were a lot of fond memories of Hugo because there were so many show people and because the town people interrelated with us, correlated with us. It wasn't a problem that we were circus people. My brother was probably one of the most popular kids in school. He played football, was top honour's everywhere, and everybody liked him.

These positive feelings of belonging did not necessarily require that circus children always excelled in school. For instance, another interviewee said,

> I hated school. It's not that I was dumb or stupid or anything. My mother left me here one year in 1960 with a lady named Ruby Doyle. I called her Aunt Ruby and I used to make straight Fs. I've gone to school with everybody in Hugo, Oklahoma, 'Oh Lucy? Yeah! I know her!' I have class pictures with everybody in Hugo! And I love every one of them.

While this interviewee did not finish school, and other circus people, particularly older individuals, had parents teach them reading, writing, geography, and arithmetic, such interviewees were aware of and appreciated this positive relationship with Hugo schools. As one of them explained, 'The school worked with us so good, because it is a circus town and they understood'.

More recently, owners have wanted to provide an avenue for circus families to have their children with them on the road. Owners of the Kelly Miller and Carson Barnes have accredited schools *in* the circus. The superintendent of the Hugo school system provides and pays for an accredited teacher in the circuses to teach the younger children. As one former circus owner recalled, 'I wanted the same curriculum, the same lessons that they had in the Hugo system'. The children are counted present for all the days that they are with the circus – as long as the circus school achieves the lessons and maintains the standard – indeed, all of children are consistently on the A-B Honour Roll. School takes place in the commissary in the morning and is off limits to anybody but the school. The past owner of Kelly Miller explained,

> I only had like three teachers in the twenty-five years that I had the show. I think what attracted them more [than the travel] was the fact that they we were so serious about education for our kids. Not just my kids, I'm talking about my employees' kids—but in providing education for the kids that they revelled in that. I think they kind of enjoyed the fact that they were part of something unique and unusual. And the successes that we enjoyed were obvious.

He continued that the superintendent once explained, '"I never have any trouble with [Kelly Miller] kids." Our kids are very serious about school, very good in school, and very well behaved'. Thus, as these examples show, schooling for many children in the circus occurs on the road *through* Hugo schools as well as *in place* in Hugo schools.

Moreover, circuses created the Hugo High School Foundation (and continue to donate funds to Hugo schools) and a local-circus themed mural, painted by a circus person, adorns an exterior wall of the elementary school. These representations in part constitute the constellations of mobilities that make home (Cresswell 2010). As Ellingsen and Hidle (2013: 254) explain the enactment of home has a public function and is 'part of the public area and is, thus, part of our cultural understanding'. It is in this shared cultural understanding, which includes different modalities (Ralph and Staehel 2011) or constellations of mobilities (Cresswell 2010), where a sense of home repeatedly emerges for circus people through various intertwining and networked material practices and movement between the road and Hugo associated with school lessons, student living arrangements, extracurricular activities, friendships, and teachers.

Funerary activities

I now turn to funerary activities, using the examples of Showmen's Rest Cemetery and Carson Barnes circus owner D.R. Miller's passing to further demonstrate that home is created on the road and in Hugo together through entwining mutual practices. Showmen's Rest, a cemetery for circus and other showmen and showwomen, is part of the larger Mt. Olivet Cemetery in Hugo. Granite posts with elephant statuettes delimit the special area while in the centre a large performing elephant sculpture is displayed; the engraving on its base reads, 'A Tribute to All Showmen Under God's Big Top'. Though circuses may contain many circus families, they also have individuals who have no family. As one circus person noted, 'The circus kind of ended up being their family and their home, and they spent their whole lives here'. It is from one of these sometimes described 'gentlemen drifters', John Carroll, that Showmen's Rest came to be. Carroll had received an insurance settlement long before he died, and in the early 1960s when he did pass, he left it all to circus owner, D.R. Miller. Miller's daughter recalled,

> So he got the idea of making this place where circus people would he buried, because a lot of times circus people, like I say, don't have roots, and they would be buried in Timbuktu. Nobody would ever know who they were or know this rich history that they had or anything about them. So he thought it would be cool to have this area where circus people could be buried and that there would always be somebody that would come and visit that would be able to tell stories about that person or have a connection. It was just going to be a place where they wouldn't he forgotten.

And though the John Carroll fund provides a plot and small marker if the person has no means to have done so, some folks have bought plots for their entire circus family. In fact, only a few plots remain, and the circuses are attempting to create an expansion plan.

Thus with the material representation of the circus in Showmen's Rest, the circus is forever part of Hugo and forever home to some. Significantly, it is because of often life-long or long-term interactions and relationships in and with Hugo that makes Showmen's Rest home, where as one circus person explained, 'my family's buried here and I'm just kind of connected'. This may be further gleaned through the example of a prominent showman's headstone, who built 'quite a home in the 50s' in Hugo, becoming somewhat of a tourist attraction. His headstone, in part, includes an exact replica, 'stone by stone' of the archway from his home in Hugo. Moreover, as his niece and now owner of the home and circus explains, 'this home has been an important part of our life because we come back here every year; we have parties on holidays, invite circus people from the community; this home has always been kind of a gathering place'. Most headstones, however, in words and symbols refer to the circus world on the road with engravings such as 'Gone to Lay on the Next Lot', 'Queen of the Bareback Riders', 'We had a good life but the season ended', and 'Showman til the End'. Circus imagery includes, for example, circus tents, elephants, trapezes, and circus trucks. Thus, in the end, circus people buried in Showmen's Rest are rooted in the route and in Hugo, where, as Ralph and Staeheli (2011) explain, home may be rooted but not in one place, and I would add not only through one modality.

Exploring the death of a senior circus owner illustrates how home is situated through localized modalities as well as broader constellations of mobilities, where the sociality of home as process is paramount. At 83, D.R. Miller died when he was visiting his circus on the road in McCook, Nebraska. His daughter explained that,

> Just before the band was to strike up for the four-thirty show ... but—it was almost like it was full-circle [because that was the town he saw his first circus as a little boy] ... And the weight that that story took off of my shoulders, I can't even describe to you how it felt ... from that little boy seeing his first circus to this famous circus owner seeing his last circus. It was a very moving experience for me and for my family.

The circus was headed to towns in Colorado to perform, so they had a service in the tent between shows. His daughter continued,

> It was a wonderful service. We gave our show, we had full capacity people, which my father would've loved, we ran them out, and we all came in, and he was brought into the tent by a young male elephant pulled in on a wagon, and he was placed on elephant tubs, which are the big tubs that the elephants perform on in the ring ... just like I think he would've enjoyed. Our minister from Hugo flew in and some friends flew in from all over, and we actually had a service, right there.

However, D.R. Miller did not want to be buried while his circus was touring, he wanted to be buried after his circus came 'home' to Hugo. So, he was put in cold storage until November, when the circus tour was over. Then when the circus 'came home', they had a huge funeral. Circus owners from all over the United States flew in for the funeral in Hugo, which was covered around the world. They set the circus tent up at the fairgrounds, with the circus seats, rings, and lighting. He again was placed on the elephant tubs in the centre ring, but this time in a 'shiny red coffin with brassy gold trim'. The procession to the cemetery included a circus parade with camels, elephants, horses, a band, and historical circus wagons. Many representatives from Hugo and the circus world spoke. Moreover, Hugo schools and businesses closed for the event. Hundreds of people from Hugo stood on the sidewalk some holding 'signs thanking him for all the fun memories of the circus and the good times'. In D.R. Miller's funeral on the road and in Hugo, the feeling of belonging for circus people is shown in part to be socially defined and practiced but subjectively felt by Miller's daughter as well as by circus people as most of those interviewed described his funerals in heartfelt detail (Ralph and Staeheli 2011: 523). The constellations of mobilities work through different spaces, places, and material and social practices as well as through different scales in various ways, including the personal, the circus tent on a lot, the streets of Hugo, and (inter)nationally.

Conclusion

This chapter argues that 'the road' may be understood as home place for many people who are part of Carson & Barnes, Kelly-Miller, and Culpepper

Merryweather circuses that winter in Hugo. However, as illustrated in the second analysis section, home is more complicated for them as intertwining mutual material practices, movement, and representations associated with schooling and funerary activities illustrate. Through nuanced constellations of mobilities, particularly concerning logistics of and between routes and place (Cresswell 2011), these circus people 'belong' on the road and in Hugo, as indicated by many circus people.

Probyn (1996) and Ralph and Staeheli (2011) provide insight into this sense of belonging, where there is *being* in one realm but a *longing* for another realm. While Ralph and Staeheli (2011) explain home for migrants as a tension between mobility and stability, I argue that home for these circus people is stable within mobilities, moments of stillness, and ephemeral moorings through different temporal and spatial scales. This is a 'productive tension' that Cresswell (2011: 717) refers to in the logistics of mobilities and 'break[s] from the bi-local and multi-local approach' (Nowicka 2007), where home is instead constituted as an enfolding of the road *and* Hugo through *dynamic* but stable lived experiences. To be sure in these experiences, nodes in the network of home are in process (Nowicka 2007; Molz 2008) as circuses move a small town every day and winter in place.

Notes

1. The oral histories were completed by Tanya Finchum and Juliana Nykolaiszyn of the Oklahoma Oral History Research Program at the Oklahoma State University. Funding for the oral histories was provided by the Library of Congress American Folk Life Center Archive Green Fellowship, which was awarded in 2011 to Finchum and Nykolaiszyn.
2. Though Christensen (2013) does not explicitly state that she draws from mobilities literature, her analysis exemplifies such an approach.

References

Adey, P. (2006) If mobility is everything then it is nothing: towards a relational politics of (im)mobilities. *Mobilities*, 1(1): 75–94.

Andrews, G.J. (2004) (Re)thinking the dynamics between healthcare and place: Therapeutic geographies in treatment and care practices. *Area*, 36(3): 307–318.

Bammer, A. (1992) Editorial. *New Formations*, 17: vii–xi.

Bissell, D. and Fuller, G. (2011) Stillness unbound. In D. Bissell and G. Fuller (eds) *Stillness in a Mobile World*. New York: Routledge, pp. 1–17.

Blunt, A. and Dowling, R. (2006) *Home*. New York: Routledge.

Casey, E. (2001) Body, self, and landscape: A geophilosophical inquiry into the place-world. In P. C. Adams, S. Hoelsher, and K. E. Till (eds), *Textures of Place: Exploring Humanistic Geographies*. Minneapolis: University of Minnesota Press, pp. 403–425.

Cassiman, A. (2008) Home and away: Mental geographies of young migrant workers and their belonging to the family house in Northern Ghana. *Housing, Theory & Society*, 25(1): 14–30.

Chen, S. (2012) Making home away from home: A case-study of archival research of the Nanyang emigration in China. *Durham Anthropology Journal*, 18(2): 59–71.

Christensen, J. (2013) 'Our home, our way of life': Spiritual homelessness and the socio-cultural dimensions of indigenous homelessness in the Northwest Territories (NWT), Canada. *Social & Cultural Geography*, 14(7): 804–828.

Clifford, J. (1997) *Routes: Travel and Translation in the Late Twentieth Century.* Cambridge, MA: Harvard University Press.

Cresswell, T. (2010) Mobilities: Catching up. *Progress in Human Geography*, 35(4): 550–558.

Cresswell, T. (2011) The vagrant/vagabond: The curious career of a mobile subject. In T. Cresswell and P. Merriman (eds), *Geographies of Mobilities: Practices, Spaces, Subject*, Surrey, England: Ashgate. pp. 239–253.

Cresswell, T. (2012) Mobilities II: Still. *Progress in Human Geography*, 36(5): 645–653.

Cresswell, T. (2014) Mobilities III: Moving on. *Progress in Human Geography*, 38(5): 712–721.

Datta, A. (2008) Building differences: Material geographies of home(s) among Polish builders in London. *Transactions of the Institute of British Geographers*, 33(4): 518–531.

Ellingsen, W. G. and Hidle, P. (2013) Performing home in mobility: Second homes in Norway. *Tourism Geographies*, 15(2): 250–267.

Gilroy, P. (1993) *The Black Atlantic: Modernity and Double Consciousness.* London: Verso.

Gustafson, P. (2001) Roots and routes: Exploring the relationship between place attachment and mobility. *Environment and Behavior*, 33(5): 667–686.

Halfacree, K. (2012) Heterolocal identities? Counter-urbanization, second homes, and rural consumption in the era of mobilities. *Population, Space, and Place*, 18(2): 209–224.

Hannam, K., Sheller, M. and Urry, J. (2006) Editorial: Mobilities, immobilities, and moorings. *Mobilities*, 1(1): 1–22.

Hay, R. (1998) A rooted sense of place in cross-cultural perspective. *Canadian Geographer*, 42(3): 245–266.

Lagerqvist, M. (2013) 'I would much rather be still here and travel in time': The intertwinedness of mobility and stillness in cottage living. *Fennia*, 191(2): 92–105.

Latour, B. (2005) *Reassembling the Social: An Introduction to Actor-Network Theory.* Oxford: Oxford University Press.

May, J. (2000) Of nomads and vagrants: Single homelessness and narratives of home as place. *Environment and Planning D: Society and Space*, 18(6): 737–759.

Molz, J. G. (2008) Global abode: home and mobility in narratives of round-the-world travel. *Space and Culture*, 11(4): 325–342.

Nowicka, M. (2007) Mobile locations: Construction of home in a group of mobile transnational professionals. *Global Networks*, 7(1): 69–86.

Paris, C. (2011) *Affluence, Mobility and Second Home Ownership.* New York: Routledge.

Ralph, D. and Staeheli, L. (2011) Home and migration: Mobilities, belongings, and identities. *Geography Compass*, 5(7): 517–530.

Relph, E. (1976) *Place and Placelessness.* London: Pion Limited.

Robertson, L. (2007) Taming space: Drug use, HIV, and homemaking in Downtown Eastside Vancouver. *Gender, Place & Culture: A Journal of Feminist Geography*, 14(5): 527–549.

Robinson, C. (2002) 'I think home is more than a building': Young home(less) people on the cusp of home, self, and something else. *Urban Policy and Research*, 20(1): 27–38.

Robinson, C. (2011) *Beside One's Self: Homelessness, Felt, and Lived.* Syracuse: Syracuse University Press.

Somerville, P. (1992) Homelessness and the meaning of home: Rooflessness or rootless-ness? *International Journal of Urban and Regional Research*, 16(4): 529–539.

Teo, S. Y. (2011) 'The moon back home is brighter?' Return migration and the cultural politics of belonging. *Journal of Ethnic & Migration Studies*, 37(5): 805–820.

Tuan, Y. F. (1977) *Space and Place: The Perspective of Experience*. London: Edward Arnold.

Ursin, M. (2011) 'Wherever I lay my head is home: Young people's experiences of home in the Brazilian street environment. *Children's Geographies* 9(2): 221–234.

Vannini, P. (2011a) Constellations of ferry (im)mobility: Islandness as the performance and politics of insulation and isolation. *Cultural Geographies*, 18(2): 249–271.

Vannini, P. (2011b) Mind the gap: The *Tempo Rubato* of dwelling in lineups. *Mobilities*, 6(2): 273–299.

Veness, A. R. (1993) Neither homed nor homeless: Contested definitions and the personal worlds of the poor. *Political Geography*, 12(4): 319–340.

7 Time and space to run

The mobilities and immobilities of road races

Julie Cidell

Event mobilities may have originally been conceptualized as the travel necessary to get to a face-to-face event that requires time-space synchronization, such as a concert or political rally (Urry 2004). However, it is also the case that some kinds of mobility are only possible in the context of an event. This chapter considers road races for runners, specifically half marathons, as events that generate unique mobilities and immobilities because of their temporary nature. This generation occurs through gathering people for the event, carrying out the event itself, and dispersing during and afterwards.

Running as a form of recreation or exercise has grown exponentially since the 1970s. Unlike other sports that require long training, expensive equipment, or teammates, there are relatively low barriers to entry in running. Runners therefore run the gamut from those who run a few miles a few times a week to ultra-marathoners who run a hundred miles at a time. Within the same event, they can also range from those who are running their first race at that distance to elite runners who are competing at the international level. For runners of all levels, participating in a road race can be a way to set goals with regards to training and performance. A road race is an event in which the distance runners travel ranges from a mile (1.6 km) to 26.2 miles (a marathon, or 42km). As the name implies, these races often use spaces that are usually reserved for cars, turning them over to people to run or walk on for the duration of the event. While the 5K or 3.1 mile distance is the most popular in the US, the half marathon is second in popularity. Since 2003, the number of half marathon finishers has quadrupled from 480,000 to two million people running in over 2,200 races per year (Running USA 2014).

Unlike other events that require corporeal travel for participation, road races take place not in reserved spaces such as concert halls, sports stadiums, or large open spaces, but on city streets. Road races therefore demonstrate that some kinds of mobility are only possible in the context of an event, when the required trans-gression of normal places and spaces is temporarily sanctioned by the temporal and spatial bounds of the event (Cidell 2014). At the same time, the event might in turn constrain or temporarily halt normal, everyday mobilities within that same limited time and space. The nature of the road race also means that it is a participant-dependent event: unlike a professional sports competition that could take place without an audience, a road race would not happen without runners. In this sense, the runners are both performing and spectating at the same time. While an audience does exist in the sense of those who cheer on the runners, the primary participants are the runners: the event's existence depends on its participants, but participants' mobility also depends on the event.

In this chapter, I draw on two concepts – event mobilities and bodily mobilities – to explore the unique mobilities and immobilities engendered by the participant-dependent event known as the half marathon. I do so through a frame-work that identifies three different stages of the event: gathering, eventing, and dispersing. The research for this project was done through participant observation in two such events: the 2014 Detroit Free Press/Talmer Bank Half Marathon, one of very few road races to cross an international border, and the 2015 United Airlines New York Half Marathon, which runs through Central Park and Times Square. Both events involve the disruption of central city traffic for the temporary race course, requiring runners to move quickly in order to minimize disruption. Both events also draw participants from great distances in order to participate in the unique mobilities they allow. Through these cases, we will see how road races as events both create and close off mobilities for participants and passers-by before, during, and after the event's limited (but repeated) time-space duration.

Event mobilities and bodily mobilities

One of the earliest pieces on mobility and the social outlined five main obliga-tions that explain why physical proximity remains important in an age of digital communication: 1) legal/economic/familial (e.g., attending a wedding or meeting a court date), 2) social (e.g., visiting friends), 3) objects (e.g., signing a physical document), 4) places (e.g., seeing the Grand Canyon for oneself), and 5) events (Urry 2003). In this case, the last is in fact the least, for very little has been written about event mobilities (until the current volume, that is). Familial, social, and object obligations have been expanded upon by Urry and others, and the concept of a sense of place has been explored by geographers in great detail. The event obligation, however, needs further expansion.

Common examples of events that necessitate physical presence are concerts, film premieres, or mega-events like the Olympics or the World Cup (Urry 2003). Even if one can watch a live or recorded presentation of the event (and many times the number of people do so as compared to attending in person), such an experience does not compare to physically being there in the moment. Mobility to and from concerts, sporting events, or theatre productions is of interest to tour-ism scholars because of the competition involved in attracting leisure travellers to spend their funds in particular locations, or because of the short- and long-term environmental and infrastructural impacts of a large number of visitors (e.g., Getz 2008; Hallmann et al. 2010; Blin 2012). However, most of these events could take place even without an audience, as exemplified by the Major League Baseball game in early 2015 played in Baltimore, Maryland, before an empty stadium because of civil unrest within the city. However, there are other kinds of events which could not exist without the coming together of many people into a specific space at a specific time. Political rallies or protests, farmers' markets, trade fairs or conferences, and festivals or fairs, to name a few, depend upon the bodily participation of a large number of people in order to exist as events (Mitchell and Scott 2008; Duffy et al. 2011; Bathelt and Spigel 2012; Cudny 2014). There is rarely a recording or live broadcast of these events, and even though they may repeat on a weekly or yearly basis, they then become different events based on the people who attend.

This kind of participant-dependent event can therefore be connected to work on bodily mobilities, 'when the body comes to life through intense proximity and where virtual travel would be irrelevant' (Urry 2001: 242). Such outdoor experiences require being in a particular place, using not only the kinesthetic sense of feeling one's body in motion, but incorporating the sights, sounds, and smells of a particular location: rock climbing, cycling, hiking, skiing, etc. (Spinney 2006). By definition, these practices are out of the ordinary and therefore can perhaps be considered forms of resistance because they involve going where most people do not go or pushing one's physical limits. Unlike concerts or sporting events, but like conferences or festivals, there is no virtual substitution or reliving of the event: physical presence is required. At the same time, however, 'such bodies in nature are subject to extensive forms of regimentation, monitoring and disciplining – by regulatory organizations, expert systems, technologies, moral guardians' (Urry 2001: 242). There's a kind of freedom in going outside the norm, but there's also a danger in being policed by formal or informal means. Events take place within circumscribed spaces and times, and it may be impossible to visit the same location when the event is not on.

Road races can therefore be thought of as a combination of bodily mobilities and event mobilities. On the one hand, running is often celebrated as an activity that almost anyone can do anywhere and at any time with minimal physical equipment. Running can be a quotidian practice, something done every day upon waking up, during the lunch hour, or even as a commute (Cook et al. 2015). Recent research in this area includes how people learn to become runners: adapting their bodies, incorporating electronic devices, and eventually (or not) claiming the identity of 'runner' (Shipway and Jones 2008; Little 2015). On the other hand, road races are very specific kinds of events that may require a great deal of travel, intense logistical considerations on the part of organizers as well as participants, and sharp demarcation in time and space. They involve experiencing places in a different way than normal, even differently from how one might run through the same city or town outside of the event (Sheehan 2006). Furthermore, road races as events afford different kinds of mobilities that are simply not possible outside of the time-space of the event, such as traversing infrastructure that is normally off limits to non-motorized travel, while temporarily foreclosing or altering other regular, automobile-based, mobilities (Cidell 2014).

This latter point is the focus of this chapter. This work is based on participant observation from two different half marathons: Detroit in 2014 and New York City in 2015. The Detroit Free Press/Talmer Bank Half Marathon and the accompanying full marathon offer the rare opportunity to cross an international border as part of a road race and to travel on two major pieces of infrastructure that are normally closed to non-motorized traffic: the Ambassador Bridge and the Windsor Tunnel. The United Airlines New York Half Marathon travels regular city streets that can nearly all be traversed by pedestrians on any given day, but the closure of Times Square to vehicular traffic is something that otherwise only happens for New Year's Eve. Both events therefore offer the opportunity to consider not only the characteristics held in common across road races – street closures, participant travel, and the running itself – but the 'intense proximity' that being able to inhabit familiar infrastructure in unfamiliar ways enables for runners in these events (Urry 2001).

The mobilities and immobilities of road races

In considering the relationship between bodily mobilities and event mobilities, I break them down into three stages: gathering, eventing, and dispersing. The first and last of these are found in most types of events: in order for an event to take place, people and objects have to move to the site where the event is to occur, and dispersion within and from the event location occurs before, during, and after. In the case of a road race, however, the event *itself* consists of different (im)mobilities that would not occur outside of the race day and time. Note that these three stages do not follow a strict timeline: gathering and dispersion are part of pre-race, race, and post-race activities. Furthermore, all three stages occur at multiple scales, starting from the body but moving outwards to national or even international scales. At the same time, all five of Urry's interdependent mobilities are present here: bodily movement of people, objects in motion, and imaginative, virtual, and communicative travel (Urry 2004). It is no wonder that coordinating such events is a full-time job, planned a year or more in advance by professionals. In this section, I consider these three stages of event mobilities at a road race, based on Urry's five interdependent mobilities.

Gathering

In the largest sense, gathering refers to bringing together the people and objects that are necessary for a road race to take place. This includes the logistics of event organization, largely handled by companies whose main role is event planning and execution, but also with the help of hundreds or thousands of volunteers (for example, 2,200 volunteers in the case of New York). It also includes the runners themselves, many of whom are travelling a considerable distance to run a distance that they could easily accomplish at home.

Getting to the race requires multiple, interdependent mobilities (Urry 2004). There is obviously the corporeal movement of bodies, which includes getting to the physical starting line on the morning of the race, but also getting to the race in the broader sense. Runners have literally thousands of options to choose from when deciding where and when to race, with imaginative and virtual travel being key parts of their decision-making. Websites for races post not only course maps to give potential runners an indication of where they could be running, but many also post video run-throughs so runners can virtually travel the course before deciding to participate. This can help runners decide if the course is scenic enough, appropriately challenging with regards to elevation change, passes major landmarks that might be of interest, or traverses infrastructure that would otherwise be inaccessible. Major running magazines like *Runner's World* post yearly lists of top 'destination races' and include advertisements from some of the 2,200 different events to entice runners to travel (e.g., Fox 2015).

For major events like the Detroit and New York City races, runners do indeed come from a wide variety of places. Figures 7.1 and 7.2 show the home locations of all of the finishers of the 2014 Detroit Free Press/Talmer Bank Half Marathon and the 2015 United Airlines New York Half Marathon, respectively. Table 7.1 shows local, national, and international participants in these two races as compared to an additional half marathon in each metropolitan area that does not traverse so noteworthy a course and therefore does not have as large of a draw. (Note that Lansing is more than 60 miles from most of the Detroit metropolitan area, which is why it appears to draw participants from a larger area.) Previous research on why people travel to road races has found that there are a variety of reasons: contributing to charity, group camaraderie, visiting a new place, or 'collecting' destinations (e.g., running a half marathon in all fifty states) (McGehee et al. 2003; Ogles and Masters 2003; Funk et al. 2007). Surveys or interviews were not done with runners in the Detroit and New York events, so it is not known for certain why they chose this race. Nevertheless, comparing the out-of-town percentage of the major races to the smaller events indicates that generally speaking, more people do travel for big-name events that traverse unique locations.

For a major race like the Detroit or New York half marathons, runners do not simply show up at the posted start time. They must attend the race expo that usually runs 2–3 days before the race, where they pick up the bib that they will pin to their clothing containing the chip to keep their official time, the souvenir t-shirt that is usually part of the registration fees, and whatever other materials the course organizers have included. While all of the runners are gathered together for registration, they also pass by booths selling running clothing, energy gels or other food, advertising upcoming races in the same area, or other products and services of interest. There is a certain kind of energy from thousands of people having travelled to the same place for this event, amplified by loud music as well as large maps and virtual run-throughs of the course projected on the walls. Even if everyone is not there at the same time the way they will be at the starting line (and race materials may be picked up by a proxy), there is a sense of gathering together for the event.

Nevertheless, getting to the starting line requires a specific set of mobility practices as well. Even local runners might not be familiar with the exact race location, and street closures and parking restrictions on event day can make even familiar parts of the city difficult to navigate. Race websites will usually post information about travel to the start and finish lines (if they differ), which

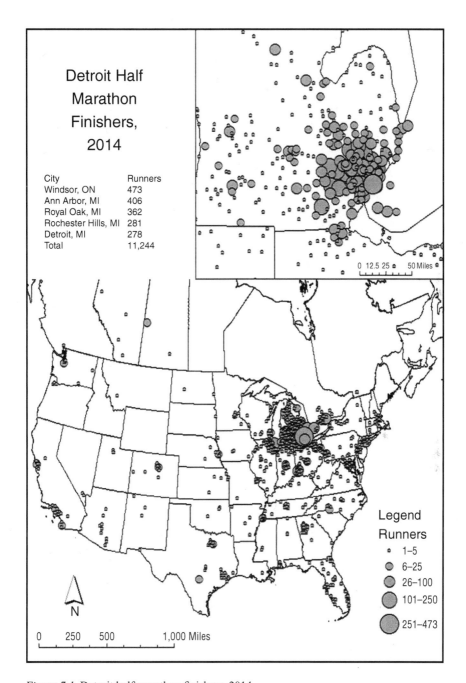

Detroit Half
Marathon
Finishers,
2014

City	Runners
Windsor, ON	473
Ann Arbor, MI	406
Royal Oak, MI	362
Rochester Hills, MI	281
Detroit, MI	278
Total	11,244

0 12.5 25   50 Miles

Legend
Runners
· 1–5
○ 6–25
○ 26–100
○ 101–250
◯ 251–473

N

0   250   500   1,000 Miles

Figure 7.1 Detroit half marathon finishers, 2014

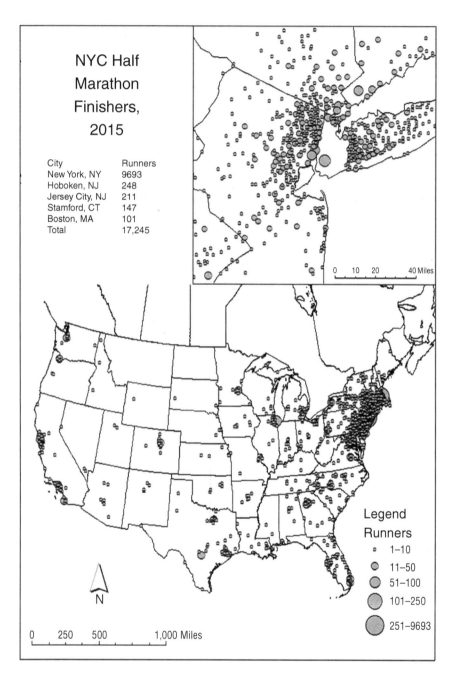

NYC Half
Marathon
Finishers,
2015

City	Runners
New York, NY	9693
Hoboken, NJ	248
Jersey City, NJ	211
Stamford, CT	147
Boston, MA	101
Total	17,245

0   10   20   40 Miles

N

0   250   500   1,000 Miles

Legend
Runners
○ 1–10
○ 11–50
○ 51–100
○ 101–250
○ 251–9693

Figure 7.2 NYC half marathon finishers, 2015

Table 7.1 Hometown of finishers in Detroit and New York Half Marathons as compared to nearby, smaller events. A distance of 60 miles was chosen to represent a travel time of about an hour.

Event	Total runners w/data	US/Canada	Within 60 miles
2014 Detroit Half	10,195	99%	86%
2014 Lansing Half	1,555	100%	82%
2015 NYC Half	19,433	91%	74%
2015 Queens Half	996	97%	85%

involves public transit information (if available), where to park or drop off a runner, and the availability or requirement of shuttles. Increased security at major events after the Boston Marathon bombing may require a security check for runners, as with the metal detectors outside Central Park for the New York race, which requires additional time before the start. Communicative travel via emails, texts, or phone calls is necessary for runners hoping to meet up with each other at the starting line. Many runners carry smartphones with them and are thus able to be in contact throughout the entire journey. This includes meeting up with friends and family after the race, which leads us to the next stage: dispersion.

Dispersing

Dispersion includes moving people and objects away from the event location in an orderly fashion after it has concluded, which is a key part of race logistics. For example, runners have to be immediately directed away from the finish line to make room for others coming through. The 'finish line' itself is dispersed across space, including the actual point where the race and its timing stop, but also where foil blankets are distributed to suddenly-chilly bodies, where complimentary food and drink are handed out, where race medals are awarded (to winners as well as to all finishers), where official photographs are taken, and where runners stretch and recover. All of these stops are optional, and so the spatial layout of the finish line area has to include them in such a way that keeps people moving through the space on their way to leaving the area entirely.

However, dispersion is also part of setting up the event in the first place. Large races like these, with nearly 20,000 finishers, can take over half an hour for everyone to cross the starting line. This means that even though runners have all been gathered together for the race, they also have to be dispersed to some extent to make the logistics work. When registering for the race, participants must enter their expected finishing time within a five-minute window. They are then assigned to a specific 'corral' at the starting line with others who are expected to run at the same pace. This keeps the elite runners at the front, slower runners at the back, and minimizes passing along the race course. A 'wave start' allows multiple corrals to move at once while reducing overall crowding, walking slowly and then more and more quickly until they reach the starting line and can finally break into a run. Latecomers can join slower corrals without penalty, since their race time does not start until they cross the starting line, although they will have to weave their way through slower runners.

During the race, non-participants have to be kept away from the race course in order to minimize interference with runners. Particularly for a road race, which almost by definition uses roadways that are normally traversed by vehicles, traffic needs to be sent away from the race location. The two races profiled here may be extreme examples, but they illustrate how in order for runners to be mobile in the streets, others' mobility must be briefly curtailed or redirected, even if they are not participants. While race courses are designed to provide a good experience for runners, they therefore also have to take into account the displacement of the usual users of the space. For example, the course for the United Airlines New York Half Marathon includes a loop through Central Park before exiting to the south down Seventh Avenue, traveling through Times Square, turning west on 42nd Street, and following the West Side Highway down to the tip of Manhattan. It is the only event for which Times Square closes to vehicular traffic other than New Year's Eve and therefore has a considerable impact on traffic within the city. Similarly, the Detroit Free Press/Talmer Bank Half Marathon (run in conjunction with a full marathon) is the only event to cross the Ambassador Bridge and Windsor Tunnel between the US and Canada, requiring a closure of the tunnel and partial closure of the bridge. In both cases, roads have to be shut down and traffic re-routed well before the start of the race. Even with communicative travel to the public over all types of media well in advance, some drivers inevitably will not be aware of the event. Both of these races therefore have a maximum finishing time of three hours, or a 13:45-minute-mile pace, in order to minimize traffic disruption. Runners that cannot meet this pace will be picked up by van or allowed to continue running on the sidewalk while the cones or barriers are removed and the streets returned to their regular users. Vehicular traffic can only be kept out of its rightful place for so long. This brings us to the race itself, which I describe under the heading of 'eventing'.

Eventing

Road races involve unique mobilities because runners are usually traveling in places where pedestrians are not allowed: down the centre of the street, across a bridge, etc. This may be part of why a runner chooses a specific race, to be able to experience a place in a unique way as a sanctioned transgression of space (Cidell 2014). For example, it is possible to traverse nearly the whole course of the United Airlines New York Half Marathon on foot via sidewalks. But the event allows runners to travel down the middle of the street, which is an especially striking experience when coming into Times Square. At the same time, mobile runners displace mobile vehicles, with several square blocks of Midtown Manhattan being cordoned off to protect the runners. At the one point on the race course where runners and cars were in close contact – runners westbound on 42nd Street and cars eastbound – the runners were clearly moving faster than the gridlocked cars. To reduce vehicular congestion, as mentioned above, runners are required to keep moving at a pace that will enable the streets to return to their normal use within three hours.

The Detroit Free Press/Talmer Bank Half Marathon involves even greater transgressions, namely crossing the Ambassador Bridge and Windsor Tunnel on foot. Neither piece of infrastructure is open to pedestrian traffic on any other occasion, so the race presents a unique opportunity for travel. While the bridge was half-open during the race, with runners on one side and vehicular traffic on the other going eastbound or westbound at specified intervals, the tunnel was completely closed to vehicles. The course was designed so that the bridge would be traversed early in the race and could be completely reopened to traffic an hour and forty-five minutes after the race start (an hour and twenty-five minutes for those who are the last to cross the starting line). This time limit is necessary given the key role that the bridge plays in international trade and in connecting cross-border manufacturing operations. Indeed, most of the vehicles observed crossing the bridge at 7:30 a.m. on Sunday morning during the race were freight trucks.

Another specific mobility only possible within the context of the Detroit Half Marathon was crossing the international border without stopping. The border check was performed in advance: runners had to include their passport number when registering and show their passport when picking up their materials at the race expo. (A US-only half marathon course was available for runners without a passport.) During the race itself, runners had to make sure that border guards could see the race bib pinned to their shirt front in order to pass the border controls. Runners were strongly advised to carry their passport with them during the race in case of emergency, but it was not required. This type of international mobility is obviously limited in that runners had to stay on the race course, and there were law enforcement officials stationed along the course within Canada, reinforcing Urry's notion of the monitoring and disciplining of mobile bodies. But this fast-moving border crossing is also a type of travel that is clearly not possible without the sanctioning of the event.

The bodily movement of people has unique aspects during a road race, but so too does the movement of objects – specifically, runners' gear. Both races were run under relatively cold conditions, around 40°F or 4°C at the start of the race. While slightly cold temperatures are good for running, they are not good for standing around at the beginning of a race or standing or walking while sweaty at the end of the race. At the same time, runners do not want to be burdened by carrying multiple layers with them along the race course. Major events like these therefore offer a gear check, where runners leave items that were necessary to get them to the starting line or will be needed after they finish. When the start and finish are close by, as in Detroit, the bags containing runners' gear simply sit and wait to be claimed. In a race like New York, however, where the start and finish are several miles apart, the gear itself has to be moved. Runners therefore face additional time constraints in gathering at the start line, because all gear has to be checked in well before the starting time so that trucks can carry it to the finish line and prepare it for claiming. This is another way in which road races are different from other kinds of events involving mobility: normally, people and their belongings are not moving differently through the city. The need to keep runners as unencumbered as possible during the event while still having access to objects they need pre- and post-race engenders this separate travel of objects.

Finally, there is communicative and imaginative travel during the event. The electronic chips that keep track of runners' starting and finishing times also enable that information to be broadcast live via the race's website. Friends and family, whether they are race spectators or are 'watching' from home, can keep track of a runner's time at intervals along the way via a website or email alerts. A runner carrying their smartphone with them might have their own apps that broadcast information on their location and pace; some of these apps allow two-way communication, with followers sending encouragement via Facebook 'likes' or comments. The United Airlines New York Half Marathon took this a step farther by encouraging participants to link their bib number to their Facebook page so that real-time results could be posted. This race also took advantage of its corporate sponsorship to introduce a kind of imaginative travel: along the race course, roughly every mile, United Airlines banners proclaimed the distance in miles to one of the international destinations they serve from New York, with the distances shrinking as runners progressed along the race course. This advertising might have prompted runners to think of traveling to the destinations mentioned, but it also encouraged them to imagine how the finish line was getting closer.

Conclusion

The study of running as a form of mobility is only just beginning (Cook et al. 2015). As a daily or near-daily practice engaged in by millions of people around the world, it is certainly worth considering alongside walking and cycling as a common way of apprehending and experiencing the world. Similarly, of the original categories of obligation that explains why we travel (Urry 2003), event mobilities have been under-studied compared to social, economic, or place-based obligations. This chapter has drawn together these two elements via road races, specifically half marathons, as a way to demonstrate that not only do events depend on multiple kinds of mobility, but certain kinds of mobility can only take place within the context of events.

There are three stages through which event mobilities come to matter: gathering, eventing, and dispersing. I have shown that multiple kinds of mobility matter to each of these stages – not only corporeal travel of people, but object travel, virtual and imaginative travel, and communicative travel. Runners have to physically get themselves to the start line on the morning of the race, which might involve navigating an unfamiliar city or a city made unfamiliar by temporary road closures. For the races examined here, 15 to 25 per cent of participants came from more than an hour's travel, some from hundreds or thousands of miles away. Virtual and imaginative travel were used to help them select the race in the first place and to arrange their personal logistics on and before race day. Objects in the form of traffic cones, bananas and bagels, t-shirts, loudspeakers, and water cups also have to be brought to the race site in order to enable a smooth event. Similarly, dispersion of runners and non-runners alike is a key part of race logistics, all intended to keep people moving as quickly as possible whether they are participating in the race or not. This includes a swift exit from the finish line area, which will likely involve communication with friends or family members, but also the dispersion of the race course itself: removing cones and barriers so that the streets can once again be used by vehicles.

While gathering and dispersing are part of any event, other mobilities are specifically relevant to the road race. The foremost of these is travelling on foot in places that normally only vehicles are allowed to go, from everyday city streets to major pieces of infrastructure such as international bridges. Such travel may require limits on participants in the form of documentation prior to the race and/ or being able to maintain sufficient speed so that key infrastructure is not blocked for *too* long. The separate travel of runners and their belongings through the space of the city is also unique to road races, as objects that are necessary before or after the race are undesirable during the event itself. Finally, the communicative travel that makes it possible for friends and family to track runners at a distance is a unique form of participation that plays a role in encouraging runners' progress along the course.

Road races continue to grow in terms of number of events and participants, which makes this a fruitful area of study for those interested in tourism, mobilities, transportation, and urban geography. The case studies in this chapter are only two of over two thousand and might represent extremes in terms of the size of the event and the extent to which runners are transgressing non-pedestrian space. Additionally, races of longer or shorter lengths might provide different perspectives, such as the New York Marathon that uses the Verrazano-Narrows Bridge for many hours, to 5K races held on runways at Dulles and O'Hare International Airports that briefly alter aeromobility, not automobility. Nevertheless, the results presented here offer a number of avenues for further research, including the different experiences of locals versus visitors; participants versus spectators versus frustrated drivers; and beginners versus experienced runners. Finally, road races remind us that while events are a certain kind of obligation that inspire or require mobilities, they also *enable* mobilities that could not otherwise take place, including experiencing the city and even international borders in new ways.

Acknowledgments

Thanks to Marci Uihlein and Charles Fogelman for their thoughts on an earlier version of this chapter. Any remaining mistakes are my own. This research was not externally funded.

References

Bathelt, H. and Spigel, B. (2012) The spatial economy of North American trade fairs. *Canadian Geographer*, 56(1): 18–38.

Blin, É. (2012) Sport et événement festif. La ville à l'heure des marathons et des semi-marathons [Sport and the festive event. A new era for the city: Marathons and half-marathons], *Annales de Geographie*, 121(685): 266–286.

Cidell, J. (2014) Running road races as transgressive event mobilities. *Social and Cultural Geography*, 15(5): 571–583.

Cook, S., Shaw, J., and Simpson, P. (2015) Jography: Exploring meanings, experiences and spatialities of recreational road-running. *Mobilities*, DOI: 10.1080/17450101.2015. 1034455.

Cudny, W. (2014) Festivals as a subject for geographical research. *Geografisk Tidsskrift*, 114(2): 132–142.

Duffy, M., Waitt, G., Gorman-Murray, A. and Gibson, C. (2011) Bodily rhythms: Corporeal capacities to engage with festival spaces. *Emotion, Space and Society*, 4(1): 17–24.

Fox, K. (2015) Bucket list: 10 destination half marathons. *Runner's World*, available online at http://www.runnersworld.com/races/10-best-destination-half-marathons Accessed 24 June 2015.

Funk, D., Toohey, K. and Bruun, T. (2007) International sport event participation: Prior sport involvement; destination image; and travel motives. *European Sport Management Quarterly*, 7(1): 227–248.

Getz, D. (2008) Event tourism: Definition, evolution, and research. *Tourism Management*, 29(2): 403–428.

Hallmann, K., Kaplanidou, K., and Breuer, C. (2010) Event image perceptions among active and passive sports tourists at marathon races. *International Journal of Sports Marketing and Sponsorship*, October: 3–52.

Little, J. (2015) 'My tracker is my best fitness partner': Running, technology and environment in the disciplining of women's bodies. Paper presented at the Association of American Geographers' annual meeting, Chicago, IL.

McGehee, N., Yoon, Y. and Cárdenas, D. (2003) Involvement and travel for recreational runners in North Carolina. *Journal of Sport Management*, 17(2): 305–324.

Mitchell, R. and Scott, D. (2008) Farmers' markets as events for local cultural consumption: the Otago Farmers' Market (Dunedin, New Zealand). In Hall, C. and Sharples, L. (eds), *Food and Wine Festival and Events Around the World: Development, Management and Markets*. Oxford: Butterworth-Heinemann, pp. 286–299.

Ogles, B. and Masters, M. (2003) A typology of marathon runners based on cluster analysis of motivations. *Journal of Sport Behavior*, 26(1): 69–85.

Running USA (2014) 2014 Running USA annual half marathon report. Available online at http://www.runningusa.org/half-marathon-report-2015 Accessed 24 June 2015.

Sheehan, R. (2006) Running in place. *Tourist Studies*, 6(2): 245–265.

Shipway, R. and Jones, I. (2008) The great suburban Everest: An 'insiders' perspective on experiences at the 2007 Flora London Marathon. *Journal of Sport & Tourism*, 13(1): 61–77.

Spinney, J. (2006) A place of sense: A kinaesthetic ethnography of cyclists on Mont Ventoux. *Environment and Planning D: Society and Space*, 24(3): 709–732.

Urry, J. (2001) Transports of delight. *Leisure Studies*, 20(2): 237–245.

Urry, J. (2003) Social networks, travel and talk. *British Journal of Sociology*, 54(2): 155–175.

Urry, J. (2004) Connections. *Environment and Planning D: Society and Space*, 22(1): 27–37.

8 Necromobility/choreomobility

Dance, death and displacement in the Thai–Burma border-zone

Tani H. Sebro

> The event is that no one ever dies, but has always just died or is always going to die, in the empty present of the Aion, that is, in eternity.
>
> (Deleuze 1990: 63)

> When normal people die they just put the body in a coffin and don't burn them. Only the monk is burned [...]. No, there is no music and dance for laypeople.
>
> (Sai Awn, research collaborator, personal interview, Chiang Mai, March 2015)

Deep in the emerald green mountains of upland Southeast Asia, in a quaint, small town hugging the Thai–Burma border, the air dances and the ground palpitates with movement. The township, consisting of about 100 households and 300 people, has in the course of three months transformed itself into a vast festival space to accommodate the roughly 4,000 pilgrims who are descending upon the tranquil valley today.[1] Rice paddies have been drained and turned into open dirt fields, dozens of temporary bamboo and tin shade buildings constructed – minivans, trucks and motorbikes keep arriving – all brimming with people. Some have driven for hours; many have travelled for days from as far away as Chiang Mai, Bangkok and the Shan State in Burma, traversing perilous roads and dozens of military checkpoints. The steady beat of the *mong* (bossed gong) resounds throughout the valley, the market is teeming with activity, and revellers dance as they pass through the open spaces, clad in their finest traditional attire. Contrary to the festal atmosphere in the valley today, the worshippers have not come to celebrate, but rather to sense, witness and participate in the final ritual journey and cremation of a much-loved Tai monk who has passed way. The death-event, a culmination of lives past and present, will be demarcated through an elaborate series of funerary rituals and ceremonies. The deceased monk, most commonly referred to as Luang Pho Taa Sreng (The Venerable Bright Eyed Father), who is remembered throughout the Tai nation for his ability to see 'more than ordinary people', despite being completely blind since the age of three.[2]

In what follows, I theorize this funerary-event, as well as other eventual becomings that I encountered during my fieldwork in Northern Thailand among Tai exiles from the Shan State in Burma, in terms of both the *necromobility* and *choreomobility* of death in the Thai–Burma border-zone.[3] The space of the border-zone is at once a scene of serenity and seeming stillness as you move about the picturesque mountains of Mae Hong Son Province, but it is also the stage of one of the largest and longest-running displacement situations in the world (Campbell 2013). It is estimated that approximately 2.3 million migrants and another 120,000 official refugees from Burma live in Thailand, most of whom settle or work in the permeable border-zones of Central and Northern Thailand (Labovitz and Chantavanich 2013; Naing 2014). The Tai, a heterogeneous group of peoples also known as the Shan, identify themselves as being a part of an imagined Tai nation and reject subjugation by the Burmese military (Jirattikorn 2008). Tai peoples are currently experiencing an intense fracturing of their sense of sovereignty as a nation in lieu of ongoing hostilities between the Tatmadaw (Burmese Military) and Shan rebel army groups. Many have fled to neighbouring Thailand, where they enjoy no official protections as political or economic refugees. I call upon conceptualizations of the event as a 'knotting of politics' (Badiou 2013), as well as the event as 'chaotic multiplicity' (Deleuze 2006: 86) or even rupture (Žižek 2014), while also attending to the kinds of necropolitics (Mbembe 2003) that have set into motion the assemblage of bodies (both living and dead), performance (dance, music and theatre), and meaning (merit-making and the belief in spirits) surrounding the funerary processions for Luang Pho Taa Sreng, the deceased monk who was blind, yet could see.

I wish to make three modest interfusions into what has been called the *mobility turn* or the *new mobilities paradigm* in lieu of the death-event.[4] The first being an expansion of *necromobilty* as a concept, to include not only the mobilities arising in the context of death, decay and burial (Jassal 2014), but also the mobilities of after-lives, future-lives and of lives considered precarious. Drawing upon Michel Foucault's (1998) concept of biopower, necromobility is understood here in relation to *necropower*, which is the sovereign's ability to decide who may to live and who must die (Mbembe 2003). Necromobilities however, refers to the *dispositifs*, or apparatuses of control, that govern the movement of bodies after death and in relation to death-events. The second interfusion I am seeking, allocates the *choreomobility* of the political, meaning the choreographed – patterned, calculated and directed – movements of bodies (both dead and living) through spaces and through times. By inviting the possibility of choreomobilities, this research attends to the ways dance and performances become constitutive of events by forging cultural consistency out of political disorder. The last interfusion is less conceptual and deals rather with the manner and methods by which we study mobilities and events. I argue that through an ethnochoreological, meaning-embodied, yet materially grounded and historically situated analysis of movement (Buckland 1999; Foster 2008, 2009, 2010), we may be able to inch closer to mapping the criticality of death and performance in mobilities research.

New lines of flight, or directions of thought, have been made possible by the proliferation of research attending to *homo mobilus* (mobile human), rather than *homo stasis* (motionless human) after the mobilities turn. Pivotal moments within the turn include a critique of the 'a-mobility' of conventional social science research, that fails to see the central role that automobility, technological mobilities and the materiality of urban mobilities plays in the intensification of how bodies and things move spatially and chronologically in relation to one another (Sheller and Urry 2006; Simmel 1997), and the unpacking of the notion of 'potential mobilities', to be used instead of biological terminologies such as motilities (Kellerman 2006). Cresswell and Merriman (2001) draw our attention to the geographies of everyday bodily rhythms, which is based upon Henri Lefebvre's premise that '(E)verywhere where there is interaction between a place, a time, and an expenditure of energy, there is rhythm' (Lefebvre 2004: 15, quoted in Cresswell and Merriman 2001: 3). Thus, the mobilities turn provides us with important embodied and critical methodologies for scoping movement, such as *rhythmanalysis* (Cresswell and Merriman 2001; Edensor 2010) and mobile, or even 'itinerant ethnographies' that are adaptive to the migrations in place, media and judgement of diasporic peoples (Schein 2002: 231).

In order to place the concepts of necromobility and choreomobility in the context of fieldwork, I draw upon my experiences as an ethnochoreologist (an ethnographer of dance, movement and choreomobility) in Upland Southeast Asia. I spent three months during the summer of 2012, and another six months from autumn 2014 to spring 2015 conducting ethnographic research and receiving dance and theatre training from Tai cultural practitioners in Northern Thailand. My research comprises over 60 interviews, oral narratives and life histories, conducted primarily in Chiang Mai and Mae Hong Son provinces. This ethnochoreography summons a vast and, at times, unwieldy cacophony of voices and movements – primarily those belonging to Tai peoples, who have fled from the Shan State in Northern Burma and resettled in Thailand. Their experiences in the border-zone vastly differ: some finding ease and economic security in Thailand, while others lead lives that can only be described as precarious. They are governed by the politics of clandestinity and exile, and far too many 'are subjected to conditions of life conferring upon them the status of living dead' (Mbembe 2003: 39–40), in particular those who face deportation from Thailand and political persecution in Burma. But for others, life as a migrant offers the possibility of new opportunities and mobilities. Most of the fieldwork was conducted in Chiang Mai province in Northern Thailand, but as a mobile ethnographer, I also travelled to other provinces for interviews and 'events'. The ethnographic work I present here is primarily based on my time spent in Mae Hong Son Province in a small township, which will remain unnamed, where the burial rituals of Luang Pho Taa Sreng were held in January of 2015. I, along with thousands of pilgrims travelled there, through dozens of military checkpoints and across perilous roads in order to bear witness, but more importantly for Tai religious practitioners, to make merit within the context of a Theravada Buddhist death-event.

Necromobility: the death-event

In fact, funeral rites can be seen as essentially a kind of communal merit making for the deceased; it is, one might argue, what Shan funerals are archetypically about.

(Eberhardt 2006: 52)

Mobilities and events are seemingly antagonistically knotted. Mobility entails processes of flow, movement and becoming, whereas the event, as it is normatively thought, is a thing of stagnation, framing and rupture. The 'death-event' – which refers here to the disassemblage of things, lives or ideas – presents an ontological problem for normative framings of the event. There is a notion of finality and of 'being no more' after death, thus movement and mobility is no longer possible in death. Through a discussion of the kinds of necromobilities that arise through and after Luang Pho Taa Sreng's death-event, I argue here that the event is multiplicitous (Deleuze 2006) and that in the context of migrancy, war and violence, as well as within the cosmology of Theravada Buddhism, the death-event becomes revelatory of complex beliefs in the after-life, which are intertwined with the Tai peoples' aspirations for obtaining sovereignty for the Tai nation – freed from the bonds of belligerent empires, colonies and states. When Gilles Deleuze asks, '[w] hat are the conditions that make an event possible?' he solutions that '[e]vents are produced in a chaos, in a chaotic multiplicity, but only under the condition that a sort of screen intervenes' (Deleuze 2006: 86). For Deleuze, the screen is a kind of membrane – or a plane of consistency upon which chaos unfolds. This notion of the event is close to Badiou's (2013) idea of something seemingly unified appearing out of a multiplicity. However, for Badiou (2013), the multiplicity appears as a knotting. Within this multiplicitous knotting, a political consistency emerges:

> In fact, we could argue that there is politics when three things form a knot: the masses who all of a sudden are gathered in an unexpected consistency (events); the points of view incarnated in organic and enumerable actors (subject-effects); a reference in thought that authorizes the elaboration of discourse based upon the mode in which the specific actors in question are held together, even at a distance, by the popular consistency to which chance summons them.
>
> (Badiou 2013: 51)

Badiou's (2013) conception of politics as knotting, and events as masses gathered in 'unexpected consistency', is grounded in Jacques Lacan's (1978, 1993, 1998) notion of the event as a puncturing of the seemingly stable forces that underpin one's existence. What emerges is an instability of relational forces between people, things, time and I might add, movement. The psychological trauma of the event, reveals society as an 'appearance' of a layer of reality with endless layers preceding and succeeding it in an unbroken lineage of being and becoming. Jane Bennett (2004) sees the Lacanian notion of the political as an event that disrupts the prevailing social order and by so doing uncovers the social and political system that underpins its 'order'. For Bennett, 'the "political" here refers to those irruptive events that reveal politics to be a masking of the restless and stubbornly diverse quality of "the real" or that which always exceeds actuality and eludes symbolic expression' (2004: 48). The death-event becomes a refraction of orderly life – a refractive prism through which subjects are now able to see their lives, and the appearance of reality, in new light.

The vessel of death

> There is, by definition, something 'miraculous' in an event, from the miracles of our daily lives to those of the most sublime spheres, including that of the divine.
>
> (Žižek 2014: 1)

Death is often referred to as a journey – a journey where divine vessels usher the deceased into the afterlife. For Tai Theravada Buddhists, the death of a monk sets into motion elaborate funerary rituals and ample opportunity for laypeople to make merit, or to do good deeds that will improve their *kam* (karma). This was the case for Luang Pho Taa Sreng, the blind monk whose body was laid to rest in an ornate vessel called a *lerm* – a kind of coffin chariot or palanquin. Placed within a silver casket and enclosed within the *lerm*, the body of Luang Pho Taa Sreng would undergo its final rite before incineration – a three-day literal 'tug-of-war' that ended in the body of the deceased monk finally being brought to the pagoda where it would be burned. The ritual called *poy lerk lerm*, is reserved only for great monks who are highly regarded for both their teachings and extraordinary abilities. Sometimes called *khruba* (holy man), Luang Pho Taa Sreng could purportedly see objects in a room and sense the presence of a certain persons despite being blind. He was also loved for his engaging *dham* (darma teachings) talks. An abbot from Shan State told me that: 'He can create great stories in his *dham* talks. He would tell stories about Shan religion. He could make up to seven people come alive – he could create their voices. He became famous in Shan State. Usually only old men come to listen to the dham talks, but with this monk everyone would come to hear him tell the stories.'

The spectacle of *poy lerk lerm* involves sometimes up to a thousand merit-makers. The *lerm*, or palanquin, containing the deceased monk is placed atop two large tree-trunks, and once attached, thick rope, made by merit-makers, is fastened to each end of the *lerm*. The rope, measuring about 200 metres, is then pulled in opposite directions by the funeral attendees across the open dirt field of the festival space. This tug-of-war continues for three days and Dee, a Tai teacher and former monk, explains, 'Poy lerk lerm is an ancient Tai ceremony that is only used when a monk dies. When we do this ritual it means that this person was worshipped and revered. Each part wants to help him, every part wants him, and so they pull in opposite directions.[5] The descriptions of the ritual varied slightly and some also claimed that half the participants want the monk to stay in this realm, and the other half want to help usher the monk to the next realm where he will be reborn, or become again (*punabbhava*). But all agreed that participating in the *poy lerk lerm* ritual is a way of making *kuso* (merit). Some merit-makers, after having joined in on a pulling session, even cut off small pieces of the pulling rope as a token, or religious souvenir, to remember the ceremony by.

As Nancy Eberhardt explains in her study about the life-cycle in Tai culture and cosmology; 'In their stories, sermons and everyday talk, Shan [Tai] depict a universe in which every purposeful action you perform registers on the cosmos and eventually returns to you' (2006: 48). Thus, a person's demise is never the

Figure 8.1 The ritual of Poy Lerk Lerm involves a 'tug-of-war', or pulling the chariot containing the deceased monk in opposite directions, signifying the worshipper's
simultaneous desire to keep the monk in the current realm and also to usher
him to towards rebirth. Image taken by the author in Mae Hong Son Province,
Thailand, 2015.

final event, but rather a continuation of the karmic cycle of *samsara* – an endless
cycle of death and rebirth whereby one's reincarnation depends on the accumu-
lated acts throughout time – this is also referred to as *kam* (karma, meaning
action). For Tai peoples there is mobility in death. The spiritual conception of
rebirth and afterlife in Tai culture speaks to a cosmological plane where the realm
of beings also includes the entities of the deceased. Especially important is the
Tai conception of *khwan* (soul) and *phi* (spirit), which illustrate the mobility of

the afterlife in Tai cosmology. Each living being, human or otherwise, contains within its body a *khwan*. Upon the death of the physical body, the *khwan* is transformed into a *phi*, a process that can take up to a year (Eberhardt 2006: 52). Proper preparations and ceremonial rites ensure the safe passage of the soul into a spirit, so that the spirit does not linger and haunt the living, but may instead find a new body within which to dwell. However, there are many cases where the spirits of the deceased refuse to leave.

Waan, a Tai dancer who is often hired to perform at festivals, events and funerals explains that there are various signs that the deceased have yet to reincarnate. She performed for the funeral of one monk in particular, whose spirit had yet to reincarnate:

> In Vieng Heng, when a monk died, there was suddenly an unusual amount of water flowing from a tree by the temple. The water was flowing from the branches of the tree and no-one knew why or where it was coming from. So some villagers went to see a *sa-le* (holy man, fortuneteller). He told them it was the dead monk. His *phi* does not want to go and he is crying.[6]

In contrast to the elaborate rites evoked at the death-event of monks, when Sai Awn's father passed away in Shan State, it was a somewhat uneventful affair. The family kept the body for one day and then quickly buried it. Seven days later they had a small funeral. The family gathered, ate food and read the 'dham', or Buddhist scripture. When asked if they had any commemorative ceremonies for his father, he lamented, 'No, there is no music and dance for laypeople'. Sai Awn's father died when Sai Awn was just a young boy, in 5th grade. He said of this father, 'He was not a very hard working person, he liked to travel and drink. The most important person in my life was my mother'. Sai Awn was not sure why his father passed away, but that it was likely because he drank too much. His alcoholism and subsequent death devastated the family: 'After he passed away, our family was not strong. There was no one to take care of us, so we had to move'. But Sai Awn did go to the temple three months after his father's passing, and after *Kao Pansaa* (Theravada Buddhist lent), in order to sleep there and follow the Buddhist precepts. This was a way for Sai Awn to make merit – to accumulate good deeds in the karmic cyclical system *samsara* (birth and rebirth) – on behalf of his father, himself and his family. Thus with the presence of death, though being a time of dissolution and end, new avenues also arise for religious practitioners to improve upon their own karma, a word translated by one Buddhist research collaborator as 'action'. By committing to doing good deeds, making merit and following scripture, practitioners significantly improve their chances of being reborn into a new and better life, after death.

There is no equality in death. Those who lead spiritually devoted lives or lives of prominence, wealth or fame, can achieve relative immortality. Those who lead ordinary lives receive little funerary fanfare. Sai Awn explains, 'When normal people die they just put the body in a coffin and don't burn them. Only the monk is burned'. In Zygmunt Bauman's (2013) book *Mortality, Immortality and Other Life Strategies*, he considers immortality as being 'the great de-equalizer':

> The amount of public mourning and the intensity of public manifestations of memory became symbolic expressions of relative social placement at the same time as they were major stakes at the game of domination. Thanks to social rituals, all members were immortal, yet some were clearly more immortal than others. Society promised immortality as an interest on mortal life properly lived.
>
> (Bauman 2013: 52–3)

The spectacle of Luang Pho Taa Sreng's funeral contrasts sharply with Sai Awn's father's funeral. Yet both offer opportunities for the living to engage in acts that I argue are necromobile – acts designed to improve upon the merit of the deceased as well as the merit-maker upon his or her own demise. For many Tai peoples who have fled from the violence and war that ravaged the Shan State during the past five decades, becoming upwardly mobile in the course of one's present life-cycle is difficult, therefore religious piousness and frequent acts of merit-making becomes a salient way of ensuring a better rebirth. Acts such as making a religious offering (*bucha*) in order to receive an amulet with Luang Phoo Taa Sreng's image or participating in the tug-of-war ritual *Poy Lerm* are all deeds that register upon the cosmos, they are acts that serve you in the next life. The collective merit-making rites seen at Luang Pho Taa Sreng's funeral reveals the ways in which Buddhism can 'police' both crowds and individuals towards performing communal religious goals (Ranciere 2004: 29). The ritual performance of death and burial are also a part of a larger political project whereby Tai nationalism is reified through collective investments in merit-making, dance, song and drama.

Choreomobility: the dance-event

> When all is said and done, theatre thinks, in the space opened between life and death, the knot that binds together desire and politics. It thinks this knot in the form of an event, that is, in the form of the intrigue or the catastrophe.
>
> (Badiou 2013: 73)

Although, the funerary processions and preparations have been going on for three months, today is the culmination of the proceedings and the villagers' labour. Today, the steady beat of the *mong* (bossed gong) sounds throughout the valley, greeting pilgrims as they arrive. The pulsing pace of the *mong* is overlaid by the irregular striking of the *glong* (long drum), the ubiquitous sound that accompanies every Tai festival and sets the rhythm for the performances and dances that follow. Men, and sometimes women, take turns beating the *glong*, while passersby stop to dance, and onlookers approvingly clap or beat their thighs as they watch. There is excitement in each person's step, everyone in their finest wares and smiling eagerly, despite the sweltering heat and dust-filled grounds. There is a bouncy castle for the kids, men selling balloons, merit-making stations where you can *bucha* (make an offering), about 50 temporary shops self-organized around the festival grounds, selling traditional costumes, CDs, DVDs, amulets, books, T-shirts, hats and noodles. The Tai monastic funeral, known as *Poy Sang Kyo Murn Jao*, is akin to what Badiou calls a 'perishable spectacle': 'a spectacle is itself perishable by nature. It can certainly be repeated a good number of times. However, everything in it, or almost everything, is mortal' (2013: 58–59).

On the eve of the first day of the festival, a group of women, all dressed in coordinative Tai traditional attire, take command of the area of the festival grounds where musicians are playing. One woman walks up to the man playing the *glong* and asks to have a turn. What ensues will be two hours of a female-led impromptu dance and music fête. The women begin by overtaking a small corner of the festival ground, drawing a few dozen onlookers. Soon their enthusiasm, and skill, draws over 300 onlookers. More musicians arrive with their instruments, having been summoned by the rhythm, energy and commotion of the scene. The dancers move to a wider space within the festival and a large circle of bodies ensnares the performance. The inner ring of the circle becomes a moving wheel of dancers and its nucleolus a groups of musicians steadily maintaining the rhythmic pulse of the crowd. The multitude moves from being a 'chaotic multiplicity' to being in unison, to finding their corporal rhythm – what Deleuze and Guattari (2001) call the *refrain* – that which holds things together.

Figure 8.2 Tai women initiate an impromptu dance performance during the funeral of Luang Pho Taa Sreng. Image taken by the author in Mae Hong Son Province, Thailand, 2015.

Waan, a 25-year-old mother, performer and Tai cultural practitioner tells me that before her performance for Tai National Day, she receives dozens of letters from military officers telling her about their lives, lamentations and hopes for the future. She uses these letters to write dramatic operas to be danced and acted out on stage during the festival. This way, the desires, intrigues and concerns of the audience are presented in an ephemeral stage-show, uniquely formed by the dancers, singers and actors themselves to produce maximal affects. Dance is evoked in nearly all contexts of Tai religious, cultural and even political life. Theravada Buddhist holidays and temple festivals produce spaces for drama, dance and performance. But dance is especially significant as a nationalist enterprise during Tai National Day, commonly celebrated in February of each year in the Shan State Army's (SSA) military encampment at Doi Tai Leng, located on the Thai–Burma border in Mae Hong Son Province. Groups of performers are hired by festival organizers to perform customized dramas, dances and songs. Thus the Tai festival performance varies depending on the setting, preference of the organizer and socio-political milieu of the event. Sai Awn explains that, 'At the funeral you will have a *ta sai* (band) – a group that will come to sing and cry about the monk. They will tell the story about *khun phii* – the spirit that comes to take away the body. They will play traditional music and cry.' Dramatic performances at Tai events produce dramatic affects – kinesthetically linking a fractured nation through rhythms and refrains.

One of the answers emerging when we attempt to think of dance or movement practice as political is the concept of *kinesthetic empathy*, understood here as the somatic understandings of repetition and difference through observation and experience. It is the desire to invest energy into the refrain, it is the act of placing oneself within the assemblage, and it is the relay between practice and theory that attract bodies in the bodies–movement–politics nexus. It is the process that allows bodies and concepts signification as culture, tradition or habit. Here I turn to Susan Leigh Foster (2010), who has made significant contributions to an understanding of the politics of dance, and in particular, the politics of kinaesthetic empathy and kinaesthesia during her investigation of how concepts like empathy and sympathy gain traction within dance and performance studies. Kinaesthesia, is the way in which the body observes and responds to movement, placements and affects, and kinaesthetic empathy reveals to us 'the many ways in which the dancing body in its kinesthetic specificity formulates an appeal to viewers to be apprehended and felt, encouraging them to participate collectively in discovering the communal basis of their experience' (Foster 2010: 218).

The politics of kinaesthetic empathy harken a new mode of thinking about biopolitics, one that is not just bound to the apparatuses of the State, but that see the political as a somatic conditioning of the body through movement and practice; we can call this the politics of *choreomobility*. Considering the affects of the death-event as choreomobility provides us with pause to ponder the *dispositifs*, or mechanisms of control, that regulates the social body (Foucault 1980), in relation to displacements. André Lepecki (2013) distinguishes between chorepolicing and choreopolitics, where choreopolicing is understood in terms of Jaques Ranciere's concept of 'police', which defines life as a policed construction, or a controlled and governed mobilizations of bodies through time and space:

> The police is thus first an order of bodies that defines the allocation of ways of doing, ways of being, and ways of saying, and sees those bodies are assigned by the name to a particular place and task; it is an order of the visible and the sayable that sees that a particular activity is visible and another is not, that this speech is understood as discourse and another noise.
>
> (Ranciere 2004: 29)

Choreopolitics however, attends to the body's will to freedom in range, purpose and form of movement. Dance mobilities have been understood in terms of the policing of bodies within the context of choreography and performance. However, the metaphor may be extended beyond the realm of the stage to comprise how life is choreographed much in the same way as a performance – through the careful staging of bodies through space and time (Cresswell and Merriman 2011).

Conclusions: an epitaph

> Instead of considering reason as the truth of the subject, we can look to other foundational categories that are less abstract and more tactile, such as life and death.
>
> (Mbembe 2003: 14)

Mobility is not a phenomena exclusive to the living, vibrant mobilities also arise after the death of the body. In fact, the life of the body as an assemblage of vital parts lingers in perpetuity after the death of the living being. Death continuously occurs throughout our seemingly alive bodies. Our cells, once alive and filled with vibrancy, are in a constant process of death, disassemblage and reassemblage. As our cells die and pass through or flake off our bodies, we generate new cells that are fed by our consumption of external organizms and inorganic materials; decayed plant fibres, meat, oxygen and hydrogen dioxide. We die and become reborn at every instant. This cycle has no beginning and no end; there is no rupture, only accelerations and decelerations in decay and multiplication. Our senescence – the process of aging – is the constant threat to our fleeting lives. As our cells cease to divide by mitosis and we disassemble. But we do not disappear, we shift into new form: energy is never lost, it only moves. The rule of *kam*, or karma, captures this transversal flow of life force, whereby nothing is ever lost, but always cyclical, mobile, caught in the wheels of samsara (death and rebirth). In this way we must be careful not to privilege the assemblage, without also attending to the always-accompanying disassemblage. There is no final death, only reincarnation.

The object of this journeying into the world of festival, performance and death among displaced Tai peoples, is to explore and critique the idea of the death-event, which is the event that becomes framed posthumously as the end of a life, as having finality, fixity or boundedness. Rather than as a closed circuit or a thing of finality, I see the death-event, and indeed any event, as a practice through which one's becomings – as an individual, as a group or as a people – are rendered visible. By looking at the event, in this case, a funerary event, both as process and performance, an ontology of the necropolitics of being, both in this life and in lives beyond, may arise. In addition to examining death-as-event, I wish also to call attention to the many preventable and unreported deaths – due to violence, illness or displacement – that imperceptibly haunt Tai exiles in the border-zone. The precarity of life and death is sensed by the researcher through my engagement with Tai migrants, as a dancer, ethnochoreologist and mobile ethnographer. Dance, I argue, like Deleuze and Guattari's (2001) refrain, is a space creator – providing the possibility of living in a world where things may be repeated without strict felicity to an essence, origin or territory. By attending to the expressive and performatic mobilities arising in the midst of violence, war and displacement in the Thai-Burma border-zone, we come closer to an ontology of exile.

Notes

1. Following the student uprisings of 8/8/88 and subsequent elections, an unelected junta illegitimately sized power in Burma. The military junta calling itself The State Peace and Development Council (SPDC) changed the nation's name from Burma to Myanmar. Most nations and organizations, including the United Nations, now use Myanmar. I however, continue to use Burma as that is how the vast majority of the Tai research community in Thailand refers to the nation.
2. I am grateful for support from The École française d'Extrême-Orient, the College of Arts and Sciences, and the Department of Political Science at the University of Hawai'i at Mānoa to conduct this dissertation research in Northern Thailand from 2014–2015.
3. Scholars referring to the Tai peoples of Upland Southeast Asia most commonly use the word Shan. Shan however, is an exonym that the Tai peoples themselves largely reject. The Burman ethnic group used the word Shan, a cognate of Siam, to refer to the Siamese (Thai) people, with which the Tai are linguistically and culturally similar, but historically distinct. The term Tai refers to the hetereogenous group of peoples who are descendants or speakers of the proto-Tai language and include the Tai Yai, Tai Lue, Tai Dam and many other Tai/Dai ethnic groups. I use Tai in order to honour the wishes of my research collaborators from the Shan State in Burma, a vast majority of whom responded that they prefer foreigners to use the endonym Tai, rather than Shan when referring to the peoples of Shan State and its diaspora.
4. I must stress that my contribution to the field of mobilities studies in lieu of the death-event, will be very modest. I prefer to consider it an infusion of concepts already posited elsewhere, and expanded upon here in the context of my experiences, encounters and engagements in the Thai–Burma border-zone.
5. Personal Interview, Chiang Mai, March 2015.
6. Personal Interview, Chiang Mai, March 2015.

References

Badiou, A. (2006) (1988) *Being and Event*, trans. O. Feltham, London: Continuum.
Badiou, A. (2009) (2006) *Logic of Worlds*, trans. Alberto Toscano, London: Continuum.

Badiou, A. (2006) The Event in Deleuze. *Parrhesia: A Journal of Critical Philosophy.* Translated by J. Roffe. Accessed Online (Dec 4, 2011): http://www.lacan.com/baddel. htm. The original French text is 'L'événement selon Deleuze', in A. Badiou, *Logiques des mondes.* Paris: Seuil.

Badiou, A. (2013) *Rhapsody for the Theatre.* London: Verso. [Edited and introduced by Bruno Bosteels. Trans. Bruno Bosteels and Martin Puchner.]

Bauman, Z. (2013) *Mortality, Immortality and Other Life Strategies.* Chichester: Wiley.

Bennett, J. (2004) The force of things steps toward an ecology of matter. *Political Theory,* 32(3): 347–72.

Buckland, T. (1999) *Dance in the Field.* St. Martin's Press.

Campbell, C. (2015) Is the world's longest-running civil war about to end? *Time.* Accessed 13 March 2015. http://world.time.com/2013/11/06/is-the-worlds-longest-running-civil-war-about-to-end/.

Cresswell, T. (2006) *On the Move: Mobility in the Modern Western World.* Taylor & Francis.

Cresswell, T. and Merriman, P. (2011) *Geographies of Mobilities: Practices, Spaces, Subjects.* Ashgate Publishing, Ltd.

Deleuze, G. (2006) *The Fold.* A&C Black.

Deleuze, G. (1990). *The Logic of Sense.* Columbia University Press.

Deleuze, G. and Guattari, F. (2001) *A Thousand Plateaus.* Continuum.

Eberhardt, N. (2006) *Imagining the Course of Life: Self-Transformation in a Shan Buddhist Community.* University of Hawaii Press.

Edensor, T. (ed.) (2010) *Geographies of Rhythm: Nature, Place, Mobilities and Bodies.* Ashgate.

Foster, S. L. (2008) Movements contagion. The kinesthetic impact of performance. *The Cambridge Companion to Performance Studies.* Ed. Tracy Davis. Cambridge: Cambridge University Press, pp. 46–56.

Foster, S. L. (2009) *Worlding Dance.* Basingstoke: Palgrave Macmillan.

Foster, S. L. (2010) *Choreographing Empathy: Kinesthesia in Performance.* Abingdon: Routledge.

Foucault, M. (1980) *Power/Knowledge: Selected Interviews and Other Writings, 1972–1977.* Harvester Press.

Foucault, M. (1998) *The History of Sexuality: The Will to Knowledge: The Will to Knowledge v. 1.* Translated by Robert Hurley. New Ed edition. Harmondsworth: Penguin.

Jassal, L. K. (2014) Necromobilities: The multi-sited geographies of death and disposal in a mobile world." *Mobilities* 1 (3): 486–509.

Jirattikorn, A. (2008) *Migration, Media Flows and the Shan Nation in Thailand.* (doctoral dissertation) Retrieved from ProQuest Dissertations and Theses.

Kellerman, A. (2012) Potential mobilities. *Mobilities* 7 (1): 171–183.

Labovitz, J. and Chantavanich, S. (2013) Assessing potential changes in the migration patterns of Myanmar Migrants and their impacts of Thailand. *International Organization for Migration,* Country Mission in Thailand. Accessed 3 March 2015: http://th.iom.int/index.php/migration-resources/migration-research/Assessing-Potential-Changes-in-the-Migration-Patterns-of-Myanmar-Migrants-and-Their-Impacts-on-Thailand-(English-Language)/.

Lacan, J. (1978) *The Seminar of Jacques Lacan Book XI (The Four Fundamental Concepts of Psychoanalysis 1964–1965),* trans. Alan Sheridan, New York: W.W. Norton & Co.

Lacan, J. (1993) *The Seminar of Jacques Lacan Book III: The Psychoses 1955–1956,* trans. Russell Grigg, London: Routledge.

108 *Tani H. Sebro*

Lacan, J. (1998) *The Seminar of Jacques Lacan Book XX (Encore 1972–1973)*, trans. Bruce Fink, New York: W.W. Norton & Co.

Lefebvre, H. (2004) *Rhythmanalysis: Space, Time and Everyday Life*. A&C Black.

Lepecki, A. (2013) Choreopolice and choreopolitics: Or, the task of the dancer. *TDR: The Drama Review*, 57(4): 13–27.

Mbembe, A. (2003) Necropolitics. *Public Culture*, 15(1): 11–40.

Naing, S. Y. (2014a) Burmese refugees criticize Thailand's push for quicker repatriation. *The Irrawaddy* [Online]. Available: http://www.irrawaddy.org/burma/burmese-refugees-criticize-thailands-push-quicker-repatriation.html.

Naing, S. Y. (2014b) Repatriation thwarted by militarization in Eastern Burma: Report. *The Irrawaddy* [Online]. Available: http://www.irrawaddy.org/burma/repatriation-thwarted-militarization-eastern-burmareport.html.

Ong, A. (1999) *Flexible Citizenship: The Cultural Logics of Transnationality*. Durham: Duke University Press.

Rancière, J. (2004) *Disagreement: Politics and Philosophy*. Minneapolis: University of Minnesota Press.

Schein, L. (2002) Mapping Hmong media in diasporic space. In F. Ginsburg, L. Abu-Lughod, B. Larkin (eds). *MediaWorlds: Anthropology on New Terrains*. Berkeley, CA: University of California Press, pp 229–244.

Sheller, M. and Urry, J. (2006) The new mobilities paradigm. *Environment and Planning A* 38(2): 207–26.

Simmel, G. D. (1997) *Simmel on Culture: Selected Writings*. London: SAGE.

Žižek, S. (2014) *Event: A Philosophical Journey Through A Concept*. Brooklyn, NY: Melville House.

9 Mobility slogans

Rhetoric, movement, and #WeAreHere

Lisa C. Braverman

Sitting in front of the Google map, it looks like most others, with a notable exception. Tiny blue bubbles with white Jewish stars are clustered within it; the clusters are particularly dense in North and South America, Western Europe, and Israel. Instructions on the left side of the screen read:

> In honor of Holocaust Memorial Day, we asked our social media followers to: "Post a photo of yourself together with a Holocaust survivor on Facebook, Twitter, or Instagram with the hashtag #WeAreHere. Also be sure to include his or her name, age, and place of residence."
>
> Here are the results: an interactive map with pictures of Holocaust survivors from all over the world.
>
> If you would like to contribute to our map, please send us photos to idfnewmedia@gmail.com.

Below these words, the same blue and white Jewish star bubbles appear next to individuals' names. One may click on 'Zaida Morry' to learn that Mr. Morry was originally from Poland, is 94 years old, and currently lives in Melbourne, Australia. Henriette Cohen is 97 years old, lives in France, and survived Auschwitz and Bergen-Belsen; Tsipora, who survived Auschwitz, uses only her first name and resides in Israel. Despite the request for current photographs with Holocaust survivors, recently-deceased survivors populate the map as well; one survivor's family outside Chicago noted that their matriarch passed away (at the time of writing) yesterday. While each and every Holocaust survivor's story is important – not only those featured on the map – this chapter investigates other elements of this map and text. In particular, I explore the mobile aspects of the #WeAreHere slogan and the ironies associated with a project of this nature. I hazard that mobilities studies, rhetorical theory, and irony illuminate one another in unique and important ways.

Working towards a fuller integration of mobilities studies and rhetorical theory, this chapter advances the notion that there exist 'slogans of mobility', elaborated upon below. Created by the Israeli Defense Forces in April 2014, the map and slogan serve as moments of mobile activism. Regarding mobility as distinct from rhetorical movement or motion insofar as the former is intractably political and relational, this chapter draws upon the work of Adey (2009) and Cresswell (2010), among others, with the intent of defining relationships between language, violence, and politics as radically mobile. As the Holocaust was in large part a crime of forced movement signified by a strong relationship between geographic location and danger, the strengths and ironies of promoting Holocaust commemoration through Jews' self-reporting of their own locations are examined. This event is thus analysed as a moment in which mobility is heavily implicated and rendered more enticing, through rhetoric, in an attempt to excite activist support. I begin by offering a short overview of rhetorical theory, and then discuss how rhetorical theory has, by and large, taken account of movement. I argue rhetoric's treatment of movement is incomplete, and could more fully appreciate the radical place of politics in the study of mobility. Similarly, mobilities studies would do well to explore the potentialities of rhetorical theory. Mobility slogans help frame event mobilities; in this case, the #WeAreHere slogan brings events of the Holocaust into contemporary social media discussions. This slogan performs an activist truth: victims of the Holocaust survived and remain present.

Mobilities and rhetoric

A practice and art dating from ancient times, rhetoric is generally regarded as the study of persuasion. In his *Rhetoric*, Aristotle elaborates upon rhetoric as finding all available means of persuasion, and notes that 'its [rhetoric's] function ... is not to persuade but to see the available means of persuasion in each case ... for neither is it the function of medicine to create health but to promote this as much as possible; for it is nevertheless possible to treat well those who cannot recover health' (2007: 36). Rhetorical theory thus advocates critical analysis of a variety of texts – speeches, photographs, signs, and the like – as well as social movements and moments of activism. Ideographic rhetoric, a meditation on the slogans borne from the intermingling of ideology and rhetoric, is of the most interest to an exploration of mobility slogans.

Ideographs, McGee (1980a) argues, are terms mistaken for the technical language of political philosophy; ideographs are slogan-like or 'God' terms that signify the collective commitments of specific populations. From an ideological standpoint, McGee's conception of the ideograph troubles the ready acceptance of (US) cultural signifiers such as 'freedom' and 'justice'. The term 'liberty', for example, encapsulates a spirit rather than an entirely reified principle (McGee 1980b). As artefacts of both rhetoric and ideology, however, ideographs take on the characteristics of paradoxically reified objects as they are made to appear as though they have maintained a fixed and stable meaning throughout time, yet are malleable enough to account for shifting social practices. In their study of the term 'equality', Condit and Lucaites (1993) explain how the ideograph was figured to take account of radically unequal practices such as slavery and racism. 'Slavery and racism', they note, 'thus solidified each other into permanence. Slavery could not be eliminated without creating a free African-American population that Anglo-Americans considered intolerable. Anglo-Americans could not revise their estimates of Africans as long as they remained in bondage' (1993: 67). Following the work of both McGee and Condit and Lucaites, McCann (2007) examines the 'victim' ideograph within the context of the Illinois death penalty commutations. Arguing that the instantly-identifying 'victim' label was, in this case, variously applied both to convicted inmates and those who were slain, McCann highlights the 'historical, material relations' to which 'ideographs' meanings [are] necessarily connected' (2007: 386). Both of these examples touch upon the peculiar relationships between ideographs and violence, arguing that ideographs may work to sediment culturally specific ideologies and practices of violence. As mobility slogans emerge as early-stage, potential ideographs, I seek to investigate how they reify and challenge the genocidal violence they attempt to articulate. More broadly, such slogans help bring event mobilities to the fore as instances that can and should shape public culture.

What, then, is a mobility slogan, and how does it intersect with rhetorical theory and mobilities studies? I define 'mobility slogans' as succinct words and phrases that explicitly reference political movement or lack of movement. They serve as calls to action, make moral prescriptions, and offer assumptions about who and what may move, should move, and who should be moving whom. With regard to violence in the public sphere, these slogans appear with budding frequency. In addition to '#WeAreHere', slogans such as 'Bring Back Our Girls', '#WithSyria', and 'The Lost Boys' reduce and disseminate ideas about violence and the human costs of war. With the possible exception of 'The Lost Boys', the aforementioned slogans serve partly as calls to action, both capturing the idea of and calling for political movement. While rhetoric has theorized movement, especially through the language of social movements, I argue both rhetorical theory and mobilities studies would be better served by becoming more highly integrated.

Rhetorical studies have long valued theories of kinetic movement, though less than they perhaps should. Often, instead of movements of the body, rhetorical theory has focused on the public address dimensions of historical and social movements (Lucas 1980). To be sure, these different types of movement are not mutually exclusive, yet there exist fundamental differences between acts such as moving one's body and analysing a temporal period of collective, concerted, and rhetorical action. One crucial difference in this case is the notion of scale, another, the fully unresolved splits between physical movements, social movements, and their accompanying studies. The importance of the corporeal is not lost in the study of rhetoric by any means, nor is it absent in studies of the rhetoric of social movements. This chapter aims to consider different ways bodies, and moments of activism, are conceptualized as (im)mobile in an anti-genocide slogan. Building off Griffin's (1952) meditations on rhetoric and historical movements, rhetoricians ignited fierce debates about the nature of movement studies in rhetorical theory.

Rhetorical movements

Defining a movement as 'some combination of events occurring over time which can be linked in such a way that the critic can make a case for treating them as a single unit', Sillars (1980: 107) argues that movement studies extend the field of rhetoric beyond that of biography. Such studies are not without their pitfalls, however: Sillars cites movement studies as being too linear, inappropriately oriented towards cause-and-effect thinking, and far too dependent upon intent as a basis for judgement. Insofar as he recounts movements as moments awaiting critical reflection and a complex interrelation between messages and craftsmanship, his position does not sufficiently account for kinetic, bodily movement.

Sillars' (1980) work remains far from the most sceptical of movement studies in rhetoric, however. Zarefsky (1980), in fact, found movement studies slippery enough to include scepticism in the very title of his thoughts on the matter. He calls us to ask ourselves whether a distinctiveness of social type has been established when we undertake the study of a social movement. His work builds upon critiques by Michael Calvin McGee that suggest social movements are not necessarily distinctive sites for theoretical enquiry. According to McGee (1980a: 236–237), 'movement' remains a mere analogue 'comparing the flow of social facts to physical movement' and thus is not a phenomenon. Social movements, according to McGee, allow us to maintain notions of morality, can lead to logical fallacies as movements are propelled by history itself, and should be a conclusion rather than a premise with which to begin research. I argue that mobilities studies – and relatedly, mobility slogans – provide a useful theoretical framework through which we may conceptualize both the materiality and ideological ephemerality of collective movement, physical or otherwise perceived. While McGee's argument that the rhetoric surrounding movements is a way to bestow social flows with a physical component is compelling, the theoretical use of mobilities studies combines the social and physical dimensions of movement, rather than treating them as conceptually divided. Rhetorical theory, then, alludes to the ways in which political movement can be rendered more explicitly persuasive.

Rhetorical scholarship on movement has not focused exclusively upon the inherent value of the term 'movement'. Lucas (1980) notes rhetoricians have largely failed to account adequately for the kinetic nature of movement in rhetoric, and scholarship since has made great strides in this direction. Foss and Domenici (2001), Pezzullo (2003), and Endres and Senda-Cook (2011), for example, incorporate ideas of embodiment, materiality and place, to bring issues of kinetic movement into closer conversation with rhetorical and public sphere theories. This chapter extends this type of work.

Theoretical connections

The rhetorical life of the slogan discussed here highlights intersections between rhetorical theory and mobility studies. Such intersections combine social forces of persuasion with the myriad meanings inherent in movement. As noted by Peter Adey (2010), scholars from fields as diverse as geography, sociology, and disability studies investigate the subject of mobility as sets of lived relations to others and to the world. Whereas Adey (2010) defines mobility as movement imbued with meaning, Thrift (2006) likens mobility to a structure of feeling that can give way to resistance. From a rhetorical perspective, Burke (1945) distinguishes between 'mere' motion and action, arguing that motion yields only physical movement, whereas action is the counterpart of motion that fosters greater meaning. The two are not mutually exclusive, however, as moments of 'conscious or purposive motion' (1945: 14) serve as building blocks for further action. Although it is admittedly difficult to imagine apolitical movement, equated here with motion, without any kind of meaning, the twin emphases of relationality and potentiality in mobilities studies provide innovative ways of thinking about the relationships between rhetoric and violence. The distance between violence, the self, and the state does not remain static, and the mobilities paradigm helps account for this dynamism. In addition to the various stages and implications of movement, the study of mobility importantly accounts for some of the politics involved in the communication of that movement.

Rhetoric, mobility, and #WeAreHere

Cresswell (2010) highlights six components of a politics of mobility that I will consider in relation to the #WeAreHere campaign. These components help animate not only aspects of the relationship between rhetoric and violence, but also particularities of how emotion travels within and among political bodies and nation-states. Cresswell (2010) asks of mobile artefacts: Why does a person or thing move? How fast does a person or thing move? In what rhythm does a person or thing move? What route does it take? How does it feel? And lastly, when and how does it stop? These questions fall under the general rubric of dromology: the regulation of different types of movement. The Holocaust and movement were inseparable, and Cresswell's central questions regarding the politics of mobility pose rich theoretical conundrums for how we might understand and engage the relationships between rhetoric, commemoration, and representation.

Notions of rhetoric and mobility have been brought together in existing literature, though not to a great extent. Drawing largely from Cresswell's theory of the relationship between rhetoric and mobility, Brouwer (2007) explores ideologies of mobility as they shaped the circulation of the NAMES Project AIDS Memorial Quilt. As Cresswell (2006) claims and Brouwer elaborates, instances that implicate mobility may be conceptually divided in a few fundamental ways: (instance of mobility) as fact, representation, and/or embodied experience. As Brouwer importantly argues, '[studies] in mobility make movement the figure instead of the ground of critical analysis' (Brouwer 2007: 703). His work blends rhetoric and notions of circulation, opening up the possibility of considering a rhetoric of mobility.

Mobility slogans, and more specifically the #WeAreHere slogan, effectively collapse long, complicated arguments into movement-infused phrases. Much scholarship about rhetoric, commemoration, and genocide (e.g. Linenthal 1994, 2001; Hasian 2004; Hartelius 2013), as well as scholarship interrogating public memory and violence more broadly (e.g. Bodnar 1994; Harold and DeLuca 2005; Sturken 2007), centres on the perils and possibilities of consumption; mobility slogans begin to turn rhetorics of genocide into consumable quasi-artefacts that are able to be manipulated. Though such scholarship often focuses upon the consumption of material artefacts, it is important for the consumption of slogans and digital rhetorics as well. Hartelius (2013) and Sturken (2007), for example, critique souvenirs designed in the wake of violent events: Hartelius problematizes knick-knacks such as candles that are sold at Dachau, while Sturken focuses on kitsch – teddy bears, snow globes, and the like – that has been produced in the wake of events like the Oklahoma City Bombing and 9/11. Even in the vast body of work that addresses public memorials and memorializing, arguments often revolve around the 'taking in' of a place, or how a visitor experiences a given memorial (e.g. Blair and Michel 2000, 2007; Hasian 2004; Hess 2007). Far less attention is paid, however, to specific units of rhetoric – like slogans – that are not as readily consumed or consumable. Insofar as event mobilities are framed by global media systems, they are manipulated and perhaps rendered more persuasive prior to being consumed on the Internet.

Much of the ever-growing body of work that addresses the complex and often paradoxical relationship between rhetoric and violence deals implicitly or explicitly with questions of location. As Cresswell's germinal questions invoke moving from one place to another, this conversation invites the integration of such rhetorical study with geography broadly, and mobilities studies more specifically. The *Quarterly Journal of Speech*'s forum on the violence of rhetoric (2013) distinguishes between how violence is constructed rhetorically (the rhetoric of violence) and the physical, material, and emotional violence that can result from rhetoric itself. Although the geographic, public, and interpersonal locations of violence are not the only things that matter to this debate, they are persistently important; violence resides in words, nonverbal acts, and a combination of the two. In addition to the perceived location of violence, the magnitude of such violence excites, or fails to excite, certain emotions through rhetoric. As Vivian (2013) notes, [transnational] memories of the twentieth century confront us with genocide, but such memories render genocidal violence as something consumable. Vivian argues compellingly that slogans such as 'never again' elevate historical atrocities to the status of something that might not be possible in today's world. As we figure genocidal violence as something more distant from our present time, he cautions that we might fail to see it and other types of violence emerging in new and different forms. Mobility slogans, which function in multiple ways, exist partly to continually remind publics not only of movements, but of events and threats. Enders (1999) goes so far as to define rhetoric as a system of pain production, intimately binding rhetorical invention with violence and memory. She pays attention to space and place, elaborating upon the ancient Christian tradition of 'rogation days' during which Christian citizens would beat their bodies against rocks and other physical structures to remind themselves of the boundaries they had transgressed. Such work, along with much of the rhetorical scholarship that engages with violence (see, for example, Harold and DeLuca 2005; Stahl 2008; Achter 2010; Gorsevski and Butterworth 2011; Doxtader 2011;

Murray Yang 2011), locates violent rhetoric/rhetorical violence in specific publics and historical contexts. Mobility slogans have the potential to broaden those publics, bringing awareness of global events to diverse audiences through social media. #WeAreHere, as discussed below, both succeeds at engaging the primary targets of its rhetoric – Holocaust survivors – and spectacularly fails at reaching a broader audience. While the slogan may evoke heritage and memory for some, its generic rhetoric has left it open to be associated with too many other meanings.

Mobility encapsulates place, and places, too, are rendered rhetorical. Endres and Senda-Cook (2011) acknowledge and extend the notion that places serve as persuasive, material actors within the concept of mobility. Defining place as particular and space as general – productively flipping De Certeau's (1984) idea that space is practised place (and coincidentally falling more in line with geographers) – the authors claim that places themselves act as performers. This framework extends to social protest and beyond, building upon formative work in geography and landscape studies that suggest rich texts emerge from human-environment interactions (Sauer 1925; Jackson 1984; Daniels 1989; Cosgrove 1998).

The #WeAreHere Google map, in several senses, serves as a rhetorical imperative to mobility. Insofar as it reports hundreds of survivors' locations, and does so by enlisting the help of their loved ones, it is defiant. Not only has this particular group survived elimination, it has thrived and procreated. Moreover, the map and slogan laugh in the face of one of the Holocaust's founding premises: the knowledge of free Jews' locations signified eminent danger, and likely death. It is of no small consequence that the map was developed by the Israeli Defense Force, or that the map privileges Jewish Holocaust victims. As Israel continually asserts its right to exist and defend itself, the map and slogan serve as reminders of the genocide against the Jews.

In considering the politics of mobility conceptualized both within and external to Cresswell's framework, I examine two things that move: Jewish Holocaust survivors as they are presented on the Google Map, and the #WeAreHere slogan itself. The slogan collapses time and location rather neatly on first glance, but is in fact multifaceted when analysed more thoroughly.

Cresswell's (2010) line of questioning begins by asking why a person or thing moves. In the case of Holocaust victims, the initial answer is clear if troubling: victims were forced to move in order to be executed. Acts of genocide plumb the most despairing depths of mobility, underscoring how hurtful mobile potential can be. Despite the inhumane and violent reasons for movement in the case of Holocaust victims, the mapping campaign aims to lend a sense of levity to the atrocity. By boldly claiming that they are *here* (and there), victims and their families not only upend embodied rhetorics of the Holocaust that kept them silent and afraid, they challenge past terrors of genocide in visually and engaged manners. Whereas disappearances and forced relocations in genocides broadly, and in the Holocaust more specifically, are often characterized by an intentionally confusing, middle-of-the-night lack of publicity, survivors' willingness to show their faces on a fully public Internet domain provides a visual depiction of the

IDF-conceptualized slogan. This visuality helps collapse the already porous borders of rhetoric and mobilities; survivors exist in place, they have – with no clear exceptions – moved from the sites of their persecution, and are presented/ present themselves in the form of a statement.

In a highly mediated and digitized society, slogans such as the hashtag phrase described here move for myriad reasons. Hashtag slogans, first and foremost, are engineered specifically to move. They call attention to events such as disappearances, police violence, and systematic social injustices (e.g. #BringBackOurGirls, #SandraBland, and #BlackLivesMatter). The hashtag symbol encourages use and publicity of slogans, as well as conversations surrounding the slogan's issues. The more pertinent questions for the hashtag mobility slogan at hand, then, relate to speed and type of movement: How fast does it move? In what rhythm, and along what routes?

An investigation of #WeAreHere raises crucial questions about the nature of digital, mobile rhetorics. Despite a compelling and highly visual, albeit small, mapping campaign, perhaps the most striking insight from the slogan's campaign comes from its Twitter presence. Paired intentionally with a hashtag, '#WeAreHere' was engineered at least partly for the Twitter forum. The slogan asks to be picked up, shared, and commented upon. Perhaps obviously, however, its language is too commonplace. It moves too quickly, too freely, and with no fixed meaning tied to genocide commemoration. Searching for the hashtag on Twitter reveals several campaigns, including a social justice campaign from singer Alicia Keys and several youth engagement movements. More obviously and at times humorously, however, individuals use the slogan to declare that they are simply somewhere, be it a park, tourist site, or even a family function. While this particular mobility slogan moves at a rapid rate – dozens of new #WeAreHere posts surface daily – the transit of the anti-genocide version is stunted. The map, and renderings of the survivors themselves, is diluted in its ability to travel at least in part due to banal, unspecific language.

The routes, rhythms, emotions, and endings of mobility slogans stretch from recent and distant histories to the radical potential of the future. For #WeAreHere, the slogan germinated from a complex and painful history of persecution, the creation of the State of Israel, and the Israeli Defense Forces' desire to create a public, digital, living memorial to Holocaust victims who survived. In thinking through the relationships between mobility and rhetoric, especially the rhythms in which words move and travel and the feelings language elicit, we must also bear in mind the tropes that organize rhetoric and experiences of mobility. As the ironies of violent mobility, survivorship, and victim visibility punctuate what appears to be a partially celebratory map of Holocaust survivors, the survivors' physical and geographic mobilities are notably tempered by a lack of rhetorical mobility of their map. Perhaps even more so than the map, the #WeAreHere slogan lies in waiting, not unlike #BringBackOurGirls or #WithSyria, ready to be mobilized again should rhetoric and global events call for it. Rhetoric, infused with the language and principles of mobility, does not stop as a physical body might. It persists, changing, changeable, and full of potential.

Several layers of irony are embedded in the rhetoric of mobility that character-izes the '#WeAreHere' slogan. In addition to encouraging the formerly deadly self-reporting of a population that has been victim to perhaps the most totalizing genocide in history, the slogan '#WeAreHere' simultaneously invokes movement and a radical ability to remain stationary and constant – despite concerted, violent efforts, this is one population that will not be eradicated. It is a population that, in both figurative and literal senses, cannot be (re)moved. At the same time, the map signifies the most liberating of mobilities – the ability to survive and move, in some cases halfway around the world, despite a history of persecution.

Conclusions

Mobility slogans such as #WeAreHere invite us to consider how event mobilities are constantly framed and re-framed in global media systems. The Holocaust, for example, was an extended, traumatic event that shaped contemporary under-standings of genocide. In this particular slogan and interactive mapping activity, survivors and their descendants assert their agency through reclaiming facets of mobility that caused genocidal violence in the first place. In proclaiming and documenting their presence, Holocaust survivors extend and change a violent event. The Holocaust becomes an event that is lived and felt today, many years after its conclusion. But its inflection changes – rather than prominently featuring overtones of tragedy and pain, this mobility slogan offers steadfastness and defiance.

As hashtag mobility slogans become increasingly common in public culture, the ways in which we discuss political movement continue to evolve. These slogans call explicitly for engagement and conversation, fostering richer engagements with mobility from individuals all over the world. As political and forced movement become more far-reaching topics of discussion, mobility slogans are ways to convey short, persuasive points. They, too, travel – or notably fail to do so.

References

Achter, P. (2010) Unruly bodies: The rhetorical domestication of twenty-first-century veterans of war. *Quarterly Journal of Speech*, 96(1): 46–68.

Adey, P. (2009) *Mobility*, New York: Routledge.

Aristotle (2007) *On rhetoric: a theory of civic discourse*, [translated with introduction, notes, and appendices by George A. Kennedy]. Oxford: Oxford University Press.

Bærenholdt, J. O. and Granås, B. (2008) 'Places and mobilities beyond the periphery', In J. O. Bærenholdt and B. Granås (eds), *Mobility and Place: Enacting Northern European Peripheries*, Ashgate, pp. 1–10.

Blair, C. and Michel, N. (2007) The AIDS Memorial Quilt and the contemporary culture of public commemoration. *Rhetoric & Public Affairs*, 10(4): 595–626.

Blair, C. and Michel, N. (2009) Reproducing civil rights tactics: The rhetorical perfor-mances of the Civil Rights Memorial. *Rhetoric Society Quarterly*, 30 (2): 31–55.

Bodnar, J. E. (1994) *Remaking America: Public Memory, Commemoration, and Patriotism in the Twentieth Century*, New Haven, CT: Princeton University Press.

Brouwer, D. C. (2007) From San Francisco to Atlanta and back again: Ideologies of mobility in the AIDS Quilt's search for a homeland. *Rhetoric & Public Affairs*, 10(4): 701–721.

Burke, K. (1969) [1945] *A Grammar of Motives*. Oakland, CA: University of California Press.

Burke, K. (1984) [1937] *Attitudes toward history*. Oakland, CA: University of California Press.

Büscher, M. and Urry, J. (2009) Mobile methods and the empirical. *European Journal of Social Theory* 12(1): 99–116.

Condit, C. M. and Lucaites, J. L. (1993) *Crafting Equality: America's Anglo-African Word*. Chicago: University of Chicago Press.

Cosgrove, D. (1998) *Social Formation and Symbolic Landscape*. Madison, WI: University of Wisconsin Press, Second Edition.

Cresswell, T. (2006) *On the Move: Mobility in the Modern Western World*. New York: Routledge.

Cresswell, T. (2010) Towards a politics of mobility. *Environment and planning. D, Society and Space*, 28(1): 17.

Daniels, S. (1989) Marxism, culture, and the duplicity of landscape. In R. Peet and N. Thrift (eds.) *New Models in Geography*, Vol. 2, Boston, MA: Unwin Hyman, pp. 196–220.

Dau, J. B. (2007) *God Grew Tired of Us*. Washington, DC: National Geographic Books.

De Certeau, M. (1998) [1984] *The Practice of Everyday Life: Living and Cooking. Volume 2*. Minneapolis, MN: University of Minnesota Press.

Delgado, F. P. (1995) Chicano movement rhetoric: An ideographic interpretation. *Communication Quarterly*, 43(4): 446–455.

Delgado, F. P. (1999) The rhetoric of Fidel Castro: Ideographs in the service of revolutionaries. *Howard Journal of Communication*, 10(1): 1–14.

Doxtader, E. (2011) Contending with violent words; or, The afterthought of (in) civility. *Philosophy and Rhetoric*, 44(4): 403–423.

Edensor, T. (2011) Commuter: mobility, rhythm and commuting. In T. Cresswell and P. Merriman (eds), *Geographies of Mobilities: Practices, Spaces, Subjects*, Farnham: Ashgate, pp. 189–204.

Eggers, D. (2007) *What is the What: The Autobiography of Valentino Achak Deng*. London: Hamish Hamilton.

Enders, J. (1999) *The Medieval Theater of Cruelty: Rhetoric, Memory, Violence*. Ithaca, NY: Cornell University Press.

Endres, D. and Senda-Cook, S. (2011) Location matters: The rhetoric of place in protest. *Quarterly Journal of Speech*, 97(3): 257–282.

Engels, J. et al. (2013) Forum on the violence of rhetoric. *Quarterly Journal of Speech*, 99(2): 180–232.

Foss, K. A. and Domenici, K. L. (2001) Haunting Argentina: Synecdoche in the protests of the mothers of the Plaza de Mayo. *Quarterly Journal of Speech*, 87: 237–258.

Foucault, M. (1990) [1978] *The History of Sexuality vol. 1: An Introduction*. New York: Vintage.

Gorsevski, E. W. and Butterworth, M. L. (2011) Muhammad Ali's fighting words: The paradox of violence in nonviolent rhetoric. *Quarterly Journal of Speech* 97(1): 50–73.

Griffin, L.M. (1952) The rhetoric of historical movements. *Quarterly Journal of Speech*, 38(2): 184–188.

Harold, C. and DeLuca, K. M. (2005) Behold the corpse: Violent images and the case of Emmett Till. *Rhetoric & Public Affairs*, 8(2): 263–286.

Hartelius, J. (2013) 'Remember-Signs': Concentration camp souvenirs and the mediation of trauma. *Culture, Theory and Critique*, 54(1): 1–18.

Hasian, Jr, M. (2004) Remembering and forgetting the 'final solution': A rhetorical pilgrimage through the US Holocaust Memorial Museum. *Critical Studies in Media Communication*, 21(1): 64–92.

Hess, A. (2007) In digital remembrance: Vernacular memory and the rhetorical construction of web memorials. *Media, Culture & Society*, 29(5): 812–830. https://www.google.com/maps/ms?ie=UTF8&oe=UTF8&t=h&msa=0&msid=211579865712499896307.0004f7afd49006cfc7911&dg=feature, Accessed September 28, 2014.

Jackson, J. B. (2008) [1984] The Word Itself. In T.S. Oakes and P.L. Price (eds) *The Cultural Geography Reader*. New York: Routledge, pp. 153–158.

Johnson, D. (2007) Mapping the meme: A geographical approach to materialist rhetorical criticism. *Communication and Critical/Cultural Studies*, 4(1): 27–50.

Law, J. and Urry, J. (2004) Enacting the social. *Economy and society*, 33(3): 390–410.

Lentricchia, F. (1985) *Criticism and Social Change*. Chicago: University of Chicago Press.

Linenthal, E. T. (2001) *Preserving Memory: The Struggle to Create America's Holocaust Museum*. New York: Columbia University Press.

Linenthal, E. T. (1994) The boundaries of memory: The United States Holocaust Memorial Museum. *American Quarterly*, 46(3): 406–433.

Lucas, S. E. (1980) Coming to terms with movement studies. *Communication Studies*, 31.4: 255–266.

Marcus, G. E. (1995) Ethnography in/of the world system: The emergence of multi-sited ethnography. *Annual Review of Anthropology*, 24(1): 95–117.

McCann, B. J. (2007) Therapeutic and material hood: Ideology and the struggle for meaning in the Illinois death penalty controversy. *Communication and Critical/Cultural Studies*, 4(4): 382–401.

McGee, M. C. (1980a) 'Social movement': Phenomenon or meaning? *Central States Speech Journal*, 31(4): 233–244.

McGee, M. C. (1980b) The 'ideograph': A link between rhetoric and ideology. *Quarterly Journal of Speech*, 66(1): 1–16.

McKerrow, R. E. (1989) Critical rhetoric: Theory and praxis. *Communications Monographs*, 56(2): 91–111.

McKinnon, S. L. (2008) Unsettling resettlement: Problematizing 'Lost Boys of Sudan' resettlement and identity. *Western Journal of Communication*, 72(4): 397–414.

Mintz, S. W. (1985) *Sweetness and Power*. New York: Viking.

Morris III, C. E. (2007) My old Kentucky homo: Abraham Lincoln, Larry Kramer, and the politics of queer memory. In C. E. Morris III (ed.), *Queering Public Address: Sexualities in American Historical Discourse*. Columbia, SC: University of South Carolina, pp. 93–120.

Murray Yang, M. (2011) Still burning: Self-immolation as photographic protest. *Quarterly Journal of Speech*, 97(1): 1–25.

Myers, F. (1994) Beyond the intentional fallacy: Art criticism and the ethnography of Aboriginal acrylic painting. *Visual Anthropology Review*, 10(1): 10–43.

Nixon, R. (2011) *Slow Violence and the Environmentalism of the Poor*. Cambridge, MA: Harvard University Press.

Pezzullo, P. C. (2003) Resisting 'National Breast Cancer Awareness Month': The rhetoric of counterpublics and their cultural performances. *Quarterly Journal of Speech*, 89(3): 345–365.

Phillips, K. R. (ed.) (2004) *Framing Public Memory*, Birmingham, AL: University of Alabama Press.

Sauer, C. O. (1996) [1925] The morphology of landscape. In J. Agnew, D. N. Livingstone and A. Rogers (eds) *Human Geography: An Essential Anthology*, Cambridge, MA: Blackwell Publishers, pp. 296–315.

Sillars, M. O. (1980) Defining movements rhetorically: Casting the widest net. *Southern Speech Communication Journal*, 46(1): 17–32

Silvey, R. (2004) Power, difference and mobility: Feminist advances in migration studies. *Progress in Human Geography*, 28(4): 490–506.

Stahl, R. (2010) *Militainment, Inc.: War, Media, and Popular Culture*, New York: Routledge.

Stier, O. B. (2005) Different trains: Holocaust artifacts and the ideologies of remembrance. *Holocaust and Genocide Studies*, 19(1): 81–106.

Stuckey, M. E. (2012) On rhetorical circulation. *Rhetoric and public affairs*, 15(4): 609–612.

Sturken, M. (2007) *Tourists of history: Memory, kitsch, and consumerism from Oklahoma City to Ground Zero*. Durham, NC: Duke University Press.

Tell, D. (2008) The 'shocking story' of Emmett Till and the politics of public confession. *Quarterly Journal of Speech*, 94(2): 156–178.

Tesfahuney, M. (1998) Mobility, racism and geopolitics. *Political Geography*, 17(5): 499–515.

'The Crime of Genocide Defined in International Law' (2013, December 1) Retrieved from http://www.preventgenocide.org/genocide/officialtext.htm.

Thrift, N. (2006) Space. *Theory, Culture, and Society*, 23(1): 139–146.

Urry, J. (2007) *Mobilities*. London: Polity.

Vivian, B. (2010) *Public Forgetting: The Rhetoric and Politics of Beginning Again*. College Station, PA: Penn State Press.

Vivian, B. (2013) Times of violence. *Quarterly Journal of Speech*, 99(2): 209–217.

Wander, P. (1984) The third persona: An ideological turn in rhetorical theory. *Communication Studies*, 35(4): 197–216.

'With Syria'. (2014, September 28). Retrieved from www.withsyria.com

Zarefsky, D. (1980) A skeptical view of movement studies. *Communication Studies*, 31(4): 245–254.

10 Food sovereignty galas

Transnational activism for rich moral economies and poor livelihoods

Elizabeth Louis

Vandana Shiva walks up to the stage at Kauai Memorial Convention hall during the 'Raise Awareness, Inspire Change' campaign in Hawaii in January 2013, to a deafening applause. Shiva, a passionate and outspoken food sovereignty advocate, is widely recognized as one of the movement's most popular ideologues and has achieved a distinct celebrity persona. She speaks and organizes several food sovereignty events a year and is sought after for her celebrity status and her rousing exhortations against corporate agriculture. These events range from focusing on localized struggles such as Hawaii's anti-GMO campaign, to speaking at academic forums, as well as large international events like the Slow Food Movement and Terra Madre festivals. On this global stage there are many such food sovereignty ideologues such as Jose Bové, Anne Lappé, Eric Holt Giménez, Mariam Mayet, but none as visible or forceful as Shiva. The speaker who introduces her starts with a long list of awards and accolades Shiva has received including being named one the five most important women in Asia, one of the seven most important women in the world.

Food sovereignty is defined as the right of each person, community, and nation to define its own agriculture and food policies that will enable each entity to not just have food security, but also ensure that the food produced is environmentally sustainable, and socially just. Like other anti-globalization and social justice movements seeking to resist the reach of neoliberal globalization, food sovereignty connects territorialized struggles to transnational networks encompassing a multitude of actors and different scales of action (Routledge 2003).

Food sovereignty events in the transnational social movement arena serve as important points of juncture where discourses collide, mediate events and then are re-presented by attendees. Food sovereignty discourses are embedded in particular geohistories (Jarosz 2014), and are therefore laden with meanings specific to who is articulating them, and at what scale. At food sovereignty events the challenge of integrating transnational discourses with local discourses and realities lends itself to essentialization, where narrow articulations of food sovereignty are foisted on attendees, often losing its relevance for diverse groups of marginalized and disenfranchised of food producers, whom ironically idealogues like Shiva claim to speak for. The discourse and ideas of food sovereignty have become as mobile as the world-travelling celebrities that advocate for it. An idealized notion of food sovereignty thus becomes deterritorialized, losing its connection to local contexts, and is re-presented as a panacea for the multiple pressures that the rural areas are facing as a result of the entry of multinational corporations, austerity measures imposed by their own governments, shifts in social aspirations of the rural poor and changing climate patterns and how these are experienced among diverse populations.

Although the overarching message of food sovereignty is clearly a scathing critique against neoliberal capitalism in agriculture, food sovereignty cannot be divorced from its specific contexts, scales and histories (Jarosz 2014). Whether it is a community in Maine opposing state regulation of locally produced foods or a country seeking to promote food self-sufficiency in the face of trade policies, the contexts are vastly different and therefore require very different actions and strategies to move towards food sovereignty.

Most literature in support of food sovereignty has focused on its *potential* to confront and resist neoliberal agriculture. Critiques of food sovereignty and similar transnational movements by Akram-Lodhi (2007), Borras et al. (2008), Borras, (2010), Boyer (2010), Trauger (2014), Bernstein (2014), Byres (2004), Cochrane (2007), Bebbington (2000), Boyer (2010), Alkon and Mares (2012), and Louis (2015) among others, highlight that the ideals do not speak to the bread-and-butter struggles of many – be they small farmers or wage workers in the Global South or poor consumers in the urban US. Most conclude that food sovereignty or similar approaches are too narrow or idealistic and fail to address the deeper issues and underlying structures that make livelihoods more vulnerable. Often they are embedded in and replicate the very neoliberal processes that they seek to oppose. Therefore while Shiva and other ideologues make claims that these movements pose a serious impediment to the global corporate food regime through the creation of a global civil society (Cumbers and Routledge 2008), there is a need to examine theoretically and empirically the implications of the popular construction of food sovereignty discourses and the strategies that are based on these ideals.

In this chapter, I argue that the movement of discourses and their location within celebrity events dislocates them from their fundamental contexts and territories. This article draws on mobilities, social movement and political economy of agriculture literatures to provide a critique of food sovereignty constructions popularized by global and celebrity events. The intent is not to denigrate the progressive work that food sovereignty engages in, but rather to contribute to emerging academic debates on the subject. It underscores that popular constructions of food sovereignty need more critical examination, debate and deliberation to ensure that the critiques of neoliberal agriculture stay in touch with the lived realities and aspirations of small peasants and the rural poor in the developing world.

Food sovereignty constructions

Mobilities are concerned with the movement of people, goods, capital, and information at both large and local scales (Hannam et al. 2006). The travelling of both material and non-material things is embedded in power and politics, creating both movement and stasis (Hannam et al. 2006). Mobilities studies both displacement and relocation in all the hybrid, complex and contradictory ways that these occur. While the mobilities literature questions if movement always leads to deterritorialization, critical work on food sovereignty suggests that popular constructions of food sovereignty created and mediated by events are as rootless as the neoliberal capitalism it opposes. The connectivity afforded by neoliberalism, by the events that bring together different food sovereignty actors and supporters, has created a popular construction of food sovereignty which provides a compelling representation of another way, a better way. The process of construction is important because it belies the power and identity of those who get to frame and own the discourse of food sovereignty at these events.

Celebrity food sovereignty events propagate social constructions that portray an indistinguishable group of 'small', 'peasant' or 'family' farmers as disenfranchised, who will be emancipated from corporate control if they only practise ecological agriculture focused on food crops. This will make rural societies just and equitable, ensure food needs are met, and make environments sustainable – the opposite of what capitalism is doing to the small peasant farmer. These simplistic constructions are powerful because they seem to offer an alternative to the current corporate food regime; one that is based neither in capitalism nor in mainstream socialism, but one that speaks to the ideas of 'ecological socialism' where environmental sustainability and social equity are achieved through small farming (Cochrane 2007).

This is an ideal that is evoked when Mariam Mayet, Director of the African Center for Biosafety in South Africa, spoke at the African and US Food Sovereignty Summit in Seattle in October 2014. While not as easily recognized as Shiva, Mayet is an important player in the global food sovereignty movement. At the Summit to critique the Gates Foundation's involvement in promoting an African green revolution, Mayet eloquently appealed to the audience to 'reimagine Africa as a vibrant continent where farmers are in control of their seed systems, are proud of their knowledge systems, share seeds from generation to generation, self-reliant on the huge diversity of seeds under their control, and women play an important role in production decisions, seed selection and breeding, and now imagine displacement is taking place by a very violent aggressive Green Revolution project funded by inter alia the Gates Foundation. Peasant farming systems have been reviled by Gates [Gates Foundation] as being backward and contributing to poverty. We have already seen in the US and industrial countries where farmers are divorced from production decisions in labs and boardrooms. We will see this happening in Africa. What is going to happen when they empty out our rural areas? Where are they going to go?'

Similar to Shiva, Mayet's fears that moving to capital and chemical intensive cropping systems will further impoverish farmers and environments. Perhaps the most alarming aspect of this whole endeavour is the role of much reviled Monsanto in the Foundation's vision for the future of farming in Africa. The Foundation is an investor in Monsanto and has partnered with them to provide new hybrid seed technologies through the African Agricultural Technology

Foundation. Therefore added to the dangers of the green revolution are fears that Monsanto's predatory practices would capture Africa's gullible markets for their GM innovations.

Since the 1980s, the environmental turn in development studies has provided an alternative discourse for shaping the future of food and agriculture (Friedmann 2004). Emblematic battles such as opposition to genetically modified crops (anti-GM) and the associated concerns of concentration of resources and biopiracy is by far one of the most important issues that gives the food sovereignty ideal a very powerful appeal. Monsanto has come to symbolize all that is evil in agriculture and is the antithesis to food sovereignty. It has rallied all kinds of support for food sovereignty in the form of resources while at the same time polarizing activists and scientists.

Food sovereignty seeks to re-embed agriculture to counter the dislocating impacts of neoliberal capital that suppresses 'particularities of time and place in both agriculture and diets' (Friedmann 1992: 272). The articulation of food sovereignty by diverse actors reflects a growing concern over the deepening reach and concentration of the agrifood sector. The 'global corporate food regime' (Friedmann 1992; McMichael 2005) now exerts control over a large share of different sectors in all stages of the cycle from seed to table that include research, inputs, production, distribution, marketing and retailing (McMichael, 2005; Edelman 2005). This concentration has reordered agrarian landscapes in some very fundamental ways (Bernstein 2009) and has incorporated and simultaneously marginalized people in the Third World (Friedmann 1992) as well as in developed nations. Corporate agriculture has led to negative environmental outcomes (including climate change), the worldwide rise in obesity and related diseases, new strains of bacteria, antibiotic resistance in humans, new animal diseases transferring to humans due to factory farming practices, and the effects of harmful ingredients in processed food such as transfats (Friedmann 2004).

Food sovereignty: whose priorities?

Food sovereignty is a definitional struggle as well as material one (Trauger 2014; Alkon and Mares 2012). It is 'a manifesto and a political project, and aspires to a program of world-historical ambition' (Bernstein 2014: 1). There are two fundamental battles that food sovereignty is trying to fight – a discursive one against neoliberal corporate agriculture best represented by corporations like Monsanto, and one on the ground that relates directly to ensuring that the rural poor have food and livelihood security. Unfortunately, these two do not always align.

The discursive struggle is largely fought on the global stage through highly publicized celebrity events and the use of media, writings etc. Celebrity food sovereignty actors and the organizations they represent have the economic and cultural capital, enabling them to organize and travel to events. They are continually in the limelight and media, therefore their particular food sovereignty constructions dominate the social movements space (Nicholls 2009: 91). Events provide a concrete 'convergence space' for transnational social movement organizing (Routledge 2003), giving those with the status and the capacity to assemble, such as Shiva (MacFarlane 2009), an advantage in shaping food sovereignty discourses on behalf of all actors within the networks (Nicholls 2009).

The contested social relations and discourses within transnational social movements for food sovereignty have been examined by some (Borras et al. 2008). For transnational movements to be successful they need to have a universalist politics to provide a collective vision for achieving transnational solidarity (Routledge 2003). Even as they are able to articulate a grand narrative as resistance to neoliberalism, they are 'entangled spaces of domination /resistance' (Routledge 2003). These allow for political buy-in from very diverse actors within movements (Edelman 2005). While they attempt to represent the voices of all actors, the more disenfranchised and less mobile actors who are more tied to their places have less power to shape the discourse, therefore their voices get submerged by the more powerful ones (Edelman 2005).

While it could be argued that the collective vision of food sovereignty is embedded and emergent from local and concrete realities (Routledge 2003), this paper asks *whose* local and concrete realities does the predominant food sovereignty ideal now reflect? On the global stage, food sovereignty constructions essentialize what is a very complex and potentially radical concept, eroding its progressive agenda. This essentialized discourse of food sovereignty privileges the views of a certain select group of ideologues over the complex interests and livelihood security issues of small farmers.

Food sovereignty means different things to different people and cannot be divorced from particular ideological, political-economic, geographic and scalar contexts (Akram-Lodhi 2007, Jarosz 2014). Not only does the essentialized and popular notions of food sovereignty make it less relevant to the real livelihood concerns of the rural poor in the developing world, these discourses have material implications taking attention and resources away from the very goals espoused by food sovereignty ideologues – to improve the lives of rural peoples disenfranchised by corporate neoliberal agriculture and bring more control into their lives.

My research examined the local outcomes of transnational food sovereignty movements in the Telengana[1] region of India using a political ecology perspective. Based on 15 months of fieldwork in 2008–2009, I focused on villages where Dalit (untouchable caste) smallholders were targeted for 'food sovereignty' interventions by a prominent food sovereignty NGO on the national and transnational scene. I found that the promotion of sustainable traditional food crops as a way to achieve food security and control of the food system reflected the overarching and essentialized ideology of transnational food sovereignty movements. While some highly food-insecure farmers benefitted from the interventions, the ideology and strategies to achieve food sovereignty did not resonate with most smallholders' bread-and-butter issues and their aspirations to move beyond a subsistence livelihood. Farmers' inability to adopt food sovereignty practices were due to: (1) compulsions to participate in an increasingly monetized economy with all the opportunities and risks that markets brings; (2) changing geographies of labour; and (3) changing values and knowledge relating to traditional agriculture. Even when sustainable food-focused agriculture allowed the farmers to take care of their food needs, they needed enough income to educate their children, pay for medical expenses, to get their daughters married, and participate in an economy that was becoming an increasingly monetized (Louis 2015).

Most small farmers interpreted food sovereignty very differently from the deterritorialized discourses produced and reproduced at food sovereignty events. Rather, they spoke of control over their livelihoods in the face of a rapidly commercializing landscape and dwindling state supports. They wanted to maintain viable livelihoods from agriculture and non-agricultural related work. They wanted to adopt modern agricultural techniques such as hybrids, as well as grow traditional food crops for their own consumption. The poorer farmers depended heavily on state safety nets, such as subsidized food and summer work. Most households were not entirely dependent on agriculture and could not scrape a living from their small pieces of land. Most do not want their children to have to eke a living off the land, but rather get an education and a government, factory or service job. Education is seen as one way to escape the poverty and insecurity afforded by farming. For these farmers, food sovereignty had very little relevance.

Other local-level research on food sovereignty focused on the Global South share similar findings on the disconnections between popular ideas of food sovereignty and local livelihood realities of smallholders. Studies from Honduras for example, showed that food security concerns of peasant movements clashed with Via Campesina's food sovereignty ideals. In Nepal, and in Tamil Nadu state in South India, food sovereignty practices were found to be too narrow and ideological because they focused only on changing farming practices, when farmers needed to address their basic livelihood concerns such as access to education, healthcare, and housing. They could not address the particular challenges farmers faced within a neoliberal agrarian economy nor meet their needs and aspirations.

Therefore, the debates emerging from this growing critical theoretical and empirical body of work of food sovereignty resonates with my own arguments that idealized notions of sustainable rural livelihoods advanced by Western-influenced notions of sustainability or social justice do not resonate with rural peoples' food security concerns in the Global South nor with their desires to participate more fully in 'development'.

Hegemony and democracy

Events reflect the politics of scale in the contentious politics (MacFarlane 2009) of transnational food sovereignty movements in two ways. Universalist politics are leveraged in the creation of a common language for food sovereignty. The universalist politics occur at a transnational scale and reframe the discourse and rhetoric of resistance. They therefore *impose* a food sovereignty ideal on actors at other scales, actors who have little capacity and mobility to frame the discourse. Second, universalist politics are created by advancing ideas of the local, speaking for local constituents and promoting localized forms of agriculture. This spatial imaginary become 'emblematic instances' that essentialize peasant experiences and motivations, and decontextualizes, dehistoricizes and depoliticizes the very place-bound struggles of rural dwellers (Bernstein 2014: 2). However, because celebrities are recognized as speaking on behalf of 'small farmers', their authority and authenticity often go unquestioned even if their connections to the daily, lived struggles of the rural poor are tenuous.

While these essentialized discourses of the 'peasant way' capture the popular attention, they transform the definition of social movement participation in ways that fail to address the structural problems that celebrities and attendees seek to address in an increasingly global political economy. At my field site, small and marginal farmers could not commit whole-heartedly to the food sovereignty 'interventions' being implemented by the NGO because it constrained their ability to maintain viable rural livelihoods. These prescriptions were based on the universalist imaginaries of sustainable rural communities, very similar to Mayet and Shiva's articulations. In fact, one of the founding members of the food sovereignty NGO, who left because he disagreed with the decidedly agroecological turn in programmes that came at the cost of addressing larger livelihood issues, said that the leadership had become increasingly influenced by the environmental turn in development discourse propagated by Western organizations and funders. They put all their might behind programmes to promote traditional, subsistence agriculture. While this benefitted marginal farmers who were extremely food insecure and so poor that they did not have adequate land, capacity or assets to grow commercial crops, they became increasingly irrelevant over time. As farmers' situations improved with state development programmes, more lucrative wage work became available, and commercial crops like cotton and corn allowed even very small farmers to participate in the market economy, these programmes became increasingly restrictive for small farmers, losing their relevance in a political-economic context that was changing rapidly.

Alternatives can also be hegemonic and undemocratic, even as they emerge to right the wrongs of global agriculture. This is partly because discourses and material practices that make sense in particular places, histories and scales, are uncritically adopted in other settings. How does this speak to democracy and participation? Where does this leave the very diverse needs, aspirations and struggles of small farmers? At one food sovereignty gathering Shiva stridently exclaimed 'They [Monsanto] hijack our governments to say the only law that will be written will be a Monsanto law. We've got to reclaim our democracies, that's why it is so important you are here'. Bina Agarwal argues that while farmers' choices are not always democratic in that they are constrained by the choices afforded by neoliberal agriculture and therefore other preferable alternatives are not available, it is also important to acknowledge that the rights of choice of the disadvantaged do not always fall in line with the ideals of global movements that speak on behalf of the disadvantaged. While it is important to identify the constraints and reflect on alternatives, a particular path cannot be forced on them (Agarwal 2014). Indeed, one of the most significant critiques levelled at transnational food sovereignty movements over the last decade is that they conflate the varied concerns of different classes of producers whereby the interests of either Western influenced NGOs or richer farmers get more voice, often submerging weaker constituents' interests (Borras et al. 2008, Akram-Lodhi 2007, Louis 2015, Bernstein 2014).

Celebrity ideologues become the imagineers (Cumbers et al. 2008: 196), or the epistemic brokers (Herring 2010) and events become the sites where travelling knowledges marginalize local concerns (MacFarlane 2009). McMichael (2014) calls this a 'strategic essentialism'. If they do represent the values of some actors, it is a narrow reality, applicable only to certain contexts. I found that food sovereignty strategies have been most effective when farmers were very food insecure and socioeconomically marginalized, depended primarily on subsistence agriculture and were less integrated into the market economy. When livelihoods are secure, farmers are interested both in being able to participate in the market on more favorable terms and, in having the option to practice a more localized agriculture. At one meeting of regional food sovereignty actors that I attended in South India in 2009, one of the leaders of a food sovereignty coalition in Sri Lanka who has worked with farmers for decades, echoed this very same sentiment saying that agroecological subsistence farming by smallholders was only possible when they had no capacity to participate in the market economy and when they had no other options.

There are situations where agro-ecological farming focused on food crops has been successful in promoting food sovereignty, but this is because the institutions were embedded in an enabling political economic environment that also contributed to farmers' livelihood security. The example of the MASIPAG in Philippines could be a case in point. MASIPAG only allows participation by those committed to growing rice organically. They do this because they are ideologically opposed to chemical intensive agriculture and to the current system of corporate control. Wright (2014) claims that this is food sovereignty in action, presenting this as an ideal that is achievable. However, without the collective organization performed by the MASIPAG network, which not only improved farmers' bargaining power in the market, it also strengthened and expanded their social networks, and most importantly, increased their incomes, would this have worked? MASIPAG also provided research and extension and other services traditionally provided by the state. If joining MASIPAG did not improve farmers' incomes, would they join, even if they valued agro-ecological production? In the semi-arid Telengana region of India I found that smallholders moved away from the food sovereignty model, when it stopped making economic sense (Louis 2015). In her promotion of MASIPAG as a food sovereignty example Wright failed to analyse what historical, ideological, political, social, cultural, institutional, and environmental conditions came together to create success for MASIPAG.

Conclusion

This chapter highlights that the broader geopolitical discourse of food sovereignty produced and reproduced at celebrity events simplify, dehistoricize and depoliticize highly complex, multiscalar and highly political issues to provide a neat framing of food sovereignty. These global celebrity food sovereignty events attended by the likes of Vandana Shiva promote an idea of food sovereignty that is hegemonic. While events are organized to capture popular attention, they do so in particularly neoliberal ways by promoting an essentialized discourse of food sovereignty that fail to address the structural problems that celebrities and the attendees seek to address. The publicity afforded to events and the reach of global and social media help to concretize food sovereignty discourses that are not relevant to the struggles of the rural poor and smallholders in the Global South.

In promoting peasant farming as central to agrarian reform, food sovereignty raises important questions about the need to take seriously the environmental consequences and full social costs of industrialization and technologies that have affected millions of peasants. Their opposition to neoliberal agriculture is well founded on a huge body of empirical work. Findings from 18 months of ethnographic research in the Telengana region of India, underscore that neoliberal policies i.e. corporatization of agriculture, pulling back of the state, commercialization with a move to non-food crops, has been detrimental to small farmers, has created widespread distress and in some areas a crisis as evidenced in the more than 250,000 suicides of farmers in India.

However, celebrity food sovereignty events are responsible for promoting narrow articulations of food sovereignty that cannot adequately confront deep-rooted structural inequities that underlie endemic rural poverty. The problems of the countryside are in fact larger than the countryside and thus need both a focus on agriculture and beyond. The rural poor need intervening institutions to help build their capabilities to access all their basic entitlements, not just food and also to address structures that keep them poor and degraded. Rural development strategies that are based solely on small farms ignore the changing realities of the contemporary countryside where diversification out of farm-based livelihoods has been going on. In India, as in many other developing countries, many 'peasants' no longer can (or want to) depend only on agriculture alone. Several political economists (Nagaraj, 2008; Suri, 2006; Ghosh, 2010; Patnaik, 2005; Bardhan, 2006; Frankel, 2005) stress that reinvesting in agriculture, labour-intensive rural industry and infrastructure are important for economic development and would create employment opportunities for the rural poor which would lead to the alleviation of rural poverty. Furthermore, there is a need for investment in social infrastructure to enable the poor to actually benefit from state and market-led development. Food sovereignty practices need to be a part of a larger plan, which involves other aspects of development and a wider safety net for the poor. The 'Right to Food' campaign in India, for example, has worked to get food entitlement as a legally defensible right. They sometimes clash with food sovereignty advocates, since they are less concerned with sustainable farming practices and more with ensuring access, where food is a universal right for all. The introduction of compulsory noon meals in all government elementary schools and the National Rural Employment Guarantee Act (NREGA), are two developments that were a result of this campaign.

These framings of food sovereignty have material consequences, as programmes and funding flowing out of powerful actors to advance a particular idea of food sovereignty often fail to address the underlying structural problems faced by smallholders. Often smallholders are pressured to uphold a particular food sovereignty model that burdens them with the responsibility of making environmentally sustainable choices, when their most immediate concerns might lie elsewhere. By pushing a singular notion of food sovereignty, celebrity events are transforming the definition of social movement participation in an increasingly neoliberal global political economy.

If the idea of 'livelihood security' becomes central to food sovereignty discourses, this would force those who claim to speak for the poor to acknowledge the complexities and differences in the experiences of different classes of rural dwellers. This is the second battle of food sovereignty. This battle requires that food sovereignty ideologues also keep in mind the real needs and problems of small farmers. Right now, the idealism and environmental sustainability goals of food sovereignty advocates trump the bread-and-butter issues of small farmers. If Shiva and others are serious about 'reclaiming our democracies' they should keep their finger on the pulse of the needs of the rural poor and make food sovereignty relevant to their struggles. Food sovereignty ideologues could spend more of their time and resources on targeting and pressuring states to deliver on their mandates to provide a basic level of livelihood for the poor.

When Jarosz (2014) argues that discourses are embedded in particular geohistories, it is a call to continually engage with the dynamic nature of food sovereignty to ensure that it continues to stay relevant for the most marginalized and disenfranchised. Those who 'own' the discourse of food/seed sovereignty need to consider how programmes influenced by their ideas play out in specific localities for impoverished farmers, and the particular challenges they face in the shift toward commercial agriculture and high capital input crops.

Food sovereignty ideologues and the events they sponsor need to clarify what they are really after. Are they trying to save 'peasant' societies? Are they trying to make agriculture viable for the rural poor? Are they trying to make agriculture the engine of development? Are they trying to feed the hungry? Each of these issues may require a distinct set of policies and programmes to address them. Therein lies the challenge of integrating transnational discourses with local discourses and realities.

Note

1. The Telengana region, has long been the locus of a movement for separate statehood. That decades-long struggle recently ended when India created the Telengana state in 2014, carved out of Andhra Pradesh state.

References

Agarwal, B. (2014) Food sovereignty, food security and democratic choice: Critical contradictions, difficult conciliations. *Journal of Peasant Studies*, 41: 1247–1268.
Akram-Lodhi, A. H. (2007) Land reform, rural social relations and the peasantry. *Journal of Agrarian Change*, 7: 554–562.

Alkon, A. H. and Mares, T. M. (2012) Food sovereignty in US food movements: Radical visions and neoliberal constraints. *Agriculture and Human Values*, 29: 347–359.

Andree, P., Ayres, J. M., Bosia, M. J. and Massicotte, M.-J. (eds) (2014) *Globalization and Food Sovereignty: Global and Local Change in the New Politics of Food*. Toronto: University of Toronto Press.

Ayres, J. and Bosia, M. J. (2011) Beyond global summitry: Food sovereignty as localized resistance to globalization. *Globalizations*, 8: 47–63.

Bardhan, P. (2006). Crouching tiger, lumbering elephant? The rise of China and India in a comparative economic perspective. *Brown Journal of World Affairs*, 13: 49–62.

Bebbington, A. (2000) Re-encountering development: Livelihood transitions and place transformations in the Andes. *Annals of the Association of American Geographers*, 90: 495–520.

Bernstein, H. (2009). V. I. Lenin and A.V. Chayanov: Looking back, looking forward. *Journal of Peasant Studies*, 36: 55–81.

Bernstein, H. (2014). Food sovereignty via the 'peasant way' a sceptical view. *Journal of Peasant Studies*, 41: 1031–1063.

Borras, S. M. (2010) The politics of transnational agrarian movements. *Development and Change*, 41: 771–803.

Borras, S. M., Edelman, M., and Kay, C. (2008) Transnational agrarian movements: Origins and politics, campaigns and impact. *Journal of Agrarian Change* 8: 169–204.

Boyer, J. (2010) Food security, food sovereignty and local challenges for transnational agrarian movements: The Honduras Case. *Journal of Peasant Studies* 37, 319–351.

Byres, T. J. (2004) Neo-classical neo-populism 25 years on: Déjà vu and déjà passé. towards a critique. *Journal of Agrarian Change*, 4: 17–44.

Cochrane, R. (2007) Rural poverty and impoverished theory: Cultural populism, ecofeminism, and global justice. *Journal of Peasant Studies*, 34: 167–206.

Cumbers, A., Routledge, P., and Nativel, C. (2008). The entangled geographies of global justice networks. *Progress in Human Geography*, 32: 183–201.

Desmarais, A. A. (2007) *La Vía Campesina: Globalization and the Power of Peasants*. Halifax, Fernwood Pub.

Drèze, J. and Sen, A. (2010) *India: Development and Participation*. Oxford: Oxford University Press.

Edelman, M. (2005) Bringing the moral economy back in to the study of 21st-century transnational peasant movements. *American Anthropologist*, 107: 331–345.

Frankel, F. R. (2005) *India's Political Economy, 1947–2004: The Gradual Revolution*. New Delhi: Oxford University Press.

Friedmann, H. (1992) Distance and durability: Shaky foundations of the world food economy. *Third World Quarterly*, 132: 371–383.

Friedmann, H. (2004) Feeding the empire: The pathologies of globalized agriculture. *The Socialist Register*, 124–143.

Ghosh, J. (2010) The political economy of hunger in 21st century India. *Economic and Political Weekly* 45: 33–38.

Hannam, K., Sheller, M. and Urry, J. (2006) Editorial: Mobilities, immobilities and moorings. *Mobilities*, 1(1): 1–22.

Herring, R. J. (2010) Epistemic brokerage in the bio-property narrative: Contributions to explaining opposition to transgenic technologies in agriculture. *New Biotechnology* 27: 614–622.

Holt-Gimenez, E. and Shattuck, A. (2011) Food crises, food regimes and food movements: Rumblings of reform or tides of transformation? *Journal of Peasant Studies* 38: 109–144.

Jarosz, L. (2014) Considering food security, sovereignty and systems narratives in Colin Sage's Environment and Food. *Sociologia Ruralis* 54: 105–108.

Lal, D. (1999) *Unfinished Business: India in the World Economy*. New Delhi: Oxford University Press.

Louis, E. (2015) 'We plant only cotton to maximize our earnings': The paradox of food sovereignty in rural Telengana, India. *Professional Geographer*, forthcoming.

Macfarlane, C. (2009) Translocal assemblages: Space, power and social movements. *Geoforum*, 40: 561–567.

Martinez-Torres, M. E. and Rosset, P. (2010) La Via Campesina: The birth and evolution of a transnational social movement. *Journal of Peasant Studies*, 37: 149–175.

McMichael, P. (2005) Global development and the corporate food regime. *Research in Rural Sociology and Development*, 11, 265–300.

Nagaraj, K. (2008) *Farmers' Suicides in India: Magnitudes, Trends and Spatial Patterns*. Chennai: Bharathi Puthakalayam.

Nicholls, W. (2009) Place, networks, space: Theorising the geographies of social movements. *Transactions of the Institute of British Geographers*, 34, 78–93.

Patnaik, U. (2005) The agrarian market constraint in India after fourteen years of economic reforms and trade liberalisation. *South Asia* 28, 233–247.

Ravallion, M. and Datt, G. (2002) Why has economic growth been more pro-poor in some states of India than others? *Journal of Development Economics* 68.

Routledge, P. (2003) Convergence space: Process geographies of grassroots globalization networks. *Transactions of the Institute of British Geographers*, 28, 333–349.

Routledge, P. and Cumbers, A. (2009) *Global Justice Networks Geographies of Transnational Solidarity*. Manchester: Manchester University Press.

Routledge, P., Nativel, C. and Cumbers, A. (2006) Entangled logics and grassroots imaginaries of global justice networks. *Environmental Politics*, 15, 839–859.

Suri, K. C. (2006). Suicides by Farmers: Political Economy of Agrarian Distress. *Economic and Political Weekly*, 41, 1523.

Trauger, A. (2014). Toward a Political Geography of Food Sovereignty: Transforming Territory, Exchange and Power in the Liberal Sovereign State. *Journal of Peasant Studies* 41, 1131–1152.

Vasavi, A. (2009). Suicides and the making of India's agrarian distress. *South African Review of Sociology* 40, 94–108.

Watts, M. (1983) 'Good Try, Mr. Paul': Populism and the Politics of African Land Use. *African Studies Review*, 26, 73–83.

Windfuhr, M. and Jonsén, J. (2005) *Food Sovereignty: Towards Democracy in Localized Food Systems*. Rugby: ITDG Publications.

11 Food as a quixotic event

Producing Lebanese cuisine in London

Ali Abdallah and Kevin Hannam

'Throw a Lebanese to the sea and he will come out of it with a fish', is a common saying used among Lebanese individuals. This is a saying that refers to the difficulties that Lebanese nationals have faced and subsequently overcome as they have adapted to new circumstances, but it also relates to the importance of food (in this case a fish) for the identity of Lebanese people. Lebanese culture has consequently placed great emphasis upon food as a key but arguably quixotic event in Lebanese social life and as a significant part of its global diaspora identity.

In her foundational paper, Deborah Lupton (1994) argued that food is intimately linked to memory and meaning, specifically, the symbolic and social nature of food events are conceptualized as connected to childhood memories. Food events then can be both minor and hugely significant at a personal level as we develop a sense of taste. As Duruz (1999: 307) has noted, 'on a regular basis, a culinary map is drawn and re-drawn – one that is textured with memories' through everyday food practices. More recent research has developed these insights from a mobilities perspective, as Gibson (2007: 4) notes: 'food is good to think mobilities with'. Cook and Harrison (2007: 40) demonstrate the mobilities of Caribbean food by mapping 'out a constellation of people, plants, bugs, diseases, recipes, politics, trade agreements, and histories, whose multiple, complex entanglements and disjunctures animate this "thing" [West Indian Pepper Sauce] and its travels'. They show the complicated global biographies of foods as they make their way through various capitalist brokers such that demands for authenticity from both consumers and producers become largely erased.

However such demands for authenticity remain significant when it comes to food and food events. Authenticity in this respect is less about authenticating the product and more about the social processes and performances of authenticity (Cook 2008). Eating out and sampling different cuisines has become an everyday event for many Western and non-Western middle class consumers, who desire authenticity in both international and local cuisine (Warde and Martens 2000; Sims 2009). However, for many migrants this involves a socially constructed and imagined sense of authenticity and positive nostalgia based upon memories of their homeland (Duruz 1999). In the example examined here we focus on the

Lebanese diaspora in London and how they have sought to maintain Lebanese food as a quixotic authentic experience both for the maintenance of their own cultural identities as well as for Lebanese and non-Lebanese consumers. The chapter is structured as follows. Firstly, we review the recent literature on food mobilities. We then outline our methodological approach before examining the production of Lebanese cuisine in London and its 'quixotic quest for authenticity' (Crang 1996: 415) before reaching our conclusions regarding the Lebanese diaspora and its attempts to 'fix' its food mobilities and identity through restaurants.

Conceptualizing food mobilities

Food facilitates social interaction and enables individuals to actively maintain social networks (Warde and Martens 2000). Food is thus a signifier of belonging, cultural identity, and home. Ways of cooking and eating can be symbolic ways of drawing boundaries between hosts and guests, such that people may engage in what Appadurai (1981: 495) termed 'gastropolitics'. Food can function as a meta-phorical 'bridge' between different cultural communities (van den Berghe 1984: 393) but can also serve to reproduce 'imaginary boundaries' between cultural groups (Ahmed 2000: 116). Food is frequently hybridized through cultural contact, but as Cohen and Avieli (2004: 762) state: 'In the encounter between the foreign and local cuisines and tastes, new dishes and new cuisines often emerge. These are not and cannot be reduced to mere fusion or hybridization of strange and local elements, but include an innovative or creative element.'

'Food, taste, and eating', argues Sarah Gibson (2007: 4), 'are all implicated in differing mobilities, whether corporeal, technological, imaginative, or virtual'. She focuses on the space of the railway dining car in terms of 'eating on the move' which brings together the corporeal mobilities of passengers, the techno-logical mobilities of rail travel, and the mobilities of food as experiences of 'travelling-in-dwelling' and 'dwelling-in-travelling' (Gibson 2007: 4). Jennie Germann Molz (2007: 77) further develops the idea of culinary tourism mobili-ties which she defines as tourists' 'practices of exploratory eating, especially in which unfamiliar foods are seen as an encounter with Otherness'. She argues that such culinary mobilities are 'not necessarily about knowing or experiencing another culture but about performing a sense of adventure, adaptability, and openness to any other culture' (Germann Molz 2007: 77). The sense of perfor-mance is significant as many food events incorporate a range of cultural perform-ativities which allow different identities to be expressed. Furthermore, Gibson (2007: 15) notes that: 'eating is important for the figure of the migrant in diasporic practices of migrant home building'. We argue that diasporas frequently quixotically romanticize their home and the food from their homeland and use food as well as their restaurants as a temporary way of fixing their identity in the face of diasporic mobility. This allows connectivity between old and new memo-ries and can be utilized by them in the context of 'modernisation, dislocation and regionalisation, re-emplacing their homeland, making their locality visible and sensible' (Panyagaew 2007: 117). Moreover, diasporas make culinary maps which 'are produced by everyday inscriptions of the imagination – inscriptions that involve the senses, memories, rituals and moments of possibility – on familiar places associated with food' (Duruz 1999: 308). It is these moments of possibility that we may consider as imaginative events of food mobilities for the Lebanese diaspora in London as they seek to produce their cuisine for different audiences but also as a route back to the imagined homeland.

The Lebanese diaspora and food

According to Hourani (2007), the Lebanese government considers Lebanon as a phoenix with two wings – the resident and the migrant. Furthermore, the Lebanese diaspora has been described as:

> more a diaspora of dispersal in which the recovery of identity reflects the experience of cross-generational attrition in assimilating societies, the impact of globalisation of the terms of participation under post-modernity, as well as the destructive and meaninglessness of war that killed and dispersed without a redeeming peace. The recovery of the imaginary homeland for many Lebanese resembles the broader predicament at present time, social impermanence, fluid identities and individual uncertainty.
>
> (Humphrey 2004: 17)

The contemporary use of the term Lebanese diaspora embraces these different senses of exile. Humphrey (2004) explains that the Lebanese diaspora and its present self-consciousness was brought into existence by the displacement of people by the enduring Lebanese civil war that lasted more than fifteen years. He argues that the Lebanese diasporic experience is the product of national disintegration, the destruction of their social worlds and their experience of resettlement in migration. Khater (2001) argues that pre-World War I Lebanese emigration also had a significant impact on the political and economic development of Lebanon. He states that in addition to the money coming in from remittances, and its significance on the local economy, it is estimated that a third of migrants returned to Lebanon. Humphrey (2004) further explains that alongside the more recent refugee communities are the older Lebanese communities who experience the diaspora as a nostalgic sense of exile primarily in terms of a loss of culture and a loss of social connections with the past.

Lebanese migrants are mostly highly educated professionals who pursue goals of educational and economic improvements in their new settings and while wanting to separate themselves from other migrant groups they also participate within their host community in order to be seen as part of that community (Abdelhady 2007). Nevertheless, this has not meant that Lebanese migrants forgot their identity as they took their traditions with them when they migrated similar to other diaspora groups (Convey 2008). Abdelhady (2007) has further identified how notions of solidarity, democracy and rights are central to many members of the Lebanese diaspora and thus their emphasis on cosmopolitan citizenship informs their participation in public events through which they can express their identity.

Lebanon's cuisine, argues Saad (2011), is deeply rooted in its history and enjoys a great reputation worldwide, and particularly by European and American consumers. Abdelrahman (2007) links the growth of Lebanese cuisine to Lebanese migration and explains that the expansion of Lebanese cuisine world-wide prompted most Lebanese establishments to expand from modest beginnings as small falafel shops to high-end restaurants with evening entertainment and sophisticated food. Lebanese food and its presentation are viewed as an aesthetic experience which is enjoyed with conviviality among family members, friends and, moreover, strangers. As Monsour (2009) suggests, for the Lebanese food is central to events throughout their life course. He argues that although we may find similarity between Lebanese cuisine and other Middle Eastern cuisines, a noticeable difference puts Lebanese cuisine in a category of its own, because Lebanese food 'combines the sophistication and subtleties of European cuisines with the exotic ingredients of the Middle and Far East. The cuisine of Lebanon is the epitome of the Mediterranean diet' (Monsour 2009: 235). Monsour (2009) further explains how in Lebanon, food not only feeds the body; it is also considered food for the soul. It is seen as an embodiment of the diverse history and civilization of the country such that Lebanese 'food is largely influenced by its historical heritage, by the diversity of its relief and its climate' (Monsour 2009: 235).

Research methods

Due to the nature of the research, primary data was collected in several stages at different times between 2011 and 2013. Data was collected among Lebanese diaspora members living in London. Due to the busy lifestyles and commitments of diaspora members, three forms of qualitative data collection were applied during each visit. Thus, participant observations, interviews and focus groups were conducted as per availability of members during each visit. After determining that Edgware Road acted as the central hub of the diaspora, primary data collection began from Edgware Road and gradually shifted to various suburbs depending on the information provided from participants and the data collected. Furthermore, the combination of secondary data compiled prior to the field research, plus the observations and data gathered from the first few visits, led to the determination of questions to be asked during both the interviews and focus groups, which would answer the research questions. Questions were based on three key themes, namely, cultural identity, mobilities and hospitality; and subsequently coded and analysed in order to reveal sub-themes. In this chapter we focus primarily on the respondents' comments regarding their perceived authenticity of Lebanese cuisine in London in order to reveal the ways in which they have tried to 'fix' this perceived socially constructed authenticity (Wang 1999; Rickly-Boyd 2012) in the face of pressures of globalization.

Lebanese cuisine in London

Following Baudrillard (1994), Khechen (2007: 7) has argued that 'historic-themed developments, theatrical events, and other hyper-traditions (i.e., traditions delinked from the times and places in which they originated) are being created and re-created as stage sets and sold to consumers seeking new experiences'. We can also see in many contexts how food festivals and events have been staged and seek to re-create traditions in the face of commodification pressures (Hall and Sharples 2003; Frost and Laing 2013; Lee et al. 2015). Hall and Sharples (2003: 10–12) further point out that:

> one of the critical factors in food tourism is the spatial fixity of the product. The tourists must go to the location of production in order to consume the local fare and become food tourists. This does not mean that local production is only consumed in situ, far from it; indeed, one of the great opportunities provided by food tourism is the potential to export to the places that the visitor comes from. Therefore, food tourism is quite literally the consumption of the local and the consumption and production of place. It is for this reason that food tourism offers so much potential to reinforce local food economies, encourage the conservation of food and biodiversity, and help sustain local identities ...

Hall and Sharples (2003) make some important points which can be also applied to a study of food mobilities, diaspora and events. There is the idea of spatial fixity in terms of product but also how this moves and can be exported. They also emphasize how identities are significant in terms of being sustained by the consumption and production of food. In terms of the Lebanese diaspora we can see their desire to maintain a quixotic sense of authenticity in terms of their staging of dining experiences both for their own culture as well as for their guests through the 'moorings' of restaurants. The food and atmosphere created in their restaurants are based upon remembered events which are 'a simulacrum without an original, a copy of a real without reality. It is a model built upon the model of the Lebanese village ... out of memories and collective imagery' (Khechen 2007: 12).

Lebanese citizens, migrants and entrepreneurs have arguably learned to be flexible and resilient. Their flexibility meant adapting rapidly to new cultures such as the British culture, and resilience in starting a new life, progressing and striving in their doings (*The Economist* 2013). Edgware Road in west London is the centre of London's Lebanese diaspora. The Lebanese in London have a reputation for hard work and hard-headed business sense and many of them have become wealthy working for major multinational companies or for themselves (Sydney 2012). In an interview conducted by the British Satellite News (BSN) (2007) George Asay, the chief executive of the Arab – British Chamber of Commerce stated that the:

> Lebanese have traditionally been merchants and entrepreneurs over the years and it is not surprising today to see that there is a large number of Lebanese

entrepreneurs in London. If you look at all the large British, American and European companies, you will find that there are lots of young Lebanese working there and contributing to the success of these institutions. Some of them have done extremely well, became branch managers or have moved on to open their own companies here in the UK and in Europe. So, the Lebanese in general are extremely hard working and contribute to the economy wherever they are.

The pursuit of career success has led to two types of Lebanese migrants, each of which perceives career success form different perspectives. These two types have been labelled as the 'Early Traditional Migrant' and the 'Modern Recent Migrant'. The Early Traditional Migrants are the migrants that left Lebanon in search of a new experience. They form older Lebanese communities who experience the diaspora as a 'nostalgic sense of exile experienced as loss of culture and loss of social connections with the past' (Humphrey 2004: 15). They brought their traditions with them, but blended in with others as they desired to be seen as unique foreigners and wanted to be part of local communities and therefore took part in everyday life. The Modern Recent Migrants are the current migrants forced out of Lebanon due to the conflict with Israel and seek to be part of an already existing community. They might change or adapt to the host's cultural beliefs but are still not sure whether they will go back to their homeland and may forget their original cultural values (Werbner 1999; Anthias 2010).

The 'Early Traditional Migrant' and the 'Modern Recent Migrant' have both played a key role in the demographical structure of the Lebanese diaspora in London. The Early Traditional Migrant sought a permanent life in the UK and strived to succeed by adapting to culture and investing in a foreign land. The Modern Recent Migrant did not intend to learn or adapt to a new culture and relied heavily on the Early Traditional Migrant who helped in securing jobs and temporary residence, and in most cases sponsored their stay and living in the UK. The hospitality industry in London was adopted by early Lebanese migrants as a means of maintaining their identity due to the difficulties of returning back home. Many early Lebanese migrants developed small food business enterprises. Adbulrahim (2009) suggests that later migrants, regardless of their class origin, became incorporated upon arrival to their host-countries in low-wage labour. They held jobs in the mainstream secondary economy or in ethnic businesses owned by other Lebanese immigrants. He argues that this incorporation is temporary as Lebanese immigrants are able to move out of low-wage labour through mobilizing social capital resources and transforming them into physical or human capital. He notes how social capital has been manifested among Lebanese migrants in the form of having access to resource-rich social relationships.

Khechen (2007) has described Lebanese cuisine as one that is related to a collective memory, cultural identity, and a perceived, yet largely imaginary, socially constructed authenticity. Farid emphasized that Lebanese migrants in London hold onto certain food traditions more than Lebanese nationals themselves:

If you visit Edgware Road you will feel that you are in Beirut but in the 1950s and 1960s. Now if you visit Beirut it is all Westernized. You will see more sushi restaurants, American, Indian and Chinese restaurants than there are Lebanese restaurants. Most of those are Lebanese owned. They want to be trendy and attract Western tourists. The Lebanese cuisine in London [has] remained Lebanese. I haven't seen or heard of any Lebanese that has established a cuisine different to the original Lebanese cuisine.

Farid had lived in London for over 40 years. He described his initial migration as a brief journey for PhD studies in London with the aim of returning home soon after. He noted his gradual integration into the host society and how the problems in Lebanon made it impossible for him to return permanently. He now returns to Lebanon for short visits but London remains his home city. He highlights above the way in which Lebanese migrants socially construct a fixed Lebanese past situated in the 1950s/1960s where Lebanese food becomes a quixotic event.

Other respondents also explained that they wanted to illustrate Lebanese traditions to the Western world and decided to open their first restaurant in London in 1991, which became so successful they soon after established another three restaurants around the city. They emphasized that Lebanese traditions were the key to their success:

We wanted to explain to the British people who we were and we did this by opening [our restaurant]. We provide the original traditions that our parents and grandparents followed. A customer that visits [our restaurant] can experience all our traditions from the moment they walk into our restaurant. After they leave they can feel that they are in the UK but when they are here we want to make them feel that they are in Lebanon. Customers liked this and wanted more.

They emphasized that they owed their restaurant's success to traditions they obtained from their upbringing in a traditional Lebanese countryside. Again, the comments made seek to construct a spatial fixity whereby customers 'feel like they are in Lebanon'. This spatial fixity adds to the sense of the quixotic event as dining experience.

Similarly, Mahmoud, the manager of another restaurant in London explained how customers like to experience original Lebanese traditions and explains that his restaurant would not have been successful if it wasn't for the traditional Lebanese experience they provided:

We make sure all our dishes are served in their original traditional format. We have singer that sings old traditional Lebanese songs while playing oud [an Arabic instrument similar to lute] and we have a belly dancer. Even the painting we have on our walls date back to the 1940s. We struggled to find such paintings but we knew our customers wanted to experience the real traditional Lebanese hospitality and we had to offer it.

Mahmoud presents the fullest, most complete example of the Lebanese simulacrum. Here the whole experience with food, music, decoration and dance come together as a whole performativity which is based upon a model of imagined past events. Respondents clearly demonstrated the perceived importance of traditional Lebanese hospitality to customers and related the success of their restaurants to the traditional experiences that they provide, but this is a highly edited and romanticized version of Lebanon.

Karim, an owner of a Lebanese café and bakery in London, explained how traditions are important not only to them but also to their customers:

> Customers want to see something different and original. They want to know that by eating in my bakery they have experienced Lebanese traditions without having to visit Lebanon. … When I first opened the bakery and café I was aiming to attract Lebanese customers that desired a real traditional café style bakery such as the ones we have in Lebanon where one can eat a mankoosha [a Lebanese type of pie] while drinking tea or coffee. The café then got popular among non-Lebanese and the majority of my customers are [now] non-Lebanese.

Furthermore, Hatim, a waiter, explained that staff members at his restaurant were constantly being trained in Lebanese traditions through videos for staff showing them how food was traditionally served, how tables were prepared and how customers were welcomed. Nevertheless, such 'traditions' are almost always subject to innovation and invention. Mahmoud highlights how his café has become more popular with the non-Lebanese as part of the growth in cosmopolitan taste. Such customers may be akin to Feifer's (1985) 'post-tourist' who knows that there is no such thing as an 'authentic' experience and are aware that things are staged, but who may still be attracted to the inauthenticity of the spectacle and the way it is commodified (Cohen 1988; Urry 1990).

Through field research in Lebanese villages Rowe (2008) has described how the memories of subtle differences abound, and survive through recipes passed down in family lines. He suggests that Lebanese people do not seem to be competitive nor comment about the differences in food as especially significant and argues that the diversity in village food has given way to acknowledging a more generic and flexible 'Lebanese cuisine' in the diaspora. He suggests that this flexible Lebanese cuisine has been used to help produce a hybrid culture for the Lebanese diaspora. Lebanese food has been mobilized, commercialized and hybridized as the diaspora has become more flexible in terms of its invented traditions based upon quixotically remembered past events.

Conclusion

The Lebanese diaspora in London embodies the Lebanese homeland through the social construction of its hospitality and food. In this chapter we have sought to highlight how the mobilities of Lebanese food traditions were central for the

Lebanese Diaspora in helping to maintain their identity in London. They have adapted Lebanese culinary heritage with a degree of Western 'exoticness' in order to form a socially constructed cultural diaspora that would be welcomed and embraced in a Western world. Entrepreneurs of the Lebanese diaspora have achieved great success by developing a hybrid Lebanese Middle Eastern cuisine. However, this cuisine, as we have seen above, is based upon a largely quixotic sense of past events and places which a given a spatial and temporal 'fix' in the space of the Lebanese restaurant. Such events are imagined and built upon a constructivist authenticity of events which are fluid, negotiable and contextual (Rickly-Boyd 2012).

References

Abdelhady, D. (2007) Cultural Production in the Lebanese Diaspora: Memory, Nostalgia and Displacement. *Journal of Political and Military Sociology*, 35(1): 39–62.
Abdelrahman, R. (2007) Belly dancing and hummus: Swedes fall for Lebanese. Available online: http://www.thelocal.se/20070614/7608 Accessed on 26 November 2015.
Ahmed, S. (2000) *Strange Encounters*. London: Routledge.
Anthias, F. (2010) Evaluating diaspora: Beyond ethnicity? *Sociology*, 32(3): 557–580.
Appadurai, A. (1981) Gastro-politics in Hindu South Asia. *American Ethnologist*, 8(3): 494–511.
Appiah, A. (2006) *Cosmopolitanism: Ethics in a World of Strangers*. New York: Norton.
Baudrillard, J. (1994) *Simulacra and Simulation*. Ann Arbor: The University of Michigan Press.
BSN British Satellite News (Online). (2007) The Lebanese community in the UK. Online at: http://www.youtube.com/user/BritishSatelliteNews?feature=watch. Accessed on 22 February 2013.
Cohen, E. (1988) Authenticity and commoditization in tourism. *Annals of Tourism Research*, 15: 371–386.
Cohen, E. and Avieli, N. (2004) Food in tourism: Attraction and impediment. *Annals of Tourism Research*, 31(4): 755–778.
Convey, P. (2008) *Diasporas*. Berkeley: University of California Press.
Cook, I. (2008) Geographies of food: mixing. *Progress in Human Geography*, 32(6): 821–833.
Cook, I. and Harrison, M. (2007) Follow the Thing: 'West Indian Pepper Sauce'. *Space and Culture*, 10(1): 40–63.
Crang, M. (1996) Magic kingdom or a quixotic quest for authenticity. *Annals of Tourism Research*, 23(2): 415–31.
Duruz, J. (1999) The streets of Clovelly: Food, difference and place-making. *Continuum: Journal of Media & Cultural Studies*, 13, 305–314.
Feifer, W. (1985) *Going Places*. London: Macmillan.
Frost, W. and Laing, J. (2013) Communicating persuasive messages through slow food festivals. *Journal of Vacation Marketing*, 19(1): 67–74.
Germann Molz, J. (2007) Eating difference: The cosmopolitan mobilities of culinary tourism. *Space and Culture*, 10(1): 77–93.
Gibson, S. (2007) Food mobilities: Travelling, dwelling and eating cultures. *Space and Culture*, 10(1): 4–21.
Hall, C. M. and Sharples, L. (2003) The consumption of experiences or the experience of consumption? An introduction to the tourism of taste. In Hall, C. M., Sharples, L.,

Mitchell, R., Macionis, N. and Cambourne, B. (eds.) *Food Tourism Around the World: Development, Management and Markets*. Oxford: Elsevier Butterworth-Heinemann.

Hourani, G. (2007) *The Impact of the Summer 2006 War on Migration in Lebanon: Emigration, Re-Migration, Evacuation and Return*. Louaize: NDU Press.

Humphrey, M. (2004) Lebanese identities: Between cities, nations and trans-nations. *Arab Studies Quarterly*, 26(1): 15–17.

Karim, J. (1992) *Lebanese Citizenship Between Law and Reality*. Beirut: Joseph al-Hajj Publisher.

Khater, A. (2001) *Inventing Home: Emigration, Gender, and the Middle Class in Lebanon, 1870–1920*. Berkeley: University of California Press.

Khechen, M. (2007) Beyond the Spectacle: Al-Saha Village, Beirut. *Traditional Dwellings and Settlements Review*, 19(1): 7–21.

Labaki, B. (2006) The role of transnational communities in fostering development. *Ethnic and Racial Studies*, 23(1): 37–61.

Lee, K., Packer, J. and Scott, N. (2015) Travel lifestyle preferences and destination activity choices of Slow Food members and non-members. *Tourism Management*, 46: 1–10.

Lowe, L. (1991) Heterogeneity, hybridity, multiplicity: Marking Asian American differences. *Diaspora* 1(1): 24–44.

Lupton, D. (1994) Food, memory and meaning: the symbolic and social nature of food events. *Sociological Review*, 42(4): 664–685.

Monsour, A. (2009) *Negotiating a Place in a White Australia: Syrian/Lebanese in Australia, 1880 to 1947, a Queensland Case Study*. PhD thesis, University of Queensland.

Ouaiss, S. (2010) *Politics, Culture and the Lebanese Diaspora*. Newcastle: Cambridge Scholars Publishing.

Panyagaew, W. (2007) Re-Emplacing homeland: Mobility, locality, a returned exile and a Thai restaurant in Southwest China. *The Asia Pacific Journal of Anthropology* 8(2): 117–135.

Rickly-Boyd, J. M. (2012) 'Through the magic of authentic reproduction': tourists' perceptions of authenticity in a pioneer village. *Journal of Heritage Tourism*, 7(2): 127–144.

Rowe, A. E. (2008) *Mint Grows Through the Cracks in the Foundation: Food Practices of the Lebanese Diaspora in New England (USA)*. Food and Migration Workshop, SOAS. London: School of Oriental and Asian Studies.

Saad, D. (2011) *Agro-Food Industries in Lebanon: A Remarkable History and a Promising Future*. Beirut: SLFI.

Sims, R. (2009) Food, place and authenticity: local food and the sustainable tourism experience. *Journal of Sustainable Tourism*, 17(3): 321–336.

Sydney (2012) Lebanon Government? Who needs a government? Online at: http://en.peninsula-press.com/uploads/reports/Libano_FP/Lebanon_report_fp.pdf. Accessed on 07 February 2013.

Tabar, P. (2010). *Lebanon: A Country of Emigration and Immigration*. Institute for Migration Studies. Beirut: LAU Press.

The Economist (2013) The Lebanese diaspora. A tale of two traders. Online at: http://www.economist.com/news/business/21573584-business-people-lebanon-fare-better-abroad-home-tale-two-traders. Accessed on 23 March 2013.

Urry, J. (1990) *The Tourist Gaze*. London: Sage.

van den Berghe, P. L. (1984) Ethnic cuisine: Culture in nature. *Ethnic and Racial Studies*, 7(3): 387–397.

Wang, N. (1999) Rethinking authenticity in tourism experience. *Annals of Tourism Research*, 26: 349–370.

Warde, A. and Martens, L. (2000) *Eating Out*. Cambridge: Cambridge University Press.

Werbner, P. (1999) Global pathways. Working class cosmopolitans and the creation of transnational ethnic worlds. *Social Anthropology*, 7(1): 17–35.

12 Afterword

Chris Gibson

As I write, the world rumbles to the sound of eventful mobilities. Once unfathomable numbers of people are fleeing to Europe (from Syria, Afghanistan, Somalia, Eritrea and elsewhere) in search of safety and hopeful futures. It was estimated there would be more than a million refugee arrivals to Europe by sea, by the end of 2015. I open the weekend newspaper travel section (a small Saturday morning ritual in our household) to see page after page advertising cruise ships of unprecedented opulence traversing ever more ambitious itineraries – a world apart from those other seafarers, on cramped and precarious boats, seeking refuge amidst brutality and hardship. In other news, 25,000 personnel from the Mexican Army, Navy, and Federal Police were this week mobilized to evacuate tourists and residents from affected towns as Hurricane Patricia, the strongest ever recorded in the Western Hemisphere, made landfall. On a brighter note, more than 400,000 visitors were expected in Britain for the Rugby World Cup, catalyzing an estimated £1 billion in economic activity. And with less fanfare (but no less cultural significance), this week more than 2,000 indigenous athletes from 30 countries have gathered in Palmas, Brazil, for the World Indigenous Games. Mobility is the leitmotif of our age. And events – wars, escapes, evacuations, border crossings, encounters with authorities, embarkations, carnivals, media stories – are both the catalyst for mobilities, and the frame through which they are experienced, aggravated, and understood.

The various chapters in this distinctive book seek to bring events and mobilities into conversation, conceptually, and empirically. Mobilities are, as the editors of the book suggest in their introduction, assemblages or networks of events. Events, in turn, are momentary distillations of intersecting mobilities, 'moorings' (Hannam et al. 2006), but also exceptional disruptions to an ordinary state of affairs. Possibilities abound for politics in the interstices between such flows and disruptions – among them the hybrid identities, jostlings and negotiations of multispecies, diasporic, and multicultural worlds. Various chapters of the book chart the pleasures but also the challenges and fraught tensions in being eventful, relational or cosmopolitan, in opening up and maintaining disruptive, affirmative, choreographed, expressive and meaningful spaces. Mobilities and events do not knit together into a tight and logically woven fabric – as if mere coordinates in topographically even space. They are tussled over, 'antagonistically knotted', as

Tani H. Sebro vividly puts it, an 'instability of relational forces between people, things, time and ... movement'.

Throughout the book are careful expositions of this. Angela Montague's chapter explores the case of the Malian Tuareg Festival in the Desert, where a new generation of cosmopolitan Tuareg nomads strategically essentialized their own cultural narrative in order to capitalize on the opportunities of exoticism, but saw that strategy falter when an otherwise successful, hybrid modern/traditional music festival became antithetical with the 2012 imposition of Shari'a law. Younger Tuareg sought alternatives, while older, rural nomadic Tuareg spoke instead of building wells and finding jobs. That festival was adjourned, but for a time it nevertheless productively collided competing discourses of tradition and modernity, cultural preservation and hybridity – catalyzing new mobilities of people, ideas, sounds and celebrations.

Mobilities, as that example well attests, become understood as meaningful within systems and categories of knowledge. These can take the form of highly mobile political slogans that unite diasporic and networked communities across the world, from Holocaust survivors (Chapter 9) to food sovereignty campaigners (Chapter 10), and Lebanese migrants, for whom the 'constructivist authenticity' of food ties culinary heritage to the task of making sense of new circumstances (Chapter 11). Mobile ideas, and the events that frame them, are frequently narrated as linking moments in time and space.

But of course, much of the narrating of eventful mobilities is retrospective – retrieving origin stories in diaspora, telling stories of travel adventures to friends and relatives, media outlets covering mega-events, or packaging up stories of refugee movements for syndicated audiences. Retroactivity is present too when ethnographers switch on their voice recorders to capture oral narratives for research purposes. The problem persists of how to capture, in spoken or written form, unfolding embodied experiences of eventful mobilities – to grasp that which is in constant fluid motion.

It is perhaps no surprise, then, that musical analogies and examples resonate throughout this book – for music itself embodies the most fluid and the eventful. It is in one sense nothing more than sound waves, pulses of audible air that engage and excite, while also enacted via eventful musical performances, festivals, and expressions. Throughout the book we travel with orchestras and see glimpses of mobile performing lives on and off the stage (Chapter 3); we go along for the ride with Karl Spracklen and fellow metal fans at the graphically-named Bloodstock (Chapter 4); we fall into the choreographed refrain and steady beat of dancers at a Tai funeral ceremony on the Thai-Burma border (Chapter 8), and are treated to the hybrid sounds of the Malian Tuareg Festival in the Desert (Chapter 2). Mobilities are fluid performances that unfold in time and space, just as notes pour forth in a song, simultaneously interrupted by staccato moments, and confined by spaces of stillness in between. Noise, movement, flow. Then silence.

* * *

There are inevitably themes that evade total capture in any book, and among them here is arguably more sustained dialogue on the visceral, in its more eventful manifestations (though we get some sense of this in Chapters 4 and 8). Also lurking in the silent corners of the book are those uneventful dimensions of mobilities – the humdrum moments traversing to and from events, the view along the way. What does it mean to be moving, in between the punctuation of strings of events?

As Anna de Jong (2015) has elsewhere described, getting there is as much of the story as the destination. Mobilities are not merely a procession of events connected in fleeting moments, but journeys where much is accrued unconsciously along the way, in the spaces in between the eventful. Being mobile is sometimes all about craving an 'undifferentiated flow'. She asks, 'what holds individuals "in place", so to speak, when attachment takes place through movement'? (2015: 2). Exploring Dykes on Bikes traversing 600 miles from Brisbane to attend the Sydney Gay and Lesbian Mardi Gras Parade, de Jong (2015: 4) attends to the visceral dimensions of mobilities, hence motorcycle riding

> brings senses into being; for example, one has to remain aware of their own riding body, how it is positioned on the road, its positionality towards other riding bodies, and other driving bodies—in this sense riding bodies open up and connect in different ways, at different times, for different reasons.

Building on Bissell and Fuller's (2011) notion of 'stillness unbound', there appears a certain kind of stillness (and privilege?) associated with merely being on the road, as thoughts drift, as the body feels the twists and turns and bumps of the highway rolling on. It seems hardly eventful, yet for many, being on the road is an event in itself.

Focusing on the visceral mobile body also tells us much about what mobile bodies leave behind, and why. De Jong (2015: 5) describes this as a 'longing' or 'yearning' to move but also to belong, a 'felt, visceral experience – an emotional affiliation that exists between individuals and collectives, individuals and things, and individuals and places – an essence that emerges through movement which correspondingly generates association'. Thus mobile bodies en route to or amidst events may be in search of belonging or escape, finding places and times to restore and nurture relationships, or leaving behind the drudgery of menial jobs, difficult divorces and, the stress of overloaded busy lives or, more forcefully, trauma or persecution.

Much hangs on the tension between the ordinary and extraordinary, as the editors of the collection suggest in their opening chapter. For the extraordinary, perhaps nothing eclipses Tani H. Sebro's immersion in a funeral ceremony on the Thai–Burma border, a region afflicted by military conflict that has seen millions migrate or flee for better futures elsewhere. There, the eventful and mobile combine in the choreographing of bodies (live and dead) to make sense out of indescribable chaos and conflict, and personal loss.

On the ordinary, questions resonate on the mechanics of mobility, the lived daily experience of mobile labour – and the labour of movement. For events – from festivals to disaster evacuations – are nothing without stallholders, food trucks, 'carnies' (carnival labourers), emergency workers, portable toilet transporters, PA technicians, crowd marshals. In Angela Montague's chapter, a significant logistical task was the trucking of water, toilets, electricity and provisions into the Malian desert for a festival, where many of Mali's own permanent citizens live without such basics. In Julie Cidell's chapter an event that itself encapsulates what it means to be mobile – road running – involved all manner of technical-logistical arrangements and, ironically, *immobilities*. Networks of intricate technologies, barriers, rules and conventions prevail, so that people can be mundanely mobile within the eventful confines of a half-marathon.

One might add to these distinctly eventful mobilities (and the working bodies that support them) a new and increasingly diverse population of long-distance commuters and distance labourers (health workers, miners, environmental scientists and sex workers) whose eventful mobilities involve intensities of interspersed intimacies and absences: grateful reunions and painful departures, regular goodbyes and welcomes home at airports, train stations and home driveways (Yeoh and Huang 2010; Skilton 2015). Future research would do well to explore the emotional labour of such mobilities and the events that punctuate them – the drudgery and sadness, the strained intimacies and disorientations of short stays, the relentless welcoming and departing – as well as the intense energies and deadline-driven stress of eventful mobile work (in the case of, say, emergency workers and festival crews). Roots and routes are made amorphous when mobile labouring, enveloping one's life. In this collection, Rebecca Sheehan's chapter on circus workers provided the most poetic insight along these lines: how a distinctive community of circus workers make 'home' while constantly on the move, but then 'winter' in a remarkable place, Hugo, Oklahoma, where school curriculum, housing and community expectations have adjusted to accommodate circus workers' seasonal lives. While 'home' is associated with stillness, with second homes and migrant places, 'the travel itself is rarely examined as a constituent of home'. Yet in increasing numbers, people live lives on the move for work, with movement the omnipresent constant. Relationships with other people, rather than concrete places, are means to emotional sustenance and belonging.

Focusing on mobile working bodies in turn brings us around full circle, to everpresent questions of power, coercion, and resistance. For all the novel theorizing around mobilities (and the presumed hyper-mobility of the current age), much stays the same. Focusing on the ordinary labour of mobile bodies reveals the things that are unmoored as much as those that depend on eventful moorings in time and space. Hence the mobilities of food sovereignty come together in celebrity events and discourses that risk unmooring their own arguments from the lived experiences of peasants for whom food livelihoods are a matter of daily survival (Chapter 1). As chapters throughout this book deftly show, the coming together of events and mobilities puts a new spin on perennial questions of struggles for prosperity, security, meaning and identity.

References

Bissell, D. and Fuller, G. (2011) Stillness unbound. In D. Bisselll and G. Fuller (eds.) *Stillness in a Mobile World*, New York: Routledge, pp. 1–17.

de Jong, A (2015) Dykes on bikes: mobility, belonging and the visceral. *Australian Geographer*, 46: 1–13.

Hannam, K., Sheller, M. and Urry, J. (2006) Mobilities, immobilities and moorings. *Mobilities*, 1: 1–22.

Skilton, N. (2015) Re-imagining geographic labour mobility through 'distance labour'. *Australian Journal of Public Administration*, 74: 364–369.

Yeoh, B.S.A. and Huang, S. (2010) Transnational domestic workers and the negotiation of mobility and work practices in Singapore's Home-spaces. *Mobilities*, 5: 219–236.

Index